PIKE PLACE ★ MARKET ★ COOKBOOK

PIKE PLACE ★ MARKET COOKBOOK

Recipes, Anecdotes, and Personalities from Seattle's Renowned Public Market

BRAIDEN REX-JOHNSON *Foreword by Tom Douglas*

SASQUATCH BOOKS
SEATTLE

Printed in the United States of America
Published by Sasquatch Books
Distributed by Publishers Group West
10 09 08 07 06 05 04 03   6 5 4 3 2 1

Cover design: Stewart A. Williams
Cover & interior illustrations: Spencer Johnson
Interior design: Kate Basart
Copy editor: Sherri Schultz

1. Beet Salad with Fresh Basil Dressing
   Reprinted from *Feeding the Whole Family: Whole Foods Recipes for Babies, Young Children and Their Parents*, by Cynthia Lair, Copyright ©1998 Moon Smile Press, www.feedingfamily.com
2. Grilled Halibut with Lemon Herb Splash and Honey-Berry Vinaigrette
   Copyright ©2002 Kathy Casey DISH D' LISH
3. Spicy Cherry Catsup and Winter Spirits
   Reprinted from *The Chukar Cherry Recipe Collection*, Copyright ©2001 Chukar Cherry Company, Inc.
4. Wild Mushroom Terrine with Apple-Rosemary Vinaigrette
   Reprinted from *A Harvest Celebration: Delectables from Distinguished Northwest Chefs*
   Copyright ©1995 The Market Foundation

Library of Congress Cataloging in Publication Data

Rex-Johnson, Braiden, 1956–
Pike Place Market cookbook : recipes, anecdotes, and personalities from Seattle's renowned public market / Braiden Rex-Johnson ; illustrations by Spencer Johnson.
       p.   cm.
   Originally published: 1992.
Includes index.
ISBN 1-57061-319-2
   1. Cookery, American. 2. Cookery—Washington (State). 3. Pike Place Market (Seattle, Wash.) I. Title.
TX715.R439 2003
641.59797'772—dc21   2002191121

Sasquatch Books
119 South Main Street, Suite 400
Seattle, WA 98104
206/467-4300
www.sasquatchbooks.com
books@sasquatchbooks.com

◆◆◆◆◆◆◆◆◆◆◆◆◆◆◆◆◆◆◆◆◆◆◆◆◆◆◆◆◆◆◆◆◆◆◆◆

As always, for Spencer and Bo-Bo, with thanks and love.

The journey just keeps getting better and better!

◆◆

Acknowledgments

A project of this size and scope is never accomplished by just one person—it's a team effort, and without the help of the following people, the revised edition of the *Pike Place Market Cookbook* could never have become a reality. My heartfelt thanks go to my editor at Sasquatch Books, Suzanne De Galan; my literary agent, Anne Depue; the Sasquatch marketing staff (Kim Foster, Gina Johnston, Susan Quinn, and Sarah Smith), and production and graphics team (Joan Gregory, Dana Youlin, Stewart Williams, and Kate Basart). Thanks also to Gary Luke, editorial director at Sasquatch Books, for believing this book was worth updating and encouraging me from the beginning.

Other important people in the book-writing process included members of the Pike Place Market Preservation and Development Authority (PDA): Michele Catalano, Pike Place Market Basket CSA program manager; Scott Davies, public information specialist; Cheryll Davis, marketing and communications assistant; Andrew Krueger, director of marketing and communications; Daniel Lieberman, executive director; Sue Gilbert Mooers, communications specialist; and Mark Musick, former farm program coordinator. Christine Stefferson, communications consultant to the Pike Place Market; Sharron Shinbo, Market resident and PDA Council member; and Paul Dunn, Market resident and president of Friends of the Market also provided valuable input and sound advice as I wrote this book. Many thanks!

My family is a constant source of inspiration and support, especially Mr. and Mrs. A. C. Johnson, Dr. and Mrs. E. B. Rex, the Rex family contingent in Orlando, and Spencer Johnson, my partner in life, sous-taster extraordinaire, and fellow bon vivant.

Most especially and heartily, my deepest gratitude goes to the cookbook's contributors . . . the small independent business owners, highstallers, fishmongers, chefs, and Marketgoers who so generously and graciously shared their recipes, cooking expertise, and stories with me. This book is a reflection of them.

Contents

Foreword

I f there were a single description for what Braiden Rex-Johnson means to the Pike Place Market, Patron Saint would be it. I know most people love the Market. They love the singers, whether they're praising Jesus or crooning for world peace. They love the food, hungry shoppers who gravitate to Russian apple cinnamon rolls, bags of hot doughnuts, and steaming pork *hum bao*. They love to browse the vendor stalls and frolic among stunning photographs of Mount Rainier flanked by tie-dyed baby bonnets and Indonesian flower farmers. That's all well and good. We need all of you who love the Market. The vendors live for you. The Market thrives with your presence.

But a Patron Saint looks out for the Market in a different way. She understands its good and bad days. She delights in its successes, never abandons it for flashier friends like one-stop grocery stores, or avoids it with convenient excuses like a rainy day or a deep chill. A Patron Saint understands the Market's nooks and crannies. She can see beauty under peeling paint or political muscle. She absorbs and appreciates the vibrant scents from summer fruit and flowers, yet relishes the quiet doldrums of the inevitable off-season that rolls around each winter.

A Patron Saint knows that when the tourist, shopper, or vendor goes home for the day, the Market is still alive, still sheltering the neighborhood and its people. Because the fact is that this nine acres we call the Pike Place Market has a heartbeat, a breathing capacity, a role to play. It has a kind of gravity—drawing to it the rest of the city and keeping it centered on what's important: good food, nourishment, energy, social character, and awareness. If there is a heart and soul of Seattle, I suggest that the Pike Place Market is it; and people like Braiden Rex-Johnson are its soul keepers. They preserve and celebrate the energy that ultimately moves beyond a transaction. Braiden, like others before her, passes on the history of the Pike Place Market much in the way of an Indian song over a campfire, enlightening future Market celebrants to its rich tales and enduring charm.

Twenty five years ago, on one of my first trips to the Market, I met Pasqualina Verdi, a true "garlic gulch" vendor from South Seattle's Italian farming community. She patiently explained, in broken English, her classic recipe for sweet basil pesto, balanced with the bitterness of flat leaf Italian parsley. Finding that recipe in Braiden's book was like finding a piece of my cooking heritage.

The recipes in the *Pike Place Market Cookbook* are an important step in continuing the traditions of the Market. As you read the book, take to heart Braiden's stories of the vendors from every ethnic background. Follow the trails she has scouted for each ingredient.

When you're done cooking your way through Braiden's book, take a moment to reflect on the history of the Market, and your part in it. Make a date with your honey, or your kids, or both, take that morning stroll on the well-worn bricks of Pike Place, and watch the Market come alive. Cradle a hot steamy latte and soak up the spirit that is the Pike Place Market. After all, the Market is going to need more Patron Saints and soul keepers . . . why not you?

—Tom Douglas

◆◆◆◆◆◆◆◆◆◆◆◆◆◆◆◆◆◆◆◆◆◆◆◆◆◆◆◆◆◆◆◆◆◆◆◆◆

Preface to the New Edition

The opportunity for an author to revise and update her favorite book after it has enjoyed a successful 10-year run is a rare and exciting one, and when the subject is the Pike Place Market, the joy grows exponentially.

But at first, I'll admit, the task seemed a bit daunting. After all, as I said in the first edition of the *Pike Place Market Cookbook*, "the Market is ever changing," and my preliminary research showed that a full 30 percent of the businesses featured in the original book had changed hands, seen their owners move on, or, in a few sad cases, lost their owners to death. Many of the longtime farmers had retired; a new crop of younger farmers had sprouted in their place. The Kaleenka morphed into Le Pichet, Cucina Fresca became Michou, Gourmondo transformed into Sesto's, and Café Sophie became Avenue One, which (very sadly) closed after five memorable years. Campagne spawned Café Campagne; Vivanda and Emerald Kettle opened for business. And on and on . . .

But on a cool January day in 2001, I made an interesting and reassuring discovery. As the sun broke through the billowy clouds to burnish the Market buildings with a rich copper light, I strolled the more obscure corners of the Market at a leisurely pace. I didn't rush by, but stopped to really look at the businesses and the food they served. I talked to the people behind the counters, analyzing how they had changed (or not) since I had first written about them back in 1992.

And in a very heartening way, especially when the world around us seems to transform so quickly, I discovered that for as much as the Market has changed during the previous decade, so much has stayed the same.

I still enjoy the banter of the fishmongers at Pure Food Fish as I ask them, "What am I going to eat tonight?" and they make suggestions. When the ubiquitous Copper River salmon is running in the spring, they jokingly reply, "Copper River crab, Copper River sturgeon, Copper River cod."

The smell of exotic spices as I pass by The Souk always perks up my senses and sends my imagination flying off on a momentary trip to India. The display cases at Bavarian Meats still boast the plumpest sausages, huge wedges of Swiss and Emmenthaler cheese, and chewy dark-grain breads. Nancy Nipples at the Pike Place Market Creamery is always quick with a hug or a spritz of water on a hot summer's day.

The highstalls (permanent fruit and vegetable stands) have changed little, except to get more diversified and better, with the addition of two all-organic options with a myriad of unique products (Jordan Village Farms and Simply the Best). The farmer population had dwindled to a trickle in the mid-1990s, but has been reinvigorated by the introduction of Organic Farmer Days on Wednesdays and Sundays. It's a joy to see a new generation of farmers selling in the open air along Pike Place, recapturing the festive atmosphere of the Market's humble beginnings.

The Market Basket Community Supported Agriculture (CSA) program, initiated in 1997, provides farmers with a steady income during the winter, when they need money for seed and equipment

◆◆◆◆◆◆◆◆◆◆◆◆◆◆◆◆◆◆◆◆◆◆◆◆◆◆◆◆◆◆◆◆◆◆◆◆◆◆

repairs. In return, the people who take a share in the Market Basket CSA (known as subscribers) receive the freshest, just-picked-for-them seasonal produce for 20 weeks from May through October.

Doing business over the Internet is another phenomenon that has burgeoned during the past 11 years. Many savvy Market business owners now operate websites that make their wares available for sale throughout the United States and the world. A fresh salmon dinner is (almost) as available in Iowa as it is any night in Seattle!

An issue of FreshWire!, the Market's electronic newsletter (another modern innovation), described the Market as "a small, multicultural town within the city." And even as our global village shrinks, I still regard the Pike Place Market as a microcosm of the world, a delicate balance of multifaceted elements.

Judy Duff, an organic farmer from Burien, explains it eloquently when she says, "We are pulled to the Market because it is the heartbeat of life itself. Children, the elderly, and everyone in between feed the Market's diversity and vibrancy. The Market is where East meets West, where cultures of the world become the ingredients for the All-Star American Tossed Salad."

The Market is the city's "alimentary canal," and I still consider it a privilege to shop from the farmers, highstallers, fishmongers, and all the specialty food shops for the best of the Northwest's incredible bounty. As I said in the first edition to this book, "The *Pike Place Market Cookbook* was inspired by this variety of foods, which I behold on my almost-daily shopping excursions to Seattle's Pike Place Market."

Many local chefs agree that the Pike Place Market is a great source of ideas and inspiration, and the inclusion of 20 of their Market-inspired recipes (plus cooking tips!) is a new feature in this edition of the *Pike Place Market Cookbook*. And while some no longer work in the Market, many of the celebrity chefs began their careers in establishments along Pike Place; others shop at the Market on a regular basis; most have cooked during Café Organic or Summer Sundays on Pike Place (cooking demonstrations organized by the Pike Place Market Preservation and Development Authority[PDA]), or for the annual Sunset or Harvest Suppers.

The festive suppers are sponsored by The Market Foundation, which coordinates the four social-service agencies in the Market, including a food bank, senior center, medical clinic, and preschool and childcare. The Sunset Supper is a summer celebration of the Market's anniversary (August 17) during which the city's best chefs cook up their specialties for hundreds of appreciative "foodies" in the open air along Pike Place. The Harvest Supper takes place in the fall or winter months, when a more intimate group of guests descends on Kaspar's restaurant in Queen Anne for a multi-course feast prepared by Nancy and Kaspar Donier and guest chefs.

With so many creative events and activities going on, so many ethnic groups and generations working together, and so much history behind and in front of it, is it any wonder that the Pike Place Market is considered to be the epitome of American farmers markets?

Cheers to the wisdom of the Market as she looks forward to her hundredth birthday in 2007!

—*Braiden Rex-Johnson, December 2002*

Introducing the Market
What is the Pike Place Market?

First-time visitors to the Market are often overwhelmed by its multitudes of people, cacophony of sounds, plethora of aromas, and abundance of fast-paced commerce. They find it hard to believe such high levels of energy can be sustained, and ask in amazement, "Does the Market go on every day?"

The tourists' innocent question is prompted by the nature of the Market itself, which is at once part meat, fish, and produce market; part breathtaking panorama of water, mountains, and sky; part vaudeville show; part arts and crafts extravaganza; and part slice of nitty-gritty street life. And yes, it does "go on" seven days a week, with once-in-a-while interruptions for certain national holidays.

In official terms, the Market is a nine-acre National Historic District with more than 250 permanent businesses, about 100 farmers, 200 artists and craftspeople, and 500 permanent residents. But unofficially, it's so much more.

Looking beyond the surface, you might be surprised to find a bed-and-breakfast inn, housing for low-income and elderly people, an improvisational comedy troupe, a luxury hotel, child care facilities, a medical clinic, a senior center, a dentist, a tarot card reader, a food bank, a daily rummage sale, and a half-price ticket booth.

The burgeoning Washington wine industry is well represented in the Market by the Washington Wine Center (which offers educational materials on Washington wines and touring the wine country), The Tasting Room (a cooperative wine-tasting room where visitors are invited to sample some of the state's best boutique wines), the Market Cellar Winery (an atmospheric winery along Western Avenue), and wine shops such as Pike and Western Wine Shop, Pike Place Grocery & Deli, and DeLaurenti Specialty Food & Wine. But—perhaps, most important, with all these temptations available!—several cash machines are located throughout the Market.

The low metal tables in the Main and North Arcades are the stalls that farmers and craftspeople rent by the day. Craftspeople can sell only items that they make, such as jewelry, clothing, and artwork, except for five "grandfathered" vendors who were selling at the Market before the "handmade only" rule was enacted. The "handmade only" rule is strictly enforced by Pike Place Market Preservation and Development Authority (PDA) officials through visits to the artisans' studios.

Farmers, who get priority for space, sell their own seasonal farm-fresh fruits and vegetables (often representative of their ethnic origins, as in the case of the Hmong farmers), as well as farm-made products available year-round (known as value added products), such as honey, jam, cheese, and flavored vinegars. When you shop the farm tables (also known as day tables or daystalls), you have the opportunity to become part of the Market's age-old "Meet the Producer" tradition by buying and learning directly from the producer. If you need advice, don't be bashful about asking how to select, store, clean, and cook the produce you buy. The farmers you buy from will be more than happy to suggest ways to use the goods they've planted, weeded, and picked for your enjoyment.

The large permanent fruit and vegetable highstalls (located in the Main and North Arcades and along Pike Place) are run by independent produce sellers who import their goods from all over the world, and also sell local produce when in season. While you'll find fresh fruits and vegetables at all nine of them, each has developed certain specialties to ensure that customers can find exactly what they want throughout the year.

Some highstalls arrange their fruits and vegetables in ornate displays with signs such as "Don't even THINK of disturbing displays," "Fragile. DO NOT FONDLE," or "AVALANCHE WARNING. Please Ask for Assistance." Woe to the customer who touches an apple or knocks a snow pea out of place. At this type of highstall the clerk will pick out the fruits and vegetables requested from boxes and bins behind the displays. Other highstalls are less formal and allow customers inside to choose their own produce.

But if fruits and vegetables, meat and potatoes, bows and bangles were the only drawing cards of the Market, shoppers might just as easily visit their neighborhood supermarket or mall. The thing that makes the Market unique is its people—low-income seniors, downtown office workers, street people, locals who live in surrounding apartment and condominium towers, tourists, parents with children in tow, strippers who work at the peep shows along First Avenue—all shopping, working, and sometimes even living together. Shoppers are drawn here as much to mingle with the crowds, to see and be seen, and to share in the excitement as to buy a tomato or a flank steak.

In this lively community where women in fur coats and diamonds rub elbows with panhandlers in threadbare suits, where hints of perfume collide with whiffs of muscatel, diversity and spirit are encouraged, indeed, almost demanded. The Market just wouldn't be the same if it were transplanted to a sleepy town or a slick suburb.

Families with long histories in the Market add to the comforting sense of continuity and timelessness found here. There's the Manzo family, whose antecedents emigrated from Italy, began farming in south Seattle at the turn of the century, came to the Market to sell their produce, and ended up owning several highstalls up and down the Main Arcade. The Genzales started as Market farmers in 1922 and today run one of the Market's most popular highstalls, with three generations working side by side. Sol and Irving Amon's father Jack began selling seafood along Pike Place in 1911. Jack bought Pure Food Fish in 1956, and Sol and Irving have owned and operated the atmospheric fish market since 1959.

Count Mike Verdi among the farmers. His mother, Pasqualina, commenced selling at the Market in 1955. She became known as the "queen" of the Market for her feisty nature and the strong

✦✦✦✦✦✦✦✦✦✦✦✦✦✦✦✦✦✦✦✦✦✦✦✦✦✦✦✦✦✦✦✦✦✦

Italian heritage of cooking she passed on to countless customers. Clarissa and Doug Cross, second-generation blueberry farmers, first came to the Market in 1983. They were among the first farmers to create value-added products so they could sell their blueberry jams and syrups year-round, a tradition they carry on to this day.

Is it any wonder that this microcosm of the world has become the most visited landmark in the Pacific Northwest, enjoyed by almost 10 million locals and tourists each year? In her book *The Farm Market Cookbook*, Judith Olney says, "Pike Place is probably the most stimulating and sensuously appealing market in America," and those of us who love it would quickly agree.

History of the Market

It was unseasonably rainy on the evening of August 16, 1907, and August 17th didn't dawn much better. Rain soaked the cobbled and planked streets of Seattle and turned unpaved roadways into little more than muddy trails.

As H. O. Blanchard, a farmer from Renton, wheeled his wagon over the planks of Western Avenue and up onto Pike Place, he didn't know what would await him—who, if anyone, would be waiting to buy his fresh produce at the newly designated public market, begun as an experiment by the Seattle City Council because both farmers and consumers were angry over high food prices.

H. O. was not to be disappointed. About 50 shoppers, most of them women, elbowed aside the single policeman stationed to maintain order, stampeded the farmer's wagon, and bought out his entire load before he could even pull to the curb. The following Saturday the crowds were again willing and eager to buy, and the 70 wagons parked on Pike Place sold out their goods within hours. Both Seattle housewives and area farmers embraced the arrangement that provided direct contact between consumer and producer, and, over the years, the Pike Place Market became a city institution.

It reached its heyday during the 1930s, when, during one year, more than 600 farmers were issued permits to sell. Throughout the Depression, the Market provided a welcoming environment to the city's jobless, as well as inexpensive food for the hungry.

During the 1940s, when the Japanese farmers were interned and many other growers went to work in defense plants, the Market lost nearly half its independent farmer population. Acres of prime farmland were claimed by industry, people moved to the suburbs, and the local supermarket became an accepted convenience. Even the Market's buildings crumbled from neglect; nevertheless, a few hearty farmers hung on and the neighborhood refused to die.

In the 1960s, developers planned to demolish the sagging buildings and put up office and apartment towers on the prime city acreage. But a grassroots citizens' group led by architect and civic leader Victor Steinbrueck formed an organization called the Friends of the Market to save

the beloved landmark. An initiative was put on the ballot on November 2, 1971, and the people of Seattle responded by voting to make the Market an historical district where uses, as well as designs, were preserved.

Strict guidelines were written by the Market Historical Commission, nicknamed "the conscience of the Market." According to *The Pike Place Market: People, Politics, and Produce,* the Commission agreed to always consider the following when evaluating applications for use or development:

1. The Market is a place for the farmer to sell his produce.
2. The Market is a place for the sale of every kind of food product.
3. The Market is a place where citizens in the low and moderate income groups can find food, goods and services, and residences.
4. The Market is and will always be a place with the flavor of a widely varied shopping area.

The Commission encouraged 17 specific types of activity, including person-to-person sales; those offering hard-to-find goods; those involving light manufacturing; those catering particularly to the pedestrian; those offering goods for sale in a natural state, as distinguished from prepackaged goods; and those bringing together people of all backgrounds, enriching the quality of life, or relating to historical Market uses or activities.

The seven-acre historical district (which later grew to nine acres) was placed on the National Register of Historic Places and, in June 1973, the Pike Place Market Preservation and Development Authority (PDA) was mandated by the state to manage the Market in the public's interest. The Authority's mission was and is to purchase, rehabilitate, own, and manage property in the Pike Place Public Market. Over a 15-year period, the PDA renovated or reconstructed every building within the Market Historical District with the help of federal urban-renewal funds and with the philosophy that "it is generally better to preserve than to repair, better to repair than to restore, better to restore than to reconstruct."

◆◆◆◆◆◆◆◆◆◆◆◆◆◆◆◆◆◆◆◆◆◆◆◆◆◆◆◆◆◆◆◆◆◆

As it was originally built, the Market was designed to emphasize the product, not the architecture, and that remains true to this day. Its unpretentious brick, concrete, and timber structures, marquees, open stalls and tables, cast-iron columns, suspended metal lighting fixtures, and tile floors look much as they did during earlier times. The spirit of the old Market has been preserved.

An example of innovative renovation occurred in the early 1980s, when the Market needed a new floor but did not have the necessary funds. For each $35 donation, Market supporters could have their name or message imprinted on a tile. Today, approximately 46,500 tiles cover the floor in the Main and North Arcades.

The consecutive numbers along the outside edge of the walkway are row markers to help locate specific tiles. Look for Ronald and Nancy Reagan's tiles in rows 351 and 352 (just to the south of City Fish), or the tiles imprinted with the prime numbers from one to 100, given by a wife in honor of her mathematician husband (in row 38 in front of DeLaurenti's west entrance).

A less happy chapter in the Market's long history occurred during the early 1990s, when a group of New York City investors who had bought tax benefits on the Market's buildings in the early 1980s claimed they owned and could control the buildings after the tax advantages were abolished in the late 1980s. After battling in both Washington state and New York courts, the PDA and citizens' groups wrestled control from the investors after agreeing to a $2.25 million settlement, and safeguards were put in place so nothing similar could endanger the Market again.

As the 20th century drew to a close and the new millennium dawned, outside forces threatened the Market more than anything internal. These external events included violent riots during the World Trade Organization meeting in Seattle, a break in a 20-inch water main that sent 1.5 million gallons of water cascading through the lower portion of the Market (temporarily closing the Main and North Arcades), and the Nisqually Quake, which rattled the old buildings with a lively 6.8 magnitude. Nonetheless, the Market weathered all these storms and continues to maintain its authentic, quirky personality as it looks steadfastly toward the future.

When to Visit the Market

Many people want to know the best time to visit the Market, and I like to answer "any day," for the Market continually changes with the people who visit it, the farmers and craftspeople who attend, the season of the year, and the weather. No two days at the Market have ever been or could ever be alike, which is another one of its ineffable charms. As Paul Dunn, a longtime Market resident and president of Friends of the Market, says, "You don't need special events at the Market, because the 'regular' Market *is* the event."

However, depending on what you want to buy, certain days of the week are better than others. For the total "Market experience," Saturdays during any season of the year are the best overall day, when you'll encounter the biggest crowds, the largest number of vendors, and the most activity.

Saturdays in summer (when the sun and Mount Rainier are out) are particularly lively. Crafts stalls burst out of the North Arcade and run all the way down to Virginia Street. Couples hold hands, T-shirts and cutoffs abound, and music and laughter permeate the air, while visitors armed with video cameras capture these happy scenes for posterity.

If you're in search of crafts, Mondays and Tuesdays are good days because farmers, worn out from busy weekends, generally don't come. Their tables, even up to the Main Arcade, are often populated by artisans selling everything from handmade bathtub toys to handpainted velvet jackets, from sand paintings to hand-stamped leather belts.

If you want to meet lots of farmers with the widest selection of fresh local produce, Wednesdays and Sundays are your best bets. This is especially true during the growing season (roughly May through October, depending on the weather) thanks to the addition of Organic Farmer Days and Summer Sundays on Pike Place. During these two very special days each week in the Market, farmers sell along Pike Place under colorful awnings, much as farmers did in the earliest days of the Market's history.

At this central selling point, there's a festive atmosphere and a pleasant give-and-take among farmers and their customers, which makes for an easy and memorable shopping experience. On Sundays, local chefs offer free cooking demonstrations using organic produce, to the delight of appreciative crowds. Wednesdays and Sundays belong to local shoppers, who come to the Market in the single-minded pursuit of the choicest flats of raspberries, the sweetest summer squashes, or the most flavorful basil.

Beginning in spring, the farmers' crops include arugula, endive, spinach, lettuces, kale, cabbage, leeks, Chinese mustard greens, bok choy, and edible pea vines. On the farmers' tables during the summer high season, you'll find strawberries, raspberries, blackberries, blueberries, and many other kinds of berries; sugar snap, English shelling, and Chinese snow peas; Kentucky Wonder, Blue Lake, fava, and Romano beans; Walla Walla sweet onions; many varieties of corn; tomatoes; zucchini and squashes; and cucumbers.

Fall heralds the return of golden acorn, Sweet Dumpling, buttercup, butternut, delicata, and spaghetti squashes; sugar pie, miniature, and full-size pumpkins; apples; gourds; Savoy cabbage; collard greens; kale; and brussels sprouts. The winter chill blows in fewer farmers, but those who do come to the Market bring potatoes, beets, chard, kale, turnips, parsnips, carrots, and evergreen wreaths, along with preserved products (such as honeys, jams, and jellies) that are available year-round. (For a more detailed listing, see Produce Availability Chart, page 204.)

During the winter months the sky reflects a thousand different shades of gray, the air turns damp and chill, and a pearlescent light infused with yellow bathes the rain-slicked streets. The crowds are smaller and more local, the Market more solemn and reflective. During this quieter time of the year, the fishmongers, butchers, highstallers, and the few farmers who brave the Market can spend lots of time answering your questions. These can be trying times financially for owner-operated businesses, and by patronizing them during the tough winter months you'll quickly establish yourself as a much-appreciated regular customer.

The winter holidays are an especially beautiful time to visit the Market, when six-foot Noble firs festooned in white lights march across the tops of the tin roofs. Along the roof at the entrance to the Market (just above the Information Booth) you'll discover giant metal sculptures of a carrot, strawberry, and pear wrapped in multicolored lights, while a team of life-sized pink pigs bridled by Christmas tree lights "flies" atop the Main Arcade, the Market's nod to Santa and his reindeer. It's an exciting moment for kids of all ages when the giant vegetables, pigs, and fir trees are illuminated as part of the annual Holiday Tree Lighting.

During this season, customers rush around with lists in hand in search of the freshest Dungeness crabs, crown roasts of beef, local chestnuts, fresh turkeys, and sumptuous desserts for their holiday dinners, as well as that perfect present for Aunt Polly. Laden with sacks of gifts, food, and wine, they trudge through the Market as Thanksgiving, Chanukah, and Christmas draw near.

Regardless of the day or season you decide to visit the Market, you don't have to get up too early to witness it arising. Unlike farmers markets elsewhere, which begin as early as 3 A.M., business along Pike Place Market starts at a more civilized hour. On a clear day, arrive around 7 A.M. and watch the sun rise on the purple horizon and Mount Rainier come out like a snow-capped apparition in the distance, while the soothing sounds of the ferry whistles serenade you.

At this early hour the farmers unload their trucks and set out their produce in elaborate displays, while the fishmongers arrange their slippery charges over ice. The smell of coffee wafts through the air as the restaurants slowly come to life.

Later, around 9 A.M., the craftspeople's roll call takes place at the end of the North Arcade under the direction of the Market Master, who assigns spaces based on seniority and attendance. The craftspeople trundle their heavy, loaded carts over the worn brick street and set up shop in their stalls of the day. Grab a caffe latte and pastry at Le Panier for a whiff of Paris and a ringside seat as all the activity buzzes around you.

By 10 A.M., the Market is in full swing, its maze of farmers, craftspeople, and small-business owners set up and ready to serve you. Stroll at your leisure, stop to chat, buy a handcrafted memento or two, nibble a piece of baklava. Most important of all, soak up the Market's unique ambience as you partake of its endless bounty.

Appetizers

Bruschetta with Fava Beans, Pecorino Romano, and Garden Mint
Smoked Salmon Cheesecake
Mussels with Arugula, Shiitake Mushrooms, and Sugar Snap Peas
Persian Almonds
Shrimp and Shiitake Mushroom Dumplings with Sake Sauce
Cool Calamari in Spicy Tomato Sauce
Chicken Livers à la Streisand
Hot, Hot, Hot Stuffed Mushrooms
Scallop Terrine
Dungeness Crab Piquillo Peppers
Oven Kebabs
Thai Seafood Cakes with Coconut-Chile Sauce
Wild Mushroom Terrine with Apple-Rosemary Vinaigrette

Bruschetta with Fava Beans, Pecorino Romano, and Garden Mint

The Pink Door

Jackie Roberts's fond memories of her grandfather eating raw fava beans along with a wedge of cheese, a hunk of crusty bread, and a glass of wine inspired this springtime appetizer she serves at The Pink Door. Luckily, in her rendition, the favas are briefly cooked before being puréed with garlic, parsley, and olive oil to form a bright green spread.

◆ To prepare fava beans, remove beans from shells and discard shells. Bring a medium saucepan of water to a boil and add beans. Cook 30 to 60 seconds, drain, and rinse in cold water. When beans are cool enough to handle, slit one side of husk with tip of a small, sharp kitchen knife, and pop out the beans inside. Repeat with remaining beans, which should yield about 4 cups.

◆ Place beans, parsley, and garlic in a food processor and pulse until beans resemble small pebbles. With motor running, add olive oil in a thin, slow stream until it reaches a thick consistency, scraping down sides of work bowl once or twice. You may need anywhere from ¾ to 1 cup of oil.

◆ Transfer bean mixture to a medium mixing bowl and stir in ¾ cup of the lemon juice. Add additional lemon juice if necessary to reach a spreadable consistency. Stir in salt and pepper, taste purée, and add more salt or pepper, if desired.

◆ To serve, spread fava bean purée on Bruschetta. Using a clean, dry vegetable peeler, shave curls of cheese over Bruschetta and sprinkle with mint.

Makes about 3 cups

Bruschetta

◆ Preheat broiler. Arrange bread slices on a baking sheet and place 3 to 4 inches from heat source. Broil 1 to 2 minutes on each side, or until golden brown. Remove from oven and rub

4 to 5 pounds fresh fava beans in the shell

¼ cup coarsely chopped fresh flat-leaf parsley

1 large clove garlic, coarsely chopped

¾ to 1 cup olive oil

¾ to 1 cup freshly squeezed lemon juice

¼ teaspoon kosher salt, or to taste

⅛ teaspoon freshly ground white pepper, or to taste

Bruschetta (recipe follows)

1 ounce Pecorino Romano cheese

Bruschetta

¼ cup chopped fresh mint

1 loaf crusty country bread, cut into ½-inch slices

2 large cloves garlic, halved

¼ cup extra virgin olive oil

one side of each bread slice with the halved cloves of garlic, then brush lightly with olive oil.

Cook's Hint: Although your first instinct might be to use extra virgin olive oil in the fava bean purée, Jackie advises against it in this particular recipe. It is too pungent and makes the purée bitter instead of buttery smooth. A good second-press olive oil does the job and is less expensive than extra virgin oil.

TOTEM SMOKEHOUSE

The tradition of smoked seafood in the Northwest, particularly salmon, goes back to the time of the Native Americans. They often left their salmon in the smokehouse for two weeks, which resulted in a dark brown, very smoky salmon. The Indians then took the smoked salmon, dried and seasoned it, and cut it into thin strips to make "squaw candy"—something similar to beef jerky that was eaten between meals as a snack.

Today, "squaw candy," or salmon jerky, is a popular item at Totem Smokehouse—which opened in 1978 and is the only store in the Market devoted exclusively to smoked seafood. It is known not only for its smoked sockeye, king, and pink salmon products, but also for the less commonly available smoked oysters, rainbow trout, albacore tuna, and scallops. At the storefront along Pike Place, samples are abundant and the employees are helpful .

All of Totem's seafood is prepared in the traditional manner of the Northwest Coast Indians: cured in a special brine of spices and then slow-smoked over alder-wood fires with no added colors, preservatives, or sugars. Careful smoking and packaging results in the moist and tender texture and richly smoked flavor for which Totem is famous.

Smoked Salmon Cheesecake

Totem Smokehouse

This rich, savory cheesecake was created by Jane Poole, who, along with partners Mark Zenger and Rebecca Petre, operate Totem Smokehouse. Slice it thinly and serve with flutes of champagne or small glasses of iced vodka for a super-elegant appetizer, or make it the showy centerpiece of a holiday or brunch buffet table.

◆ Preheat oven to 375°F. Lightly grease a 9-inch springform pan or spray with nonstick cooking spray.

◆ In a small mixing bowl combine butter, bread crumbs, and ⅔ cup of the walnuts until well blended. Pat crust mixture into bottom and up sides of springform pan and reserve.

◆ With an electric mixer, blend cream cheese and sugar until fluffy. Add eggs and beat until smooth. Add lemon juice, garlic, and basil and beat until smooth. Pour mixture into springform pan.

◆ Bake 25 to 30 minutes, or until filling is set. Remove from oven and cool to room temperature. Refrigerate until ready to serve.

◆ About 30 minutes before serving, remove cheesecake from refrigerator and bring to room temperature. Sprinkle remaining ⅓ cup walnuts and smoked salmon evenly over top of cheesecake and cut into thin slices.

Serves 12 to 16

1 tablespoon unsalted butter, room temperature

1 cup store-bought dry Italian-flavored bread crumbs

1 cup chopped walnuts

2 packages (8 ounces each) cream cheese, room temperature

⅓ cup granulated sugar

3 large eggs

¼ cup freshly squeezed lemon juice

1 clove garlic, minced

1 cup chopped fresh basil

1 can (5½ ounce) Totem Smokehouse smoked salmon, drained, skin removed, crumbled

MATT'S IN THE MARKET

The lunchtime crowd bellies up to the counter or jockeys for one of the half-dozen tables at Matt's in the Market. With just 9 stools, 14 table seats, a surfeit of hungry diners, and a "no-reservations" policy, the place is usually packed just after it opens at 11:30 A.M.

The lucky few sit at solid wooden tables draped with blue-striped tablecloths and enjoy a bird's-eye view of the Market clock and the activity on bustling Pike Place. Jazz from owner Matt Janke's personal collection plays softly in the background; the casual mood feels more Louisiana bayou than Seattle slick.

Signature dishes at lunch include a crab-filled gumbo redolent of the traditional filé, or sassafras, powder that's used for thickening. It's spicy but not lip-searing. The Honkin' Hot Albacore Tuna Sandwich is a slab of albacore crusted with wasabi, seared rare, and served with mustard pickle relish. Don't miss the Cornmeal-Crusted Catfish or the Oyster Sandwich, reminiscent of a New Orleans po' boy.

The dinner menu changes every two to three months, inspired by what's fresh and in season when Chef Erik Cannella shops in the Market. Save room for dessert and order the bread pudding, which is studded with dried cranberries and chunks of chocolate. It would taste good paired with a glass of red wine or a port from Matt's eclectic, personally selected list.

Mussels with Arugula, Shiitake Mushrooms, and Sugar Snap Peas

Matt's in the Market

Like all recipes, this one is simply a framework for your own creative embellishments, advises Matt Janke, who suggests substituting fava beans, asparagus, mizuna, kale, or beet greens as they come into season for a variety of flavors and textures to complement the mussels and dipping broth. Penn Cove mussels, which are grown just outside of Seattle on Whidbey Island, are Matt's mussel of choice. Brothers Rawle and Ian Jefferds, who co-own Penn Cove Shellfish, have been delivering straight to Matt's door since he opened for business in 1996.

2 tablespoons olive oil

6 ounces shiitake mushrooms, cleaned, stems removed and discarded, and quartered

3 tablespoons chopped shallots

1 teaspoon chopped garlic

½ to 1 teaspoon crushed red pepper flakes

1 cup peeled, seeded, and chopped plum tomatoes (see Techniques section)

- Heat olive oil in a stockpot over medium-high heat. Add mushrooms, shallots, garlic, and pepper flakes and cook 2 to 3 minutes, or until garlic begins to turn golden and the mushrooms shrink slightly, stirring frequently.

- Add tomatoes and mussels and stir well; then add arugula, sugar snap peas, and beer, and stir well. Cover and bring to a gentle boil, then cook 5 to 7 minutes, or until mussels have opened, stirring occasionally. Discard any mussels that do not open. Season to taste with salt and pepper.

- To serve, divide mussels among individual bowls or present them in a communal bowl along with seafood forks, shell bowls, and extra napkins.

Serves 4 as an appetizer, 2 as an entrée

2 pounds Penn Cove mussels, scrubbed and debearded just before cooking

1 cup shredded arugula (Note: To shred the arugula, align the leaves and cut into ¼-inch slices with a sharp knife)

½ pound sugar snap peas, rinsed, patted dry, and strings removed

1 cup beer or dry white wine

Kosher salt

Freshly ground black pepper

STACKHOUSE BROTHERS ORCHARDS

Rodney and Don Stackhouse, brothers and second-generation orchardists, have been farming together in the fertile San Joaquin Valley of California for more than 30 years. Each day, Rodney walks through the orchards, making sure every tree is producing the perfect crop he demands. Meanwhile, Don oversees the harvest of ripe fruit and nuts so that quality is maintained throughout the processing and packaging phase.

You'll find Myrna and Keeley (wife and daughter, respectively, of Don Stackhouse) or Percy (their affable agent) in the North Arcade of the Market seven days a week, all year round. They sell almonds of all sorts, dark and golden raisins the size of your thumbnail, and dried apricots, nectarines, and peaches as big as half dollars.

Sampling is highly encouraged here, since in addition to the dried fruits, the almonds come in natural (raw), plain-roasted, hickory-smoked, garlic-onion, cheese-jalapeño, honey-roasted, cinnamon, raspberry, and orange-honey flavors.

Persian Almonds

Stackhouse Brothers Orchards

¼ cup water

1 tablespoon sea salt

2 pounds raw almonds

Enjoy these salted almonds with a glass of fino sherry, a wedge of manchego cheese, and a plate of oil-cured olives (available at The Spanish Table and some upscale grocery stores) for a satisfying combination of colors, flavors, and textures.

◆ Place water and sea salt in a small glass measuring bowl and stir until salt is almost completely dissolved. Put measuring bowl in microwave oven until ready to heat.

◆ Place almonds in a large, dry skillet over medium heat. Stir constantly 10 to 15 minutes, or until the nuts begin to crackle.

◆ Just after nuts begin to crackle, heat salted water in microwave oven on HIGH about 30 seconds to 1 minute, or until the water boils.

◆ Remove nuts from the heat and pour the salt mixture over them. Stir constantly until they turn white. Turn almonds out onto a baking sheet and allow to cool and dry in the open air, about 15 to 30 minutes. Store in an airtight container or resealable plastic bag until ready to serve.

Makes 6 cups

Shrimp and Shiitake Mushroom Dumplings with Sake Sauce

Etta's Seafood

A fellow chef dubbed Tom Douglas "an Asian man in a white man's body" because of his affinity and love for Pacific Rim cuisines. Tom is also a man who enjoys eating out, and this variation on dim sum was inspired by a meal he enjoyed at a local Chinese restaurant.

◆ Pulse shrimp in a food processor until smooth. Place shrimp in a large bowl and gently stir in green onion, cilantro, bean sprouts, soy sauce, pepper flakes, sesame seeds, and shiitake mushrooms. Cover and refrigerate.

◆ Using a soup spoon, form prawn mixture into 1-inch balls and flatten slightly with back of spoon.

◆ Heat peanut oil in a large skillet over medium heat. Cook dumplings in batches until light golden brown on both sides, adding more oil as necessary. When all the dumplings have been browned, drain off excess oil and return all the dumplings to the skillet.

◆ Add chicken stock to the skillet, bring to a boil, cover the pan with a lid or aluminum foil, and simmer 3 to 5 minutes. Dumplings are done when they are springy and firm to the touch; cut one open if in doubt. *Do not overcook*, or the dumplings will become rubbery.

◆ Lift dumplings out of the stock and arrange on a large serving platter or individual appetizer plates. Ladle Sake Sauce over dumplings and garnish with bean sprouts.

Serves 4 to 6

Sake Sauce

◆ Mix all the ingredients in a small glass dish, cover, and use immediately or refrigerate until ready to use.

Makes about 1¼ cups

1 pound shrimp, peeled and deveined

1 green onion, roots and top ¼-inch removed and discarded, remaining portion chopped

2 tablespoons chopped cilantro

2 cups mung bean sprouts, plus extra for garnish

2 tablespoons soy sauce

½ teaspoon crushed red pepper flakes

1 tablespoon sesame seeds

½ cup coarsely chopped shiitake mushrooms

¼ cup peanut oil

1 cup homemade chicken stock, or ½ cup canned chicken broth plus ½ cup water

Sake Sauce (recipe follows)

Sake Sauce

½ cup sake

¼ cup soy sauce

⅓ cup unseasoned rice vinegar

2 tablespoons Vietnamese fish sauce (nuoc mam)

1½ teaspoons red chile paste with garlic

2 tablespoons very thinly sliced green onion

Just north of the Market, next door to the Seattle Athletic Club (one of the city's prime workout spots) and overlooking Victor Steinbrueck Park, Etta's Seafood* dishes out some of the most creative and playful food in all of Seattle. It's the brainchild of Tom Douglas, a James Beard Award–winning chef who's recognized as one of the granddaddies of Northwest cuisine, and his wife and business partner Jackie Cross. The duo also own two other restaurants a bit farther uptown: the Dahlia Lounge (opened in 1989) and the Palace Kitchen (1996).

Etta's opened in 1995 in the former Cafe Sport space—coincidentally, the very restaurant where Tom debuted as a chef and served as general manager. There's a casual, clubby atmosphere and often a wait to get in, especially without reservations. But once seated in the sunny front dining room or more intimate dining room behind the bar, you get to sample some of Tom's signature dishes. These include his Tasty Sashimi Tuna Salad with Green Onion Pancakes; Dungeness crab cakes; Whole Maine Lobster Wok-Seared with Fermented Black Beans, Garlic, and Chiles; and Triple Coconut Cream Pie. Don't miss one of the best salmon dishes in town: Etta's Spice-Rubbed and Pit-Roasted King Salmon with Corn Bread Pudding and Shiitake Relish. If you have time for only one salmon dish in Seattle, this is the one to try.

As Tom explains in *Tom Douglas' Seattle Kitchen,* an engaging and heartfelt portrait of the Seattle food scene, "Etta's, named after our daughter, Loretta, showcases the best and freshest local seafood and continues the creative amalgam of traditions and flavors that is the signature of Seattle cooking."

*Just outside of the Market Historic District.

Cool Calamari in Spicy Tomato Sauce

Andaluca, Mayflower Park Hotel

Since 1999, Wayne Johnson has been executive chef at Andaluca,* the romantic, Mediterranean-inspired restaurant in downtown Seattle's venerable Mayflower Park Hotel. And since 1999, Chef Wayne and his staff have been regulars at the Market, stopping by several times a week to see what's fresh and new at Sosio's, Pure Food Fish, Don & Joe's Meats, and DeLaurenti, and on the organic farmers' tables. This recipe is inspired by the specialty classes in Mediterranean cuisine that

1½ cups water

1 pound cleaned squid, bodies cut into ½-inch rings, large tentacles cut in half

2 tablespoons olive oil

1 cup diced white or yellow onion

2 teaspoons minced garlic

1 teaspoon kosher salt

Wayne took while training at the famed Culinary Institute of America (CIA) in the Napa Valley.

◆ Bring water to a boil in a large saucepan. Add squid and cook 1 to 2 minutes. Remove pan from the heat, transfer squid to a colander, and immediately rinse under cold running water. Drain completely and transfer squid to a medium bowl. Use immediately, or cover and refrigerate until ready to use.

◆ Heat olive oil in a large skillet over medium heat and cook onion, garlic, salt, and ½ teaspoon of the pepper flakes for 3 minutes, or until onions are translucent, stirring frequently.

◆ Add tomatoes, lemon zest, rosemary, and tomato paste and stir well. Bring to a boil, reduce heat, and simmer 5 minutes, stirring occasionally. Taste and add the remaining ½ teaspoon pepper flakes, if desired.

◆ Remove sauce from heat and cool to room temperature. Place cooked calamari and parsley in a medium mixing bowl, add sauce, and stir gently to mix. Serve immediately, or cover and refrigerate until ready to use.

Serves 4 to 6

Cook's Hint: Chef Wayne likes to serve this zesty dish like a Spanish tapa (appetizer) or as a tantalizing first course for a dinner party. If serving as a first course, for pleasing visual and textural contrast, he suggests accompanying the calamari with Bruschetta (page 2) and a small pile of baby arugula tossed in a simple lemon vinaigrette. I've also tossed the spicy sauce and calamari (after rewarming) with cooked pasta for a satisfying entrée.

*Outside of the Market Historic District.

½ to 1 teaspoon crushed red pepper flakes

2 cups crushed plum tomatoes in purée (Note: Crushed plum tomatoes in purée are a canned product available at DeLaurenti in the Market and upscale grocery stores)

2 teaspoons minced fresh lemon zest

2 teaspoons minced fresh rosemary

1 teaspoon tomato paste

2 tablespoons minced fresh flat-leaf parsley

PATTI SUMMERS

I n 1984 vocalist Patti Summers and husband/bassist Gary Steele realized a long-held dream when they got off the lounge circuit and opened Patti Summers, a restaurant, bar, and live music venue at First and Pike in the Corner Market Building. Patti had visions of dressing beautifully, greeting her guests for dinner, singing both her own and other musicians' compositions to entertain her guests, and hosting famous jazz players from all over the country. But day-to-day problems kept getting in the way, from prima donna chefs to drug dealers doing business in the lounge during lunch.

Taking matters in hand, Patti and Gary cleaned up the place and Patti became chef. "I thought aïoli and calamari were towns in Italy," the flamboyant entertainer says with a roll of her expressive eyes. "If I had known when we bought the restaurant I would end up as the working chef, we never would have bought it. But today, to my knowledge, I run the only restaurant in Seattle where the entertainer and owner is also the chef."

The grotto-like space down a shallow flight of stairs at the busiest corner of the Market features "gourmet Italian dining and great music, everything from Big Band to jazz to rock, depending on the night of the week," according to Patti. There's not a bad seat in the house, and at least part of the couple's original dream survives intact—Patti and Gary have played host to such jazz luminaries as Freddie Hubbard, Bobby McFerrin, and Diane Schuur.

Chicken Livers à la Streisand

Patti Summers

This divine pâté, which is as light as a mousse and slightly sweet, is best served on a bed of green or red leaf lettuce, garnished with baby bagels, cream cheese, cornichons, cherry tomatoes, and thinly sliced sweet onion rings.

◆ Heat olive oil in a large skillet over medium-high heat and sauté chicken livers 4 minutes, stirring constantly. Turn heat to low; add onion, garlic, mace, allspice, ginger, thyme, and bay leaf and cook 3 minutes more, stirring constantly, until chicken livers darken and begin to crumble on the surface. Remove bay leaf and place mixture in a food processor or blender.

◆ Pulse mixture until chicken livers are mashed but not smooth, then add butter, whipping cream, and Cognac. Pulse again until mixture reaches desired consistency, which can range from slightly chunky to silky smooth.

◆ Spoon mixture into a 5-by-9-inch loaf pan, smooth top, and chill overnight to let the flavors meld. Cut around edges, turn loaf pan upside down, turn pâté out onto a plate, and cut into 1-inch slices. Serve on a bed of lettuce with the garnishes described above.

Serves 8

5 tablespoons olive oil

1 pound chicken livers

⅓ cup minced white or yellow onion

1 clove garlic, minced

Pinch of ground mace

Pinch of ground allspice

Pinch of ground ginger

Pinch of dried thyme

1 bay leaf

½ cup unsalted butter

½ cup whipping cream

2 tablespoons Cognac

3 to 4 large lettuce leaves, rinsed, drained, and spun dry

Hot, Hot, Hot Stuffed Mushrooms

Micks Peppouri

There's something so satisfying and slightly retro about stuffed mushrooms, but this rendition submitted by Mick family matriarch Ginger Mick takes a turn toward the wild side with the addition of hot pepper or wine jelly. In fact, part of the fun of this recipe is varying the jelly that tops the mushrooms to give them a distinctive flavor and aroma.

16 large or 32 medium button or cremini mushrooms, stem ends trimmed

2 tablespoons extra virgin olive oil

5 tablespoons unsalted butter, melted

MICKS PEPPOURI

One of the Market's great success stories, Micks Peppouri, started in eastern Washington in the mid-1970s when Walter Mick received a jar of pepper jelly, plus the recipe to make it, as a gift. The elementary school principal started experimenting with the recipe, sharing samples with friends, family, business associates, and just about anybody else who would taste them. As time went by, more and more people encouraged him to bottle and sell his pepper jelly.

In 1982, Walt and wife Ginger formed Micks Peppouri and began selling Walt's pepper jelly on the farmers' tables in the Pike Place Market. Buoyed by their success, the couple created new flavors, leased a prime permanent selling space, and started winning awards at fancy-food shows. The Micks' most stunning victory occurred in 1997, when they swept their category at the National Fiery Food Challenge, winning first, second, and third places.

Today, the Micks still make their jellies the old-fashioned way, using fruits and vegetables raised by family members in the Yakima Valley. Made of fresh, natural ingredients, the jellies contain no fat, salt, or cholesterol. In addition to the pepper jellies (which are available in eight levels of heat, from totally mild to extremely hot), their product line has expanded to include pepper jellies flavored with garlic, ginger, horseradish, lime, and cranberry. Wine jellies—the family's first product not made with peppers—are flavored with Chardonnay, Cabernet, and Merlot.

You're invited to try all these creative products at the Micks' permanent stand in the Main Arcade seven days a week.

◆ Preheat oven to 350°F. Lightly oil a 9-by-13-inch baking pan and reserve.

◆ Quickly rinse and pat dry the mushrooms; then remove the stems, coarsely dice, and reserve. With a clean pastry brush, lightly brush the mushroom caps inside and out with olive oil.

◆ In a medium mixing bowl, mix butter, bread crumbs, water chestnuts, and the reserved mushroom pieces. Add egg and cheese, and stir until completely combined.

◆ Stuff mushrooms with bread mixture and cook 10 to 12 minutes, or until tops turn golden. Remove from oven. Drizzle the tops of the mushrooms with jelly and serve immediately.

Makes 16 appetizers

¾ cup unseasoned dry bread crumbs (see Techniques section)

¼ cup chopped canned water chestnuts

1 large egg

¼ cup freshly grated Parmesan cheese

¼ cup Micks Pepper or Wine Jelly, lightly whipped with a fork

Scallop Terrine

Ray's Boathouse

In 2002, Ray's Boathouse* took home a coveted America's Classic award from the prestigious James Beard House in New York City. The award is given to long-established restaurants deeply rooted in their communities, which is a good description of Ray's. Founded in 1939 as a "boathouse," a place where locals could rent boats and purchase fishing supplies, in 1973 it opened as a restaurant and has been serving innovative treatments of Northwest seafood ever since. Executive chef Charles Ramseyer, who shared this sophisticated recipe, signed on in 1993 after cooking his way around the world from his native Switzerland. The chef and his crew are frequent participants in the Sunset and Harvest Suppers and Taste of the Nation, events that benefit the Market Foundation.

◆ Position a rack in the center of the oven. Preheat oven to 375°F. Line a 4-by-8-inch loaf pan with plastic wrap, leaving a 4-inch overlap of plastic wrap on each side, and reserve.

◆ Remove any excess moisture from scallops by rolling in a clean kitchen towel or paper towels. Place scallops in a food processor and pulse 30 seconds. Add egg white and process 20 seconds, or until mixture becomes thick and doughlike. Scrape down the sides of the work bowl.

◆ With processor running, add lemon juice, Pernod, Worcestershire sauce, and cayenne. Add whipping cream slowly, until mixture becomes smooth, scraping down the work bowl as needed. Season to taste with salt and pepper. Transfer scallop mixture to a chilled mixing bowl, cover, and refrigerate 30 minutes.

◆ Transfer scallop mixture to prepared loaf pan, spread evenly to the sides of the pan, and wrap tightly with excess plastic wrap. Place loaf pan in a larger pan that will hold it without crowding. Pour boiling water halfway up sides of the larger loaf pan, then transfer entire unit to the center of the oven.

½ pound scallops, rinsed, drained, patted dry, and with the side muscles removed

1 egg white

Juice of half a lemon

1 teaspoon Pernod or other anise-flavored liqueur

1 teaspoon Worcestershire sauce

Pinch of cayenne pepper

1 cup whipping cream

Kosher salt

Freshly ground black pepper

- Lower oven temperature to 275°F and cook 45 to 55 minutes, or until scallop meat bounces back when you touch it gently with your finger and a sharp knife inserted in the center comes out clean and warm to the touch, or the terrine reaches an internal temperature of 140°F. Remove loaf pan from water bath and allow to rest 15 minutes. Remove terrine from pan, unwrap plastic, and transfer terrine to a serving platter.

- Cut terrine into slices and serve warm. Alternatively, leave terrine whole and wrapped in the plastic, refrigerate, and slice just before serving.

Serves 6 to 8

Cook's Hint: Chef Charles notes that in order to prevent the scallop mixture from separating, it is very important that all the ingredients, the food processor blade, and mixing bowl be well chilled before starting the recipe. It is also very important to use "dry" scallops, those that have not been soaked in chemicals during processing, or the terrine will become watery and break apart. Once cooked, the terrine can be served hot with Dungeness crabmeat sauce, chive-lemon butter, or lobster sauce. If serving cold, he suggests using either a dill cream sauce or chive sour cream topped with a dollop of caviar. To vary the flavor of the terrine itself, try adding half a pound of crabmeat or shrimp and/or three tablespoons of chopped fresh chives.

*Outside of the Market Historic District.

Dungeness Crab Piquillo Peppers

The Spanish Table

Piquillo peppers are hand-picked, wood-fire-roasted, hand-peeled peppers from Spain that are often stuffed. *Picada* is a crushed nut sauce composed of almonds, hazelnuts, pine nuts, olive oil, bread, garlic, and salt. In this dish, the sweet nuttiness of *picada*, rich Dungeness crab, and sherry-laced white sauce combine with the mild tanginess of *piquillo* peppers to form an authentic tapa (appetizer) recipe.

1 tablespoon amontillado or cream sherry

½ pound Dungeness crabmeat, picked over for shells and cartilage

1 tablespoon minced fresh flat-leaf parsley

16 green or red piquillo peppers

½ cup dry white wine

- ◆ Preheat oven to 350°F.

- ◆ Pour half the White Sauce into a small saucepan over medium heat, add sherry, stir well, and cook until sauce is heated through. Remove sauce from heat and gently stir in crab and parsley, being careful not to break up crab pieces.

- ◆ With a teaspoon, separate the lips of one of the piquillo peppers, then hold between your thumb and forefinger to create a pocket. Spoon in about 1½ tablespoons of crab filling, depending on size of peppers. Repeat with remaining peppers, placing peppers in a medium baking dish, glass pie plate, or cazuela (Spanish terra-cotta baking dish) as you finish stuffing them. If using a round cazuela, place the points toward the center so they form a "rose."

- ◆ Add the remaining White Sauce to the small saucepan, add white wine, and cook over medium heat 2 to 3 minutes, or until alcohol evaporates. Stir in picada until well blended, remove sauce from the heat, then pour sauce over peppers. Bake peppers 20 to 25 minutes, or until they are heated through. If desired, sprinkle lightly with smoked paprika.

- ◆ To serve, place peppers on a colorful platter or serve directly out of the cazuela.

Makes 16 appetizers

White Sauce

- ◆ Melt butter in a small saucepan over medium heat and whisk in flour, stirring constantly. Slowly add milk, stirring well after each addition of milk. When sauce reaches the consistency of heavy whipping cream, remove from heat and add salt to taste.

Makes 1 cup sauce

Cook's Hint: If *picada* is unavailable, in a mortar and pestle crush five hazelnuts and five pine nuts, then add ¼ teaspoon minced garlic and a pinch of sea salt (Spanish recommended) and crush until blended. Add 1 tablespoon fresh or dry bread crumbs (see Techniques section) and 1 tablespoon Spanish extra virgin olive oil. Combine until the ingredients form a thick paste.

1 tablespoon Molí de Pomerí picada

Sweet, bittersweet, or spicy smoked paprika (pimentón) (optional)

1 cup White Sauce (recipe follows)

White Sauce

2 tablespoons unsalted butter

2 tablespoons all-purpose flour

1 cup whole milk

Pinch of kosher salt

THE SOUK

Webster's Dictionary defines a souk as a marketplace in North Africa or the Middle East. For the past 25 years the Soames-Dunn Building has housed its own Souk, a marketplace where silk scarves and Indian movie posters hang in the windows, and where the fragrance of exotic spices—curry, saffron, turmeric, garam masala—perfumes the air.

Seattle's Souk is a mecca for Middle Eastern, Indian, and Pakistani delicacies. In the cooler you'll find *halal* meats that have been slaughtered and prepared according to the strict guidelines of Islam. Wooden barrels hold numerous varieties of basmati rices, legumes, and lentils available in bulk. Black lemons, piled in a tall jar like shrunken heads, add a distinctive flavor to soups, lamb dishes, or rice.

Dozens of brands of chutneys and pickles; quince, date, eggplant, and fig jams; dried apricot paste from Syria; and even toiletries line the sagging shelves. Other reminders of home for Seattle's Indian and Arabic émigrés include newspapers and magazines, audio- and videotapes, and calendars in Arabic as well as in several Indian tongues.

Oven Kebabs

The Souk

These flavorful morsels may be the Pakistani answer to the ever-popular Swedish meatball. They're fun to make and go down easy, especially when paired with a spicy dipping sauce, Thai peanut sauce, or Apricot Sweet-and-Sour Sauce (page 63). Larger patties can be served as an entrée along with Pea Pullao (page 58) and a green salad.

◆ Preheat broiler and adjust oven racks so that top rack is about 3 inches from heat source.

◆ Mix all the ingredients thoroughly and form into small balls or flatten into 3-inch patties about 1 inch thick. Arrange on baking sheets and broil 3 to 5 minutes on each side, depending on desired doneness. Serve as described above.

Serves 12 or 16 as an appetizer, 8 as an entrée

2 pounds lean ground beef

¼ teaspoon ground cloves

¼ teaspoon ground cardamom

¼ teaspoon freshly ground black pepper

¼ teaspoon ground cumin

¼ teaspoon ground ginger

¼ teaspoon ground cayenne pepper

1 tablespoon plain yogurt

1 large white or yellow onion, diced

Kosher salt to taste

THE PIKE PUB & BREWERY

Visitors to Seattle (and savvy locals) are always delighted to discover there's a spacious modern brewery just half a block south of the Pike Place Market where they can watch several varieties of beer in production. This wasn't always the case.

The Pike Pub & Brewery* started back in 1989 in a cubbyhole space on Western Avenue, where Market Cellar Winery is now located. The brainchild of Charles Finkel, a beer and wine merchant and an expert on food and wine pairing, the tiny brewery produced Pike Pale Ale, Pike Kilt Lifter Scotch Style Ale, Pike Naughty Nellie's Ale, Pike India Pale Ale, and other microbrews.

Positive reports about Pike beer started to spread. Beer writer Michael Jackson named Pike as one of the three American breweries whose products he would choose if marooned on a desert isle. The reputations of a handful of small craft breweries such as Pike helped put the Northwest on the radar screen of discriminating beer lovers around the world.

As demand increased, the production facilities expanded to 20,000 square feet and moved up to First Avenue in 1996. In the new digs, you'll find a 12,000-barrel brewery, a 200-seat pub, a cigar room, and a beer museum teeming with memorabilia and nostalgia. The restaurant serves the expected pub grub—burgers, sandwiches, pizza, salads, and finger food—as well as more ambitious offerings such as the following appetizer.

*Just outside of the Market Historic District.

Thai Seafood Cakes with Coconut-Chile Sauce

The Pike Pub & Brewery

Baking these Asian-inspired seafood cakes saves some calories and lightens the flavor, but they're also delicious pan-fried in a skillet or on the griddle. Chef Gary Marx serves the cakes drizzled with a luscious sweet-hot sauce, along with a fistful of wild salad greens on the side, and pickled ginger and a lime wedge for extra color and flavor contrasts.

◆ In a large mixing bowl, stir together the bell peppers, parsley, mayonnaise, lime juice, Worcestershire sauce, egg yolks, cayenne, chile sauce, salt, and pepper until well blended.

2½ tablespoons diced red bell peppers

¼ cup chopped fresh flat-leaf parsley

½ cup mayonnaise

¼ cup freshly squeezed lime juice

2 teaspoons Worcestershire sauce

4 large egg yolks

¼ teaspoon cayenne pepper

2 tablespoons Thai sweet chile sauce (Mae Ploy brand recommended)

Gently stir in 1¼ cups of the panko plus the shrimp and crabmeat, being careful not to break up the crab. Cover and refrigerate 1 to 2 hours.

◆ About 15 minutes before cooking, preheat oven to 375°F. Lightly spray a baking sheet with nonstick cooking spray. Place flour on a small plate with a rim and season with salt and pepper. Place the eggs and water in a small mixing bowl and whisk thoroughly. Place the remaining 2 cups panko on a small plate with a rim.

◆ Scoop the crab mixture into a ¼-cup measuring cup, pressing firmly. Rap the cup sharply to remove the crab ball, then lightly dust in seasoned flour, lightly dip in egg wash, and cover with panko. Place on prepared baking sheet, press down gently to form a cake, and repeat with remaining crab mixture. It helps if you designate one hand for the wet ingredients and one hand for the dry to avoid a sticky mess.

◆ Spray seafood cakes lightly with nonstick cooking spray and bake 15 to 20 minutes, or until light golden brown and firm around the edges. To serve, divide among individual plates and drizzle with Coconut-Chile Sauce.

Makes 20 cakes; serves 10 as an appetizer

Coconut-Chile Sauce

Whisk together all the ingredients in a small mixing bowl. Serve immediately, or cover and refrigerate.

Makes about 1½ cups

½ teaspoon kosher salt, plus extra for seasoning flour

½ teaspoon freshly ground black pepper, plus extra for seasoning flour

3¼ cups panko (Japanese bread crumbs)

¾ pound bay shrimp, lightly rinsed, patted dry, and chopped

¾ pound Dungeness crabmeat, picked over for shells and cartilage, gently patted dry if moist

1 cup all-purpose flour

2 large eggs

¼ cup water

Coconut-Chile Sauce (recipe follows)

Coconut-Chile Sauce

¾ cup mayonnaise

½ cup Thai sweet chile sauce (Mae Ploy brand recommended)

¼ cup coconut milk

1 tablespoon chopped fresh flat-leaf parsley

1 tablespoon freshly squeezed lime juice

Wild Mushroom Terrine
with Apple-Rosemary Vinaigrette

Rover's

Thierry Rautureau, chef/owner of Rover's,* began his culinary apprenticeship in the French countryside at the age of 14. He's a great proponent of the Market because it reminds him of the town markets in Europe he remembers from his childhood. Since 1987, Thierry has been serving up Northwest-inspired French food at Rover's, where he specializes in exquisite five- and eight-course tasting menus. Those menus might include an innovative terrine like the one below, which the ebullient "chef in the hat" created for one of the Market Foundation's Harvest Suppers. When sliced, this beautiful appetizer reminds me of stained-glass windows.

◆ Lightly brush a small terrine mold or a 4-by-8-inch loaf pan with vegetable oil. Cut parchment paper to fit the sides and bottom of the pan, press into pan, and brush parchment lightly with vegetable oil. Set aside.

◆ Heat 2 tablespoons of the hazelnut oil in a large skillet over medium-high heat and add mushrooms. Cook 5 to 8 minutes, or until mushrooms shrink slightly and begin to lose their juice, stirring occasionally. Add 1 tablespoon of the shallots, plus half of the garlic, chives, and thyme; cook 2 minutes, stirring constantly. If vegetables start to stick, add the remaining 1 tablespoon oil. Season to taste with salt and pepper and set aside to cool.

◆ Mix goat cheese with the remaining 1 tablespoon shallots plus the remaining garlic, chives, and thyme. Season with salt and pepper, then mix with cooled mushrooms.

◆ Spread mushroom/cheese mixture evenly in the prepared pan, press plastic wrap directly onto the surface to cover, and refrigerate for at least 4 hours or (preferably) overnight to allow the flavors to meld.

2 to 3 tablespoons hazelnut oil

1 pound wild and cultivated mushrooms such as shiitake, oyster, cremini, chanterelle, boletus, morel, cauliflower, coral, or lacteria, cleaned and coarsely chopped. (Note: If using shiitake mushrooms, be sure to cut away and discard the stem, which is tough.)

2 tablespoons minced shallots

1 teaspoon minced garlic

3 tablespoons chopped fresh chives

2 sprigs lemon thyme, rinsed and leaves picked from stems (Note: If lemon thyme is unavailable, substitute 2 sprigs thyme, rinsed and leaves picked from stems plus ⅛ teaspoon finely grated fresh lemon zest)

Kosher salt

Freshly ground black pepper

6 ounces fresh, soft goat's-milk cheese (chèvre)

Apple-Rosemary Vinaigrette (recipe follows)

Sprigs of bronze fennel, for garnish (optional)

◆ To serve, unmold terrine and cut into ¾-inch slices. Arrange slices on a decorative platter, drizzle with Apple-Rosemary Vinaigrette, and garnish with fennel sprigs, if desired.

Serves 8

Apple-Rosemary Vinaigrette

◆ Place the vinegar, oils, shallot, and wine in a blender or food processor and pulse until well blended. Pour into a small mixing bowl, add the apple, stir well, and season to taste with salt and pepper.

Makes about ⅔ cup

*Outside of the Market Historic District.

Apple-Rosemary Vinaigrette

3 tablespoons apple-rosemary vinegar (Note: If apple-rosemary vinegar is not available, substitute 3 tablespoons apple cider vinegar plus ¼ teaspoon minced fresh rosemary)

3 tablespoons walnut oil

3 tablespoons canola oil

½ shallot, coarsely chopped

1 tablespoon Semillon-Sauvignon wine or dry white wine

3 tablespoons peeled, cored, and diced Braeburn apple

Kosher salt

Freshly ground black pepper

Soups & Salads

Bread Salad
Wild Mushroom Soup with White Truffle Oil
Nonna's Chicken Dumpling Soup
Triple Blue Summer Salad
Celery Root Soup
French Onion Soup with Gruyère Croutons
Beet Salad with Fresh Basil Dressing
Salmon Soup with Aïoli
Wilted Spinach Salad with Garlic, Pine Nuts, and Currants (Spinaci alla Romana)
Grilled Beef Salad with Fresh Lime Dressing
Chilled Yellow Taxi Tomato Soup
Grilled Asparagus with Hazelnut Vinaigrette and Pinot Noir Syrup
Turkish Bean Salad (Piyáz)
Winter Squash Soup
Potato Salad Puttanesca
Plum, Zucchini, and Mint Soup

Bread Salad

Sur La Table

Summertime, when tomatoes, peppers, onions, and basil are at their prime in taste and inexpensive in price, is the best time to whip up a bowl full of bread salad. Plan on spending about 45 minutes to prep this salad, to allow for the bread to soak up the vinaigrette and the flavors to meld.

◆ Preheat oven to 350°F.

◆ Arrange bread slices on baking sheets so slices don't overlap, and toast lightly. While slices are still warm, rub large whole garlic clove over one side of each bread slice, then brush both sides of bread with olive oil. Cool and cut into cubes. You should have about 4 cups of bread cubes.

◆ Toss together bread cubes, bell pepper, tomatoes and their juice, onion, and basil. The recipe should be completed to this point about ½ hour before serving.

◆ To serve, pour two-thirds to all of the vinaigrette over salad, depending on juiciness of the tomatoes. Toss and let stand at room temperature until juices have penetrated bread, about 20 minutes. Be careful not to oversoak the bread.

◆ To serve, divide salad among salad plates and garnish with fresh basil leaves.

Serves 4

Red Wine Vinaigrette

◆ Whisk together garlic and red wine vinegar, then add olive oil in a slow, thin stream, whisking constantly until dressing thickens. Add salt to taste. Use immediately, or cover and refrigerate until ready to use.

Makes about ⅔ cup

---

1 pound firm-textured bread (La Panzanella bread from DeLaurenti Specialty Food & Wine is recommended), crusts removed and cut into ¾-inch slices

1 large clove garlic

Extra virgin olive oil

1 yellow bell pepper, diced

4 ripe tomatoes, seeded and chopped into ¾-inch cubes, reserve juice

1 small Walla Walla sweet onion, cut into ⅛-inch slices

1 cup fresh basil leaves (firmly packed), kept whole if small in size, or torn into pieces if large, plus extra basil leaves for garnish

Red Wine Vinaigrette (recipe follows)

Red Wine Vinaigrette

1 clove garlic, minced

3 tablespoons red wine vinegar

½ cup extra virgin olive oil

Kosher salt

Since 1972, Sur La Table in the old Seattle Garden Center building has been a foodie's delight. With its decidedly Continental feel and flair, this delightfully cluttered kitchen shop boasts more than 12,500 items from more than 900 vendors worldwide. Here you'll find items that literally aren't carried anywhere else in the United States and perhaps the world.

From an extensive line of copper cookware directly imported from a sixth-generation family of French artisans to well-known brands such as Le Creuset (enamel-coated cast-iron cookware) and J. A. Henckels (cutlery), Sur La Table has a little something for everyone. Atop the groaning shelves you'll find small appliances, bakeware, kitchen tools, books, linens, tableware, gadgets, and specialty foods.

Among the more unusual offerings are asparagus tongs, an *herbes de Provence* mill, balsamic vinegar in a glass replica of the Eiffel Tower, porcelain escargot shells, mini cheesecake pans, and wine thermometers. Children are treated like young chefs-in-training at Sur La Table, with boutique bakery sets, kid-sized kitchen furnishings, and miniature tea sets.

The staff is knowledgeable and ready to help, and the mail-order catalog is always an event for the millions of customers who receive it. Within its pages, owner Renée Benkhe describes the unique items she's gathered during her latest buying trips to France, Mexico, Morocco, Croatia, or Vietnam.

Wild Mushroom Soup with White Truffle Oil

Cascadia

At Cascadia,* Chef Kerry Sear creates "Decidedly Northwest" prix-fixe menus that feature ingredients from the Cascadia region, which stretches north to Alaska, south to Oregon, west to the Pacific Ocean, and east to the Cascade Mountains. This lush soup, which would be perfect for an elegant

¼ cup (½ stick) unsalted butter

1 clove garlic, minced

2 shallots, thinly sliced

1 leek, white and pale green part only, cleaned and thinly sliced

dinner party, is among the seasonally changing *potages* that fill Chef Kerry's Designer Soup in a Can, a mock-Campbell's can with a potato-wafer biscuit "lid." The can is printed with instructions: "1. Remove wafer. 2. Pour into bowl. 3. And eat." Decidedly gourmet, yet playful, not unlike the dining experience at Cascadia in downtown Seattle's Belltown neighborhood.

◆ Melt butter in a large saucepan over medium heat. Add garlic, shallots, and leek, and cook 3 to 5 minutes, or until vegetables are softened but not colored, stirring occasionally.

◆ Add mushrooms and cook 3 to 5 minutes, or until mushrooms shrink slightly and begin to release their juices, stirring occasionally.

◆ Add potato and enough vegetable stock to cover. Reserve any remaining stock. Bring to a boil, then reduce heat and simmer 6 to 8 minutes, or until potatoes are soft.

◆ Remove pan from heat; then, using an immersion blender, a stand-up blender, or a food processor, purée soup in small batches. If using a blender or food processor, cover the top with a kitchen towel and process using short pulses at first so that hot soup doesn't overflow when the machine is turned on.

◆ Strain through a fine-mesh sieve placed over a large bowl, pressing out the solids with the back of a large spoon. Return soup to the saucepan, add cream, and stir well. Add the remaining stock if necessary to reach the desired consistency, bring to a simmer over low heat, and cook 3 to 5 minutes, or until heated through, stirring occasionally. Add the truffle oil, stir well, and season to taste with salt and pepper.

◆ To serve, ladle soup into individual bowls, then garnish with baguette slices.

Serves 6 as an appetizer

*Outside of the Market Historic District.

½ pound wild mushrooms, such as chanterelles, morels, and/or porcini, cleaned and coarsely chopped

1 medium russet potato, peeled and diced

3 cups homemade vegetable stock, or 1½ cups canned vegetable broth plus 1½ cups water

1 cup light cream or half-and-half

2 tablespoons white truffle oil

Kosher salt

Freshly ground white pepper

Grilled or baked baguette slices, for garnish

FRANK'S QUALITY PRODUCE

A s far back as I can remember, the Market has been a part of my life," says Frank Genzale, owner of Frank's Quality Produce, one of the Market's most popular highstalls. "My family started at the Market in 1922 as farmers. At the age of five I began helping my grandmother, Angelina, in her stall."

For the Genzale family, life in the United States began in 1921 when Frank "Cheech" Genzale, Frank's grandfather, left Italy and started working at his brother's farm in the Rainier Valley, south of Seattle. By the late 1920s, Cheech was able to buy 10 acres in Sunnydale, where he grew carrots, beets, onions, lettuce, cabbage, spinach, sweet corn, and celery. In 1929 he returned to Italy for his wife, Angelina, and their son, Tony.

The family continued to farm and sell their produce on the farmers' tables at the Market, with Angelina and grandsons Tony, Jr., and Frank doing the selling and Cheech and Tony handling the farming. Cheech died in 1973 at the age of 76, and Angelina died in 1986 at the age of 82.

Frank and Tony, Jr., started a highstall in the North Arcade together in 1972, but today Frank works with his sons, Johnny (22) and Frank, Jr. (29), and his uncles Tony and Ray (75 and 80 years young, respectively) at his produce stand on the east side of Pike Place. Brother Tony operates a produce stand in West Seattle.

"We're just a traditional Market family trying to make it down here," Frank explains. "There are no 40-hour weeks in the Pike Place Market. I'm here seven days a week, working 12- to 14-hour days. The boys work the same hours six days a week. But what sets us apart from Safeway is that we deal with our customers one at a time, bagging their tomatoes and answering their questions. We sell ourselves every time we deal with a customer."

Nonna's Chicken Dumpling Soup

Frank's Quality Produce

N onna means "grandmother" in Italian, and this beloved recipe was passed down by Frank's grandmother, Angelina, to Frank's mother, Antoinette (Anne). It takes a bit of time to prepare, but the result is well worth it . . . comfort food Italian-style, made from a recipe filled with love.

◆ Place water and chicken in a large stockpot. Add ½ teaspoon of the salt and the chicken bouillon. Bring to a boil and simmer, skimming off fatty foam that floats to surface. When chicken is

6 quarts (24 cups) water

1 chicken roaster or fryer (about 4 pounds), cut into pieces

¾ teaspoon kosher salt

3 tablespoons chicken bouillon powder, or 9 chicken bouillon cubes (1 teaspoon each)

½ cup chopped carrots

½ cup chopped celery

done, about 45 minutes to 1 hour, remove from stock, skin, debone, and cut meat into bite-sized pieces. Strain stock, then return to stockpot. Reserve chicken meat for later use.

◆ Bring stock back to a boil and add carrots, celery, onion, leek, and ¼ teaspoon of the pepper. Reduce heat and simmer 7 to 10 minutes, or until vegetables are tender. Strain and reserve stock and vegetables for later use. Meanwhile, cook pastina as package directs, about 4 to 6 minutes. Drain, rinse, and reserve for later use.

◆ Grind chicken breasts and thighs, or process in food processor. Whisk eggs in a large mixing bowl, then add the ½ cup cheese, parsley, the remaining ¼ teaspoon salt, and the remaining ¼ teaspoon pepper. Combine egg mixture with ground chicken and mix thoroughly. Heat chicken stock to boiling and drop dumpling mixture by rounded, compacted tablespoonsful into hot stock. Reduce heat, cover pot, and simmer 5 minutes, or until dumplings rise to surface of stock and are tender. Add reserved pastina and vegetables to stock and stir well.

◆ Ladle half a dozen dumplings, about ¼ cup of the reserved chicken pieces, and 2 cups of broth into each soup bowl. Sprinkle with additional grated cheese, if desired.

Makes 12 cups; serves 12 as an appetizer, 6 as an entrée

Triple Blue Summer Salad

Canter-Berry Farms

Clarissa Metzler Cross, co-owner with her husband Doug of Canter-Berry Farms, suggests trying this easy-to-make layered salad, which travels well to picnics and potlucks, during the height of local tomato season. The name comes about because it contains blueberry vinegar, fresh blueberries, and blue cheese.

◆ Arrange tomato slices in a single layer in the bottom of a stainless-steel or glass mixing bowl or baking dish, then

½ cup chopped white or yellow onion

½ cup chopped leek

½ teaspoon freshly ground black pepper

½ cup pastina (very small bits of pasta, generally used in making soup)

½ pound boneless, skinless chicken breasts

½ pound boneless, skinless chicken thighs

2 large eggs

½ cup grated Parmesan or Romano cheese, plus extra for garnish

½ cup minced fresh flat-leaf parsley

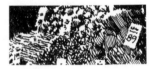

3 large tomatoes, cored and cut into ¼-inch slices

½ cup crumbled good-quality blue, Gorgonzola, or Roquefort cheese

½ cup Canter-Berry Farms blueberry vinegar or other mild fruit-flavored vinegar

6 large romaine lettuce leaves, rinsed and patted dry

½ cup fresh blueberries, for garnish

CANTER-BERRY FARMS

Five acres amid the verdant farmland of the upper Green River Valley are home to Canter-Berry Farms, where the husband-and-wife team of Clarissa Metzler Cross and Doug Cross raise both blueberries and American Saddlebred horses. Each of the eight varieties of cultivated highbush blueberries the couple grows is chosen for the unique taste and texture it will add to the blueberry jam, vinegar, chutney, and syrup Clarissa cooks up in small batches in her processing kitchen located right at the farm.

The Crosses' acreage is historic, founded as a land grant farm in the 1860s. The original homesteader hailed from France and operated his acreage as a fruit farm. In 1954, Clarissa's parents, Edith and Fred Metzler, bought the farm from the original homesteader's grandson, who had planted it in blueberries in 1947. The Metzlers planted more blueberry bushes, and soon their summertime farm became the permanent residence where they raised four daughters. In those early days, U-pick blueberries went for 15 cents a pound, and Fred would entice new customers out to the farm by offering them a piece of Edith's legendary blueberry pie.

Since 1975, the second generation of Metzlers—Clarissa and Doug—have operated the farm. In 1983 the younger generation introduced their popular blueberry products and gift packs, and were among the first farmers to sell "value-added" products at Pike Place. For six months they worked at perfecting the final formula for their chutney by giving samples to their Market customers and adjusting until they got it just right. Today you'll find them at their farm table in the Market's North Arcade five or six days a week during the summer and most weekends year-round. Here's to blueberry fields forever!

---

sprinkle with a couple of tablespoons of cheese and a couple of tablespoons of vinegar. Continue layering tomatoes, cheese, and vinegar until you run out, ending with vinegar. Let salad stand at room temperature 15 to 30 minutes. If not serving within that time, cover and refrigerate.

◆ Fifteen to 30 minutes before you want to serve, arrange lettuce leaves on salad plates and divide tomatoes and cheese among plates, drizzling with any remaining vinegar. Garnish with blueberries and mint leaves and sprinkle with black pepper, if desired.

Serves 6

Fresh mint leaves, for garnish (optional)

Freshly ground black pepper (optional)

Celery Root Soup

Salty's on Alki

Byron Shultz joined Salty's on Alki* in 1999 and quickly climbed through the ranks to become corporate chef at the seafood-savvy West Seattle restaurant renowned for its picture-postcard views of the downtown Seattle skyline, decadent desserts, and bountiful Sunday brunch. Byron lives in Pioneer Square, the historic heart of the city, and visits the Market weekly. "My favorite season, culinarily, is late fall/early winter," he explains. "I feel that the cold months challenge chefs to create outside their comfort zone. A chef who is adept at working with the limited palette these months bring is one worth watching." With its bright celery taste accented by thyme, plus the lush additions of oysters and caviar, this soup, which Byron served as a first course at one of the Market Foundation's Harvest Suppers, is a wondrous way to celebrate autumn.

◆ Heat oil in a stockpot over medium-high heat and add onions, shallot, and celery. Cook 5 to 8 minutes, or until onions are translucent, stirring often. Reduce heat as needed so onions do not brown.

◆ Add celery root, thyme, bay leaves, and chicken stock. Bring to a boil, then reduce heat to simmer and cook 12 to 15 minutes, or until celery root is tender, stirring occasionally. Remove bay leaves and discard.

◆ Using an immersion blender, a stand-up blender, or a food processor, purée the soup in small batches. If using a blender or food processor, cover the top with a kitchen towel and process using short pulses at first so that hot soup doesn't overflow when the machine is turned on.

◆ Strain soup through a fine-mesh sieve placed over a large mixing bowl, pressing out the solids with the back of a large spoon to remove as much liquid as possible. Return soup to saucepan over low heat, add crème fraîche and cream, and stir well. Bring soup to a simmer, stirring occasionally, but do

1 tablespoon vegetable oil

1 small white or yellow onion, diced

1 shallot, diced

1 rib celery, diced

1 large celery root (about 1½ pounds), scrubbed, peeled, and cut into ½-inch cubes

½ teaspoon dried thyme, crumbled

2 bay leaves

5 cups homemade chicken stock, or 2½ cups canned chicken broth plus 2½ cups water

¼ cup crème fraîche

¼ cup whipping cream

Kosher salt

White pepper

4 to 10 Kumamoto oysters, shucked

½ to 1½ ounces Beluga caviar, for garnish

Thyme sprigs, for garnish

not allow it to return to a boil or it could curdle. Season to taste with salt and pepper.

◆ To serve, ladle soup into individual bowls. Place an oyster in the middle of each bowl of soup and garnish with caviar and a few fresh thyme leaves.

Serves 6 to 8

*Outside of the Market Historic District.

French Onion Soup with Gruyère Croutons

Le Pichet

The French onion soup most Americans are familiar with features a beef stock base, but I much prefer this lighter version that hails from Lyon, France, in which chicken stock forms the foundation of the recipe. The lighter stock lets the earthy flavor of the onions shine through and gives the soup its pleasing golden color. Chef Jim suggests serving this soup with a light red wine, such as Beaujolais or Cabernet Franc, and a leafy green salad for a complete meal.

◆ Preheat oven to 350°F. Place bread slices on a baking sheet and bake 8 to 10 minutes, turning once, or until dry and crisp. Remove from oven and reserve.

◆ Melt butter in a stockpot over medium heat. Add onions and garlic, stir well, and cook 15 to 20 minutes, or until dark brown in color but not burned, stirring occasionally.

◆ Add sherry, increase heat, and cook 10 minutes, or until sherry is almost completely reduced. Add white wine, stir well, and cook 5 minutes, or until reduced by half. Add thyme and bay leaf and 6 cups of the chicken stock. Bring to a boil, then reduce heat to a simmer and cook 20 minutes to meld the flavors, stirring occasionally. Add more stock as necessary to give a pleasing ratio of stock to onions.

Six ½-inch-thick slices of hearty bread

¼ cup (½ stick) unsalted butter

2½ pounds yellow onions, peeled and cut into thin slices

½ head garlic, peeled and cut into thin slices

1½ cups medium-dry sherry

¾ cup dry white wine

1 tablespoon fresh thyme, rinsed, leaves picked from the stems, and minced

1 bay leaf

6 to 8 cups homemade chicken stock (see Techniques section)

Kosher salt

Freshly ground black pepper

¼ pound Gruyère cheese, grated

◆ Skim off any fat that rises to top of pan and discard, then season to taste with salt and pepper.

◆ To serve, preheat broiler. Spoon the soup into individual oven-proof bowls, then top with the reserved croutons and cheese. Heat under broiler until cheese turns golden and crusty.

Serves 8 to 12 as an appetizer, 4 to 6 as an entrée

Cook's Hint: In many soup and stew recipes, canned chicken, beef, or vegetable stock can easily be substituted for homemade stock with little loss in flavor or texture. However, since this recipe relies so heavily for its flavor and texture on the quality of the chicken stock, be sure to use your best homemade stock.

LE PICHET

Since it first opened its doors in the summer of 2000, Le Pichet has captured the hearts of Seattleites in a big way. It's easy to see why. The brainchild of Jim Drohman, former executive chef at Campagne (page 99), and Joanne Hearon, Le Pichet bills itself as *"bar le jour/café la nuit"* (bar by day/cafe by night). The narrow space features dark-wood tables with slate tops, a zinc bar, huge mirrors, and walls the color of Dijon *moutarde*.

Breakfast and lunch offerings include strong coffee and pastries, fresh salads, simple egg dishes and sandwiches, pâtés and terrines, and cheese plates. The dinner menu adds dishes such as Grilled New York Steak with Fried Onion Rings, Grilled Pork Sausage on a Macaroni-and-Bleu-Cheese Gratin, and—perhaps my favorite entrée—Roasted-to-Order Chicken served with Spicy Red Sauce and Haystack Potatoes. Although it takes the chef one hour to prepare and cook this dish since it's made-to-order, it's well worth the wait.

Le Pichet, which means "pitcher" in French, refers to the way the reasonably priced, predominantly French country wines are served . . . by the bottle, the *pichet* (two-thirds of a bottle), the *demi-pichet* (about two glasses), or the glass. And after a *pichet* or two at this workingman's bar/cafe, you begin to understand the secret of the good life that the French have known all along.

Beet Salad with Fresh Basil Dressing

My friend Cynthia Lair teaches at Bastyr College and is also the author of *Feeding the Whole Family* and *Feeding the Young Athlete*. Cynthia prepared this recipe for Café Organic, the Market's summertime cooking series, and loves the organic farmers who sell at the Market because they are so proud of their beautiful produce. "Carrots, beets, and greens are presented as if they were pictures of their grandchildren," she says. "The vendors glow about being a part of their creation."

◆ To prepare beets, rinse them and remove tops. Bring a large pot of water to a boil and add beets. Lower heat and simmer 1 hour, or until beets are tender. Set aside to cool. When cool, peel beets, cut them into small cubes, and reserve.

◆ To prepare beet greens, rinse them by submerging the bunch in a sink or large pot full of cold water. Shake off excess water and chop bunch into bite-sized pieces.

◆ Bring a large pot of water to a boil and add greens. Cook 30 seconds, or just until stems are tender. Place greens in a colander and run cold water over them to stop the cooking process. Squeeze out excess water and reserve greens.

◆ When ready to serve, place cubed beets, beet greens, pumpkin seeds, and green onions in a large bowl. Pour dressing over salad and toss gently to mix. Crumble feta over the top, if desired. Serve at room temperature or chilled.

Serves 6

Fresh Basil Dressing

◆ Place all the ingredients in a small jar with a lid and shake well to mix. If not using immediately, refrigerate until ready to serve.

Makes about ⅓ cup

Cook's Hint: If beet greens are unavailable, Cynthia suggests substituting raw watercress, spinach, or arugula leaves that have been well rinsed and spun dry or collard greens that have been well rinsed, coarsely chopped, and cooked until tender in the same way as described above for the beet greens.

4 large beets

1 bunch beet greens

¼ cup pumpkin seeds, toasted (see Techniques section)

2 green onions, white and pale green part only, finely chopped

Fresh Basil Dressing (recipe follows)

¼ pound feta cheese (optional)

Fresh Basil Dressing

3 tablespoons extra virgin olive oil

2 tablespoons balsamic vinegar

¾ teaspoon Dijon mustard

¼ teaspoon freshly ground black pepper

1 tablespoon minced fresh basil

EMMETT WATSON'S OYSTER BAR

Tucked back in the Soames-Dunn Building, Emmett Watson's Oyster Bar is named for one of Seattle's most crusty, opinionated, and oyster-lovin' journalists, the late Emmett Watson. The Oyster Bar started in 1976 in a tiny 210-square-foot space with eight bar stools and some of the best fresh oysters, steamed clams, and beers on tap in town. In the intervening years, Emmett's expanded its menu and seating capacity, and now offers outside dining (weather permitting) in a charming, ivy-covered courtyard.

In addition to fresh oysters on the half shell and 50 kinds of beer, Watson's serves notable seafood soups and fish 'n' chips made with true cod, oysters, and clams. The "chips," or French fries, are the good, old-fashioned kind—hand cut with the skins left on. The restaurant's oysters and salmon soup have been written up in newspapers around the world.

Watson's is the kind of place where everyone mingles happily, menu selections are hand-scrawled on brown paper bags, and the waitresses have a definite attitude. Perhaps because it embodies so much scrappy Seattle charm, the James Beard Foundation (a nonprofit organization that promotes the appreciation of American food and wine) honored the restaurant with its American Regional Classics award. Only "locally owned and operated regional restaurants with a very distinct menu and atmosphere that have withstood the test of time and are beloved in their communities" need apply. Ray's Boathouse (page 14) is another local winner of note.

Salmon Soup with Aïoli

Emmett Watson's Oyster Bar

Italy has its cioppino, France has its bouillabaisse, and Seattle has its Puget Sound Salmon Soup. With a clam-based broth substituting for the more commonly seen tomato-based broth, and the addition of salmon fillets to the mild whitefish fillets and shellfish found in many seafood soups and stews, this Salmon Soup is world-renowned.

◆ Preheat oven to 350°F. Place bread slices on a baking sheet and bake 8 to 10 minutes, turning once, or until dry and crisp. Remove from oven and reserve.

◆ Heat olive oil in a large saucepan over medium heat and sauté garlic and onion 3 minutes, or until opaque but not browned. Add clam juice, tomatoes, white wine (if used), oregano, and

Four ½-inch-thick slices of hearty bread

1 tablespoon olive oil

2 cloves garlic, minced

1 medium white or yellow onion, chopped

1 can (46 ounce) clam juice

½ can (14½ ounce) whole tomatoes, drained and chopped

2½ tablespoons dry white wine (optional)

½ teaspoon dried oregano, crumbled

Pinch of crushed red pepper flakes

Kosher salt

Freshly ground black pepper

A mixture of seafood to your taste, including 1 pound salmon fillets (skinned and cut into bite-sized chunks); ½ pound lean fish fillets, such as halibut, cod, or red snapper (cut into bite-sized chunks); ½ pound clams (scrubbed); and ½ pound mussels (scrubbed and debearded just before cooking)

Aïoli (recipe follows)

pepper flakes. Season to taste with salt and pepper. Bring mixture to a boil, then turn down heat and simmer 30 minutes, stirring occasionally.

◆ Just before you are ready to serve, add seafood. Cover pan and simmer 5 to 7 minutes, or until fish is done and shellfish opens. Remove any clams or mussels that do not open.

◆ To serve, place the reserved croutons on the bottom of four soup bowls, then divide the broth, fish, and shellfish among the bowls. Drizzle Aïoli over the fish and broth in each bowl.

Makes about 6 cups; serves 4

Aïoli

◆ In a food processor or blender combine garlic, egg, lemon juice, salt, and pepper and process about 2 minutes. Add olive oil in a slow stream until smooth and thick. Cover and refrigerate until ready to use.

Makes about ⅔ cup

Aïoli

3 cloves garlic, minced

½ large egg

1½ tablespoons freshly squeezed lemon juice

½ teaspoon kosher salt

¼ teaspoon freshly ground black pepper

½ cup olive oil

Wilted Spinach Salad with Garlic, Pine Nuts, and Currants

(SPINACI ALLA ROMANA)

Throughout his career in Seattle, Chef Don Curtiss has cooked up Mediterranean and Italian classics using fresh Northwest ingredients such as Dungeness crab, wild mushrooms, and just-picked herbs at venues such as Andaluca, Assaggio, and Prego. So it's only natural that he prepared this traditional Italian appetizer during a Summer Sundays on Pike Place cooking demonstration. "I've always felt that the Market is what makes Seattle an exciting place to be a chef. All the incredible local ingredients, the people so dedicated to growing the finest-quality products, the seasonality of the fish and seafood are basically the essence of what it means to be a chef. Our Market is the envy of every chef in the country," Don says. He's now an even more frequent Market shopper, having signed on with Kathy and John Casey at DISH D' LISH (page 128).

◆ In a large skillet, heat the ¼ cup olive oil over medium-high heat. Add garlic, pine nuts, currants, salt, and pepper, and cook 1 to 2 minutes, or until garlic becomes translucent and pine nuts turn light golden brown, stirring often.

◆ Add spinach leaves and cook 1 to 2 minutes, or until leaves just begin to wilt, stirring leaves from bottom of skillet to top so they cook evenly. *Do not overcook*, or the leaves will become limp and compressed!

◆ Add lemon juice and stir gently. Season to taste with salt and pepper.

◆ To serve, divide spinach among individual plates, drizzle with the 1 tablespoon extra virgin olive oil, and serve immediately.

Serves 4

¼ cup olive oil

2 teaspoons chopped garlic

1 tablespoon pine nuts

1 tablespoon dried currants

Pinch of finely ground sea salt, plus extra for seasoning

Pinch of freshly ground black pepper, plus extra for seasoning

1½ pounds baby spinach leaves, rinsed, drained, and spun dry

Juice of half a lemon

1 tablespoon extra virgin olive oil

Grilled Beef Salad
with Fresh Lime Dressing

Typhoon!

When summertime hits the Northwest, people head outside and cooking becomes a simpler, quicker process than in the cloudy winter months. That's when a refreshing, easy-to-make main-dish salad such as this one comes in handy. Best of all for lighter summer dining, Chef Bo Kline's zesty lime dressing achieves its delightful "zip" without the addition of fat or oil.

◆ Preheat grill or broiler.

◆ Cook steak to desired doneness (Chef Bo suggests cooking it rare). Slice thinly and arrange on one side of a decorative platter. Arrange mesclun mix on the other side.

◆ Spoon 2 to 3 tablespoons of Fresh Lime Dressing over beef and greens. Save remaining dressing for another use. Arrange green and red grape halves over salad and serve immediately.

Serves 4 to 6

Fresh Lime Dressing

Mix all the ingredients in a small nonreactive bowl. Use immediately, or cover and refrigerate for later use.

Cook's Hint: Some parts of the country have better selections of Asian sauces than others. Wherever you live, if you are unfamiliar with the often confusing array of brands and labels in foreign languages, you are generally safe buying the most expensive brand (which typically entails a modest increase in price) for better-quality ingredients.

Makes about ½ cup

---

1 pound aged top sirloin

1 pound mesclun salad mix, rinsed, drained, and spun dry

Fresh Lime Dressing (recipe follows)

½ cup green seedless grapes, cut in half lengthwise

½ cup red seedless grapes, cut in half lengthwise

Fresh Lime Dressing

¼ cup freshly squeezed lime juice

¼ cup good-quality fish sauce (Golden Boy brand recommended)

2 teaspoons granulated sugar

2 teaspoons minced garlic

2 teaspoons minced fresh Thai chile peppers

Chilled Yellow Taxi Tomato Soup

Earth & Ocean, W Hotel

During his entire career as a chef, through stints at Seattle's Dahlia Lounge, Campagne, and Carmelita, Johnathan Sundstrom has been committed to discovering the best ingredients he can find in the Puget Sound area. This dedication to quality was recognized by *Food & Wine* magazine when it named Johnathan, now executive chef at Earth & Ocean* in downtown Seattle's W Hotel, as one of the 10 best new chefs in America in 2001. As Johnathan says, "As a chef, I find that the best way to get excited about new menu items is to take a walk through the Market, looking, smelling, and tasting the local harvest. There is such a great selection and variety of local products that one can't help but be inspired." He served this refreshing savory soup at the Market's seventh annual Sunset Supper.

◆ Place tomatoes, garlic, and salt in a large nonreactive bowl, stir well, cover, and refrigerate 30 minutes to 1 hour.

◆ Pass tomatoes through a food mill with a fine-mesh plate or purée in food processor. If using a food processor, pass tomato purée through a fine-mesh sieve placed over a large mixing bowl, pressing out the solids with the back of a large spoon to force out as much tomato juice as possible.

◆ Add olive oil and vinegar, then season to taste with pepper and additional salt, if needed. Cover and place soup in freezer for 1 to 2 hours, or until it is very cold and slightly slushy in texture. Do not leave soup in freezer more than a couple of hours, or it will freeze completely.

◆ To serve, ladle soup into bowls, then garnish with crabmeat and a basil leaf.

Serves 8 as an appetizer

Cook's Hint: Johnathan advises that the best time of year to make this recipe is during August and September, when sweet, vine-ripened tomatoes from the Yakima and Okanogan Valleys arrive in Seattle farmers' markets. "Use the variety that smells the

8 cups chopped yellow tomatoes (about 1½ to 2 pounds whole tomatoes)

3 cloves garlic, minced

1½ tablespoons kosher salt, plus extra for seasoning

¼ cup extra virgin olive oil

¼ cup white balsamic vinegar

Freshly ground black pepper

¼ cup fresh Dungeness crabmeat, for garnish

8 lime basil leaves or sweet or Thai basil leaves, for garnish

best and is bursting with juice," he suggests. "And if lime basil isn't available, regular (Italian or sweet) basil or the more authoritative Thai basil make excellent substitutes." If serving this dish to vegetarians, substitute a drizzle of seasoned goat's-milk yogurt for the crab. To season the yogurt, add extra virgin olive oil, kosher salt, and freshly ground black pepper to taste. A squeeze of fresh lime juice is another enticing addition.

*Outside of the Market Historic District.

Grilled Asparagus with Hazelnut Vinaigrette and Pinot Noir Syrup

Cafe Juanita

After moving to Seattle in 1993 and working her way up the line at Place Pigalle, the Dahlia Lounge, and Brasa, Holly Smith decided to open her own restaurant. In 2000, she acquired the long-running Cafe Juanita* in Kirkland, Washington. A bushel full of glowing reviews for her rustic Northern Italian food followed, and it all started along Pike Place. "My first memory of the Market came when, as a young cook, I was sent out to procure live Dungeness crabs," Holly reminisces. "Because I was wearing a chef's coat, I looked like I knew what I was doing. In reality, I had little experience. As I awkwardly tried to wrestle the crabs out of the tank, I realized that people were watching me, enthralled that a 'real chef' knew how to accomplish such a task. Eventually, the fishmonger came to my rescue and helped get the crabs out of the tank for me."

◆ Preheat grill or broiler.

◆ Toss asparagus in olive oil and sprinkle with salt.

◆ Grill or broil asparagus 3 to 6 minutes (depending on thickness), or until just tender (do not overcook!), turning occasionally.

◆ To serve, divide asparagus among individual plates. Drizzle with Hazelnut Vinaigrette and Pinot Noir Syrup, then sprinkle with hazelnuts and serve warm or at room temperature.

Serves 4

2 pounds asparagus, hard ends removed, remaining portion rinsed, drained, and patted dry

3 tablespoons extra virgin olive oil

Kosher salt

Hazelnut Vinaigrette (recipe follows)

Pinot Noir Syrup (recipe follows)

2 tablespoons toasted hazelnuts, chopped (see Techniques section)

Hazelnut Vinaigrette

◆ Place shallot, mustard, lemon juice, and vinegar in a large bowl and whisk in hazelnut oil and olive oil a few drops at a time until the mixture turns thick and smooth, then season to taste with salt. Alternatively, place first four ingredients in a blender or food processor, pulse a few times to blend, then add oils in a slow, steady stream until sauce turns smooth and thickens slightly. Season to taste with salt.

◆ Pour the sauce into a bowl or jar. If not using immediately, cover and refrigerate for later use.

Makes about ¾ cup

Pinot Noir Syrup

◆ Melt sugar in a large, heavy-bottomed, nonreactive saucepan over medium-high heat, without stirring, until sugar turns golden. This will take 3 to 5 minutes, but watch carefully, since sugar can burn quickly.

◆ Carefully and slowly add one-quarter of the wine, which will bubble vigorously, stirring up sugar mixture from the bottom of the pan. If desired, wear oven mitts to protect your hands from splatters. Add the remaining wine, bring to a boil, and cook 20 to 25 minutes, or until slightly thickened and reduced to about ⅔ cup, stirring occasionally.

◆ Remove from heat, cool at room temperature, and place in a glass jar or bottle. The syrup will thicken as it cools, and can be stored at room temperature indefinitely.

Makes ⅔ cup

Cook's Hint: When making the Pinot Noir Syrup, Holly prefers using organic instead of nonorganic granulated sugar. She explains, "Organic sugar melts and caramelizes quickly because it contains less water, plus it's a beautiful pale golden color. I find it has a finer taste that's less sweet in some ways than regular granulated sugar." It is available at health food stores and upscale grocery stores.

*Outside of the Market Historic District.

Hazelnut Vinaigrette

1 shallot, minced

1 tablespoon whole-grain mustard

1 tablespoon freshly squeezed lemon juice

3 tablespoons sherry vinegar

¼ cup hazelnut oil

6 tablespoons extra virgin olive oil

Kosher salt

Pinot Noir Syrup

5 tablespoons organic granulated sugar or regular granulated sugar

1 bottle (750 milliliter) good-quality Pinot Noir or other red varietal, such as Merlot or Zinfandel

NO BOUNDARIES CAFE

Located in the Economy Atrium, between Studio Solstone and Tenzing Momo, No Boundaries Cafe is like a calm oasis in the midst of the Market's hubbub. Owners Mehmet Tetik and Ramazan Senturk, who hail from Turkey, treat their customers like long-lost friends. You get the sense that there really are no boundaries here, for everyone is welcomed and valued no matter their country of origin.

It all began back in 1997, when the two men were so drawn to the Market they decided to open a casual restaurant there. "I came from Turkey, where I know markets that are thousands of years old," Mehmet, the engaging on-site manager, says. "So this Market with all of its history is very important to me."

The sunny-yellow cafe offers a breakfast buffet and a wide array of sandwiches (made-to-order or ready for convenient take-away), soups, salads, and desserts. Everything is house-made with Mediterranean touches. The lentil soup is thick with carrots, celery, potatoes, and spices, while the vegetarian dolmas are pleasantly plump and briny-good. Don't miss the moussaka salad (eggplant sautéed with fresh lemon, tomatoes, and onions), tuna melt sandwich (big enough for sharing), or rice pudding (creamy sweet, cinnamon-y, and satisfying).

Turkish Bean Salad (Piyáz)

No Boundaries Cafe

The personable owners of No Boundaries Cafe, Mehmet Tetik and Ramazan Senturk, describe their bean salad as "just the kind of good, healthy, filling food that we like to prepare for our customers and our families and to eat ourselves."

◆ Rinse beans. In a large saucepan combine beans and the 8 cups cold water. Bring to a boil, then reduce heat. Simmer 2 minutes and remove from heat. Cover and allow to stand 1 hour. Alternatively, soak beans overnight in a covered pan in refrigerator. Drain and rinse beans.

◆ In the same pan, combine beans and the 8 cups additional water. Bring to a boil; then reduce heat, cover, and simmer 45 minutes, or until beans are tender but not mushy, stirring occasionally. Drain water and discard.

1 pound dry navy beans or dry great northern beans

8 cups cold water plus 8 cups water

6 tablespoons extra virgin olive oil

Juice of 1 lemon

4 plum tomatoes, cored, seeded, and diced

2 green onions, roots and top ¼ inch removed and discarded, remaining portion cut into ¼-inch slices

1 carrot, peeled and diced

2 tablespoons minced fresh flat-leaf parsley

- Place beans in a large mixing bowl, add olive oil and lemon juice, and toss until beans are well coated. Add tomatoes, green onions, carrot, and parsley and toss well. Season with salt and pepper. Cover and refrigerate 1 to 2 hours or (preferably) overnight to allow the flavors to meld.

- Fifteen to 30 minutes before you wish to serve the salad, remove from refrigerator and allow to stand at room temperature. Arrange lettuce leaves on individual plates and spoon salad into lettuce leaf "cups." Sprinkle with feta and olives.

Serves 6 to 8

Winter Squash Soup

Throughout the years, during cooking demonstrations for the Taste of Washington Farms and Organic Farmer Days, Chef Walter Bronowitz has become something of a legend among Market regulars for cooking up this thick, spicy squash soup. In his chef's whites, he has patiently stirred his bubbling cauldron, then handed out thousands of samples to hungry Market-goers. Walter, a Culinary Institute of America graduate, taught at the Culinary Arts Program at Edmonds Community College and now works as an executive chef and restaurant consultant.

- Preheat oven to 375°F.

- Lightly rub squash chunks with olive oil, arrange on a baking sheet, and bake 45 minutes to 1¼ hours, or until squash is very soft. If squash starts to brown too much, turn down heat. Remove from oven, scrape squash meat from skin, and discard skin; then mash squash meat with a fork and reserve.

- Heat the 1½ tablespoons olive oil in a large saucepan over medium heat. Add peppers and cook 2 minutes, stirring constantly. Add onion and cook 5 to 8 minutes, covered, until softened but not browned, stirring occasionally and reducing heat as necessary. Add Spice Mix and stir well.

- Add apples, stir well, then turn up heat to medium-high and cook 5 minutes, or until apples have dried out and begin to

Kosher salt

Freshly ground black pepper

6 to 8 large romaine or butter lettuce leaves

¼ cup crumbled feta

¼ cup small, brined olives, such as kalamata or niçoise

2½ pounds winter squash, such as butternut or Hubbard, cut into chunks and seeded

1½ tablespoons olive oil, plus extra for rubbing squash

2 teaspoons minced fresh Thai or other small, hot chile peppers

½ large white or yellow onion, chopped

1½ to 2 tablespoons Spice Mix (recipe follows)

¼ pound tart apples, such as Gravenstein or Granny Smith, grated

3 cups homemade chicken or vegetable stock, or 1½ cups canned chicken or vegetable broth plus 1½ cups water

Kosher salt

Freshly ground black pepper

brown and the spices give off a very strong aroma but are not burned. Stir constantly with a wooden spoon.

◆ Add stock, and use wooden spoon to scrape up all the ingredients from bottom of pan. Add roasted squash, stir well, bring to a simmer, and cook 20 minutes, stirring occasionally.

◆ Using an immersion blender, a stand-up blender, or a food processor, purée soup until smooth. If using a blender or food processor, cover top with a kitchen towel and process using short pulses at first so that hot soup doesn't overflow when the machine is turned on.

◆ Strain through a fine-mesh sieve placed over a large bowl, pressing out the solids with a large spoon. Season to taste with salt and pepper. The soup can be cooked to this point and served after completing the following step. Alternatively, the soup can be cooled and refrigerated or frozen for later use, but be sure to complete the following step before serving.

◆ When ready to serve, heat soup almost to boiling, then "temper" soup and sour cream to prevent curdling. To temper, place sour cream in a large mixing bowl. Add about 1 cup of hot soup to bowl, whisking constantly until blended. Add another cup of soup, whisk well, then add the contents of the mixing bowl back to soup pot and whisk to blend. Warm the soup, but do not bring it back to a boil, or it could curdle.

◆ To serve, ladle soup into individual bowls and garnish with croutons or fresh sage leaves as desired.

Serves 4 to 6 as an appetizer, 2 to 3 as an entrée

Spice Mix

◆ Combine coriander and cumin seeds and sage in a small glass jar with a lid and shake well. Taste and add mace, if desired.

Makes about 2½ tablespoons

Cook's Hint: Unless you are accustomed to spicy foods, use the lesser quantities of Thai chile peppers and Spice Mix the first time you make this soup, as the soup tends toward the hot side.

½ cup nonfat sour cream or nonfat Quark (a soft, unripened cheese that is available at the Pike Place Market Creamery and upscale grocery stores)

Croutons or fresh sage leaves, for garnish

Spice Mix

1 tablespoon whole coriander seeds, toasted and ground (see Techniques section)

1 tablespoon whole cumin seeds, toasted and ground (see Techniques section)

1 tablespoon minced fresh sage, or 1 teaspoon dried rubbed sage

Ground mace (optional)

Potato Salad Puttanesca

This recipe, which would be the perfect accompaniment to a summer picnic or fall tailgate party, comes from Catherine Stanford, who works as director of property development for the Pike Place Market Preservation and Development Authority (PDA). Catherine confides that working in the Market for over a decade has given her ready access to all sorts of fresh produce and specialty products, which has extended her passion for good cooking. Sometimes she even dreams of writing her own cookbook!

◆ Bring a large pot of water to a boil, add potatoes, cover, and cook 15 to 20 minutes, or just until tender. Drain water, loosely cover potatoes with a clean kitchen towel to keep them warm and soak up excess water, cover pot, and reserve.

◆ While potatoes are boiling, place sun-dried tomatoes in a small bowl, cover with hot water, and set aside for 10 minutes. Drain tomatoes, discard water, mince, and reserve.

◆ In a medium skillet, heat the 2 tablespoons olive oil over medium-high heat and cook garlic and onion 5 to 7 minutes, or until softened, stirring often.

◆ Place onion in a medium mixing bowl along with the ¼ cup extra virgin olive oil, balsamic vinegar, capers, reserved sun-dried tomatoes, and olives. Mix well, then season to taste with salt, black pepper, and pepper flakes. Reserve dressing.

◆ Cut warm potatoes into bite-sized pieces and add to a large mixing bowl. Toss gently with reserved dressing, being careful not to break up potatoes. Let salad rest 20 to 30 minutes at room temperature to allow flavors to meld, then divide among individual salad plates, garnish with quartered eggs, and sprinkle with basil. If not using immediately, cover and refrigerate the salad, allowing it to come to room temperature before serving.

Serves 6

---

2 pounds whole tiny new potatoes, scrubbed

8 large sun-dried tomatoes (not oil-packed)

2 tablespoons olive oil

5 cloves garlic, minced

1 medium red onion, chopped

¼ cup extra virgin olive oil

¼ cup balsamic vinegar

3 tablespoons capers, rinsed and drained

4 ounces (about ⅔ cup) kalamata olives, pits removed, coarsely chopped

Sea salt

Freshly ground black pepper

Crushed red pepper flakes

2 hard-boiled large eggs, quartered, for garnish

6 fresh basil leaves, cut in chiffonade (see Techniques section)

Plum, Zucchini, and Mint Soup

Le Gourmand

Bruce Naftaly is chef and owner of Le Gourmand,* a charming Northwest/French restaurant in the Ballard neighborhood, where he's been serving prix-fixe dinners since 1985. Bruce was one of the first chefs to see the possibilities of a seasonal Northwest cuisine, serving only fresh items, in season, from this area. A champion of small family farmers and a loyal Market shopper for more than 26 years, Bruce demonstrated this recipe for enthusiastic Marketgoers, who appreciated the chef's creative use of tart fruit (Shiro or greengage plums) in a savory dish.

◆ Melt butter in a large, heavy-bottomed, nonreactive saucepan over medium heat. Add garlic, shallots, onion, leek, chile pepper, and bay leaves, and cook 5 to 7 minutes, or until onions soften but do not color, stirring occasionally.

◆ Add plums, zucchini, and chicken stock, cover pan, and bring to a boil. Reduce heat, cover pan, and simmer 8 to 10 minutes, or until zucchini is soft, stirring occasionally. Add mint, stir well, and simmer 5 minutes. Remove bay leaves and chile pepper.

◆ Pass the soup through a food mill with a fine-mesh plate, or purée in small batches in a blender or food processor. If using a blender or food processor, cover the top with a kitchen towel and process using short pulses at first so that hot soup doesn't overflow when the machine is turned on. Pass soup mixture through a fine-mesh sieve placed over a large mixing bowl, pressing out the solids with the back of a large spoon to force out as much liquid as possible.

◆ Season to taste with salt and, if serving immediately, rewarm the soup, being careful not to let it come to a boil. Alternatively, transfer the soup to a nonreactive bowl, cover, and refrigerate up to 2 days before serving either hot or cold.

Serves 4 to 6 as an appetizer

2 tablespoons unsalted butter

2 cloves garlic, peeled and halved

2 shallots, peeled and coarsely chopped

½ white or yellow onion, coarsely chopped

1 leek, white part only, cleaned and coarsely chopped

1 fresh Thai or other small, hot chile pepper, left whole

2 bay leaves

½ pound tart plums, such as the Shiro or greengage varieties, coarsely chopped

½ pound zucchini, cut into 1-inch pieces

2 cups homemade chicken stock, or 1 cup canned chicken broth plus 1 cup water

¼ cup chopped fresh mint

Kosher salt

Cook's Hint: If tart plums are not available, Bruce suggests substituting underripe sweet plums. The Italian prune variety makes a particularly suitable substitution. If serving the soup cold, a bit of additional stock may be needed to thin the soup to the desired consistency. For an elegant touch of richness, add a dollop of crème fraîche or a swirl of heavy cream to individual bowls of soup just before serving.

*Outside of the Market Historic District.

Vegetarian Entrées & Side Dishes

Pike Place Market Winter Root Curry
Cheesy Tomatoes
Microwave Mozzarella Vegetable Pie
Pasta con Fagioli
Asparagus Lover with Veggies
Winter Squash Flan
Braised Red Cabbage with Apples
Pea Pullao
Butternut Squash and Oregon Blue Cheese Lasagne
Penne Caprese
Garbanzo Bean and Potato Patties with Apricot Sweet-and-Sour Sauce
Grand Central Strata
Five-Spice Grilled Corn with Roasted Red Pepper Butter
Thanksgiving Stuffing
Chutney Hollow Squash
Italian Fonduta (Cheese Fondue)
Spicy Vegetable Stew
Pasqualina Verdi's Pesto Sauce
Raspberry Snap Peas
Stir-Fried Harvest Medley
Potato Gratin

Pike Place Market Winter Root Curry

World Merchants Spice, Herb, & Teahouse

I love the technique of grinding whole spices, so I was delighted when World Merchants owner Tony Hill submitted this curry recipe. In the notes that accompany the recipe, Tony explains, "The 'problem' with using potatoes in a curry comes when you cook the dish in the authentic, slow fashion. Potatoes will dissolve after a few hours of stewing, a trick that can become your thickener in the dish, but leaves you with none of the interesting mouthfeel of the diced potatoes. In America, the underutilized root vegetables like turnips and rutabagas should be rescued from the deep, dark pantries to which they've been relegated to solve this problem. They will hold their shape and form much better than spuds for the duration of a curry's stove time. Conveniently, their flavors meld perfectly with the complexities of

2 tablespoons peanut oil

3 tablespoons clarified butter (ghee) (see Techniques section)

1 medium white or yellow onion, diced

4 tablespoons freshly ground Madras Curry Powder (recipe follows)

2 cups peeled, diced (¼-inch) turnips

2 cups peeled, diced (¼-inch) rutabaga

1 cup peeled, diced (¼-inch) carrots

WORLD MERCHANTS SPICE, HERB, & TEAHOUSE

It comes as no surprise that Tony Hill's motto is "Eat well and enjoy life!" As the creator and owner of World Merchants,* which opened in 1994, Tony trots the globe in search of the freshest and purest spices, herbs, and teas. He's journeyed to the pepper coast of India, the tea gardens of China, the jungles of South America, the Spice Islands and Madagascar, and all of the major culinary centers of Europe including Reggio-Emilia in Italy, Provence in France, the paprika fields of Hungary, and the saffron fields of Spain.

Tony, a.k.a. "The Spice Guy," is passionate about what he does; he's a walking encyclopedia of tea and spice history, techniques for use, and lore. His atmospheric shop just below the Pike Place Market features an amazing array of herbs and spices (with information note cards that detail origins, history, and interesting characteristics), in addition to a relaxing tea bar where you can stop in for a freshly brewed cup. While you're there, look for his book, a hefty compendium on spices and herbs (with recipes!) entitled *Flavor Alchemy: The Definitive Spice Guide for a Global Kitchen.*

*Just outside of the Market Historic District.

curry and leave the diner with a new appreciation for winter vegetables."

◆ Heat peanut oil and clarified butter in a stockpot over medium-high heat, add onion, and cook 5 to 7 minutes, or until onions are translucent, stirring often. Add curry powder and cook 3 minutes, stirring constantly, until curry gives off its aroma and is lightly toasted. If necessary, add a tablespoon or two of stock to keep onions from scorching.

◆ Add turnips, rutabaga, carrots, and potato, and enough stock to cover vegetables. Bring stock to a simmer, then cover stockpot and cook 1½ hours over low heat, adding stock as needed to keep vegetables covered. Uncover the pot, stir well to break up the potatoes, and cook an additional 30 minutes without adding any more stock. During the final minute of cooking, add parsley and stir well, then salt to taste.

◆ To serve, divide rice among individual soup bowls and cover with curry. Add a dollop of yogurt and serve immediately.

Serves 6

Madras Curry Powder

◆ Place all the ingredients in a mortar and pestle or a spice grinder and grind to a fine powder.

Makes about 4 tablespoons

Cook's Hint: Tony advises that this dish is a natural for the crockpot as well as the stovetop. Prepare as directed to the point where you would cover the stockpot and simmer for 1½ hours; instead, transfer the stew to a crockpot and cook over low heat for 8 hours. Finish with the parsley or cilantro and serve as described above.

For a twist on plain old rice, add a pinch of saffron or a few whole cardamom seeds to the water or stock as you bring it to a boil, then add the rice and cook as usual, being sure to remove and discard the cardamom seeds before serving.

¾ cup peeled, diced (⅛-inch) russet potato

6 to 8 cups (1½ to 2 quarts) homemade chicken or vegetable stock, or 3 to 4 cups canned chicken or vegetable broth plus 3 to 4 cups water

¼ cup minced fresh flat-leaf parsley or cilantro

Kosher salt

Cooked rice

Plain yogurt

Madras Curry Powder

1 teaspoon whole Tellicherry or other good-quality peppercorns

1 tablespoon ground turmeric

¼ teaspoon whole cardamom seeds

½ to 1 teaspoon crushed red pepper flakes

2 teaspoons whole coriander seeds

1 teaspoon whole cumin seeds

½ teaspoon ground cinnamon

1 teaspoon whole fenugreek seeds

1½ teaspoons whole brown mustard seeds

½ teaspoon ground ginger

SOSIO'S PRODUCE

Sosio's is a friendly highstall where you're invited inside to pick and choose your fruits and vegetables without getting your hands slapped because you're disturbing the displays. The owner, Susie Manzo, and her ever-reliable staff (including longtime employees Alan, Mike, Kelly, and Mark) banter and joke and point you toward what's best to buy, all the while tempting you with free samples to prove their point. During the summer, don't miss a slice of their tree-ripened peaches, which have earned the nickname "Oh My God" because of the never-failing reaction from anyone who tastes them. Insider's tip: They're so sweet and full of juice that it's best to eat them standing over the sink.

Sosio's specialties include a wide variety of seasonal mushrooms (chanterelles, morels, shiitakes, porcini, lobster, and Chicken of the Woods) and mushroom powder, heirloom tomatoes (with enticing names such as Brandywine, Early Girl, and Green Zebra), and even purple-tinged vegetables. These include the incredibly crunchy, sweet, and healthful Beta Sweet maroon carrots; purple asparagus (an import from California); and purple Peruvian potatoes (which, despite the name, often hail from local farms).

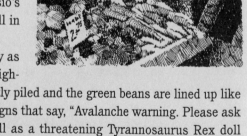

On the south wall of the stall, you'll notice a mural of an elderly man surrounded by boxes of fruits and vegetables. The man is Sosio Manzo, patriarch of the Manzo clan, who was born in Italy in 1889, came to Seattle at the age of 20, bought a farm, and began selling at the Market in 1909. One of Sosio's sons, Dan, gave up farming to set up a highstall in the Pike Place Market in 1948.

That produce stand is still in operation today as Manzo Brothers Produce. It's a more formal highstall than Sosio's, where the peaches are perfectly piled and the green beans are lined up like soldiers on parade. The produce is guarded by signs that say, "Avalanche warning. Please ask for assistance" or "Pleeza no squeeza," as well as a threatening Tyrannosaurus Rex doll designed to dissuade overeager shoppers.

Dan, Jr. and wife Susie own Sosio's, so when you're shopping the highstalls in the Main Arcade you have a better-than-average chance of buying produce from the Manzo family somewhere along the line, continuing a long Market tradition.

Cheesy Tomatoes

Sosio's Produce

B ubbling, cheesy tomatoes hot from the broiler make an easy yet elegant side dish that goes well with any sort of simply prepared fish, chicken, or meat.

◆ Preheat broiler and place an oven rack about 8 inches from heat source. Arrange tomato halves on a baking sheet without touching or overlapping. Sprinkle on herb/spice blend to taste, then sprinkle cheese evenly over tomato halves.

◆ Cook 5 minutes, or until the cheese is bubbly and golden brown.

Serves 4 to 6

6 plum tomatoes, cored and cut in half lengthwise

Johnny's Salad Elegance, Mrs. Dash, or a similar herb/spice blend of your choice

1 cup grated mozzarella cheese

Microwave Mozzarella Vegetable Pie

Sosio's Produce

Y ou can serve this "pie" as a hearty side dish or as a vegetarian meal when accompanied by crusty bread and a substantial salad. If you have any left over, put it on a prebaked pizza crust with tomato sauce and extra mozzarella cheese, and broil or bake until the cheese melts for a simple vegetarian pizza!

◆ Sprinkle the water in the bottom of a 6-by-8-inch microwave-safe baking dish, or a similar-sized dish that is at least 3 inches deep. Layer one third of eggplant, bell pepper, and onion slices in bottom of baking dish, sprinkle on 1 teaspoon herb/spice blend, then sprinkle on ⅓ cup of the cheese. Follow the same order with remaining vegetables, herb/spice blend, and cheese, ending with cheese on top.

◆ Cover dish with vented plastic wrap, then microwave on HIGH 5 to 7 minutes, or until vegetables are tender/crisp and cheese is melted. Rotate dish two or three times during cooking time. Remove from microwave, cover entire dish with plastic wrap, and let stand 2 or 3 minutes more to finish cooking. Serve immediately.

Serves 4 to 6

2 tablespoons water

2 Japanese eggplants, scrubbed, patted dry, and ends removed, cut ¼ inch thick

1 green, yellow, red, or purple bell pepper or a mixture of all four, cut ⅛ inch thick

1 yellow onion, cut into ⅛-inch slices

1 tablespoon Johnny's Salad Elegance, Mrs. Dash, or a similar herb/spice blend of your choice

1 cup grated mozzarella cheese

Pasta con Fagioli

Cannellini (or *fagiola*) beans are creamy-white kidney beans, slightly larger than navy beans and with a fluffier texture. They are used in this healthy vegetarian recipe devised by Ann Magnano, the former owner of the Market's long-running health-food store, Magnano Foods (now Ivacco Foods). After selling her business in 1995, Ann focused on other passions, such as Moonbeam Farm, her 25-acre tract on Guemes Island in the San Juans. But the siren song of the Market called her back in 2001, and now, in addition to farming and selling her organic crops at the Anacortes Depot Market and in co-ops, she volunteers her time on the Pike Place Market Preservation and Development Authority (PDA) Council. Pasta *con fagioli* (with beans) is especially good served with a fresh green salad, crusty bread, and a bottle of Chianti.

◆ Fill a large saucepan with water and bring to a rolling boil. Add cannellini beans and boil 3 to 5 minutes. Drain water, replace with the 8 cups water, and bring to a boil again.

◆ Meanwhile, heat olive oil in a large skillet over medium heat and add garlic. Cook until garlic becomes soft, then reduce heat to low and add wine and capers.

◆ Reduce heat to low under the beans, add a pinch of oregano and the sautéed garlic and capers to saucepan, and simmer 1 hour, or until beans are soft. During the last 20 minutes of cooking time, add sun-dried tomatoes.

◆ Meanwhile, heat a large pot of water to boiling for the pasta. Add pasta and boil 10 to 15 minutes, or until pasta is al dente. Drain pasta, then divide among dinner plates and spoon cannellini beans and sun-dried tomatoes on top. Sprinkle with freshly grated cheese, and garnish with fresh basil leaves.

Serves 8

½ pound dried cannellini beans

8 cups water

¼ cup olive oil

2 to 3 cloves garlic, chopped

¼ cup dry white wine

1 teaspoon capers

Pinch of dried oregano, crumbled

1 cup sun-dried tomatoes (not packed in oil)

1 pound linguine

Parmesan or Pecorino Romano cheese, for grating

Fresh basil leaves, for garnish

TYPHOON!

The husband-and-wife team of Steve and Bo Kline are the life force behind Typhoon!,* which blew into the Market neighborhood in the summer of 2000. The Klines had already established three successful sister restaurants (two in Portland, Oregon, and the other in Redmond, Washington) when the downtown Seattle branch came into being. Their space is warm and inviting, a bit like an exotic, dark-wood outpost thanks to a bamboo "jungle" at the entrance, rows of brass clocks set to different time zones, and vintage Thai photos on the walls.

Bo, a native of Thailand who acts as executive chef, draws inspiration for her dishes "from the pushcarts of the peasants to the palaces of Asia." Her menu ranges from Thai classics such as *tom kah gai* (chicken coconut soup), *pad Thai* (Thailand's best known noodle dish), and chicken in green curry to "nouvelle Thai" and "lost" dishes. The latter include historic favorites, peasant dishes, and palace dishes that Bo has researched and rediscovered.

The wine list is eclectic, with bottles from Germany, France, Australia, California, Oregon, and Washington, each chosen to complement Typhoon!'s unique cuisine. Asian and domestic microbrews are another option, but perhaps most impressive is the tea menu. With more than 128 different varieties available, there are teas shaped like tiny balls of gunpowder, sun-dried and pan-fired teas, rare white teas, and teas picked by monkeys. Typhoon! is the place to linger over $3,000-per-pound teas for a fraction of their cost when brewed by the pot. Which makes it easy to say *sanuk*, or "enjoy" in Thai.

*Just outside of the Market Historic District.

Asparagus Lover with Veggies

Typhoon!

Bo Kline, chef and co-owner with her husband Steve of Typhoon!, explains that Thai chefs love to improvise and take advantage of the freshest vegetables—so feel free to substitute whatever is fresh and in season when you make this recipe. However, the one inviolate rule of Thai cuisine is that the ingredients must be sliced bite-sized or smaller or easily cut with a spoon or fork. This is the reason natives of Thailand use a fork and large spoon as utensils, and why there are no knives offered in Thai restaurants.

½ pound asparagus, hard ends removed and remaining portion rinsed and drained

1 tablespoon vegetable oil

2 teaspoons minced garlic

- Add an inch of water to a large skillet, cover, and bring to a boil. Add asparagus and cook 2 to 3 minutes, covered, or until tender-crisp. Remove from heat, drain water, and rinse with cold water. Drain cold water and remove asparagus to paper towels to drain, patting until very dry. Transfer to a baking pan and reserve.

- Heat oil in a wok or large skillet over medium-high heat. Add garlic and stir-fry 30 seconds to 1 minute, stirring constantly. Do not allow garlic to burn. Add reserved asparagus and cook 1 minute, turning spears to coat them completely in oil. Return asparagus to baking pan, cover with aluminum foil, and reserve.

- Add mixed vegetables to wok and cook 3 to 5 minutes, stirring constantly, or until they brighten and become tender-crisp.

- Add broth, oyster sauce, sugar, soy sauce, and sesame oil and stir well.

- Mix cornstarch and water, then measure out 2 teaspoons of the liquid and add to wok. Stir well and check consistency of sauce. If too thin, add more of the cornstarch mixture. If too thick, add a tablespoon or two of water. Remove wok from heat, taste vegetables, and season to taste with additional sugar, soy sauce, and/or sesame oil as needed.

- To serve, arrange asparagus spears on a dinner plate, pour vegetable sauce over asparagus, and serve immediately.

Serves 1 as an entrée, 2 to 3 as a side dish

Cook's Hint: Although many people in the Western Hemisphere think of soy sauce as the salty brown stuff that comes in little plastic packets, in Asian countries there is a wide range of soy sauce styles. In this recipe, Bo recommends using what she refers to as a "thin" soy sauce, specifically the Kwong Hung Seng (Dragonfly) brand, as opposed to the thick, dark, almost molasses-like Chinese soy sauce. She also prefers the Lee Kum Kee brand of oyster sauce, although other brands can be used with only a slight difference in flavor.

¼ pound mixed vegetables of your choice, such as broccoli, cauliflower, carrots, button mushrooms, shiitake mushrooms, or young corn, cut into bite-sized pieces

¾ cup vegetable broth

1 tablespoon plus 1 teaspoon oyster sauce (see Cook's Hint below)

½ teaspoon granulated sugar

½ teaspoon soy sauce (see Cook's Hint below)

¼ teaspoon toasted sesame oil

1 tablespoon cornstarch

1 tablespoon water

Winter Squash Flan

IslandWood, A School in the Woods

As chef at IslandWood, A School in the Woods,* Greg Atkinson cooks for adults and schoolchildren, encouraging young culinarians to appreciate good food, its sources, and how what they eat impacts the environment. Greg is also an award-winning food writer, author of *In Season* (Sasquatch Books, 1997) and *The Northwest Essentials Cookbook* (Sasquatch Books, 1999) and food columnist for *Pacific Northwest* magazine. At a Harvest Supper that benefited the Market Foundation, Chef Greg served this savory flan (a custardlike side dish) along with grilled venison. I think it also makes an unusual and satisfying vegetarian entrée when flanked by a mixed green salad, crusty bread, and a hearty grain dish such as couscous or pecan rice.

◆ Position oven rack in center of oven.

◆ Preheat oven to 375°F and butter six 4-ounce ramekins or glass custard cups. Place cups in a baking dish that will comfortably hold all of them and reserve.

◆ Cut squash into disks or wedges and scrape out seeds, then cut away peel. Cut the peeled and seeded squash into 1-inch dice. You should have about 2½ cups of cubed squash.

◆ In a large skillet or saucepan, melt the butter over medium-high heat and cook the onion 5 minutes, or until tender and golden, stirring often. Add half-and-half and squash, bring the mixture to a boil, cover, and reduce heat to low. Let the squash simmer gently for 15 minutes, or until tender, stirring occasionally.

◆ In a blender or food processor, pulse eggs with salt, then add squash mixture. Cover the top of the machine with a kitchen towel and process using short pulses at first so that the hot mixture does not overflow when the machine is turned on. Pulse until smooth, then divide squash mixture evenly among the ramekins.

◆ Pour boiling water into baking dish around ramekins until it reaches halfway up the sides, then cover baking dish with

1 pound winter squash, such as kabocha, delicata, or acorn

2 tablespoons unsalted butter

½ medium white or yellow onion, peeled and thinly sliced (about ¾ cup)

½ cup half-and-half

3 large eggs

1 teaspoon kosher salt

buttered aluminum foil. Bake 25 to 30 minutes, or until a knife inserted in center comes out clean. Remove custards from oven and allow to stand 10 minutes.

◆ You can choose to serve the flans at once, keep them warm in a 200°F oven for up to 1 hour, or refrigerate and then reheat as needed. To serve, loosen edges of custards with a spatula or knife, slipping the point of the spatula down the sides of the custards to let in enough air to release the custards. Invert onto plates and enjoy.

Serves 6

*Outside of the Market Historic District.

Braised Red Cabbage with Apples

Uli's Famous Sausage

Uli Lengenberg suggests serving this authentic German side dish, which he fondly remembers eating as a youth, along with fresh bratwurst (see Cook's Hint below). You can serve this bright purple cabbage melange of sweet, tart, and salty flavors the same day you make it, but it will be even more delicious and aromatic if it marinates overnight to allow the flavors to meld.

◆ Heat oil in a stockpot over medium heat, add bacon, and cook 6 to 8 minutes, or until lightly browned, stirring occasionally. Add onion and cook 5 to 7 minutes, or until tender, stirring often.

◆ Add apple, chicken stock, red wine, vinegar, bay leaves, cloves, salt, pepper, nutmeg, cinnamon, and sugar and stir well. Cover and bring to a boil, then add the cabbage and stir well. Cover and cook 12 to 15 minutes, or until cabbage is very tender and the apples cook down completely, stirring occasionally. Remove from heat, taste, and add salt, sugar, or red wine vinegar as needed. If serving now, continue with the following step. If serving later, allow cabbage to cool to room temperature, cover, and refrigerate overnight.

1 tablespoon vegetable oil or lard

2 strips thick bacon, diced

1 white or yellow onion, diced

1 tart apple, such as Granny Smith or Gravenstein, peeled, cored, and quartered

1 cup homemade chicken stock, or ½ cup canned chicken broth plus ½ cup water

½ cup dry red wine

2 tablespoons red wine vinegar, plus extra for seasoning

2 bay leaves

4 whole cloves

½ teaspoon kosher salt, plus extra for seasoning

ULI'S FAMOUS SAUSAGE

The son of German restaurant owners, master butcher Uli Lengenberg has operated everything from retail shops and a catering service in Germany to deli restaurants in Taipei, Taiwan. So when The Incredible Link went up for sale, Uli took a chance and bought the already-established sausage business in the Pike Place Market's Main Arcade. This bear of a man with dark hair and a handlebar mustache hasn't been sorry.

"We're thrilled to be part of Seattle's Pike Place Market, an internationally known venue for locally made and grown products," Uli says. "We hope to bring our customers traditional and innovative sausages so good that we will see them come back again and again and again."

The *Meister*, who hails from "sausage country"—Westphalia, Germany—offers a tantalizing variety of handmade, authentic German and international sausages, such as Cajun Andouille, Garlic Chicken, and Pike Place Smoked Salmon sausage.

Whichever sausage you choose, you can be sure it is "the best of the wurst," as Uli likes to say. They're sold by the pound for take-out, or grilled sausages are available for immediate consumption at a narrow counter that faces a large viewing window where you can watch the intricate, largely handmade process of sausage-making every weekday. *Guten appetit!*

◆ Just before serving, mix potato starch with water. Cover and reheat cabbage over medium-high heat, stirring often and being careful not to scorch cabbage. Remove pan from heat, add potato flour/water mixture, and stir well. Return to heat until thickened slightly, stirring often.

◆ To serve, divide cabbage among individual plates and sprinkle with parsley.

Serves 6 to 8

Cook's Hint: The braised cabbage pairs perfectly with fresh bratwurst. To cook fresh bratwurst, Uli suggests melting 1 tablespoon of oil, butter, or lard in a skillet. Add the sausages (do not prick first!) and cook until lightly browned, turning occasionally. Add a few tablespoons of water, cover the pan, and cook 10 to 12 minutes. Take off the lid and cook 3 to 5 minutes more, or until browned as desired.

¼ teaspoon freshly ground black pepper

¼ teaspoon ground nutmeg

⅛ teaspoon ground cinnamon

2 tablespoons granulated sugar, plus extra for seasoning

1 medium head red cabbage (about 2 pounds), outer leaves removed and discarded, cored, cut in half, and cut into ⅛-inch strips

1½ teaspoons potato starch

1 tablespoon water

Chopped fresh flat-leaf parsley

Pea Pullao

The Souk

This colorful rice casserole becomes something special thanks to the addition of traditional Indian spices. It pairs nicely with Chicken Masala (page 86) or Lamb Burgers (page 98).

◆ Preheat oven to 300°F. Heat butter in a large ovenproof saucepan with a lid over medium-low heat, and add onion, peppercorns, cardamom pods, cumin, bay leaves, and cinnamon stick. Cook 5 minutes, stirring occasionally, then add salt to taste.

◆ Stir in rice until rice kernels are well coated with oil, then add water. Bring to a boil, cover, then simmer rice mixture 5 to 7 minutes, or until about half the water is absorbed. Stir in peas, bring mixture to a boil, then cover and turn heat down to simmer.

◆ When most of the water has been absorbed (about 5 minutes), put the saucepan in the oven (covered) for 15 minutes, being sure to cover the saucepan handle with aluminum foil if it is not oven-safe. Before serving, remove the cardamom pods, bay leaves, and cinnamon stick, and fluff the rice with a fork.

Serves 6

2 tablespoons unsalted butter or vegetable oil

1 small white or yellow onion, cut into ⅛-inch slices

4 whole black peppercorns

4 whole cardamom pods

¼ teaspoon ground cumin

2 bay leaves

1 cinnamon stick (3 inches long)

Kosher salt

1 cup basmati or long-grain white rice

1½ cups water

1 package (9 ounce) plain, frozen sweet peas

Butternut Squash and Oregon Blue Cheese Lasagne

Kaspar's

Since 1993, when the Market Foundation's Harvest Suppers (multi-cause gourmet dinners) began, Kaspar and Nancy Donier have been donating their time, energy, and restaurant facilities to the events. They've also been perennials at the Market's popular Sunset Suppers, participate in the Taste of the Nation, and have even cooked and cruised the Mediterranean, all to benefit the Market Foundation. Kaspar's* vegetarian lasagne is

2 to 2½ pounds butternut squash

3 tablespoons olive oil

1½ cups whipping cream

1½ cups (about 8 ounces) crumbled Oregon blue cheese

Pinch of kosher salt, plus extra for seasoning

Pinch of freshly ground black pepper, plus extra for seasoning an intriguing mix of meltingly tender winter squash, lush blue-cheese cream sauce, blanched spinach, and earthy hazelnuts. The ground nutmeg and fresh sage leaves that garnish the casserole infuse the kitchen with enticing aromas as the lasagne is baking, to create a recipe that is the essence of autumn.

◆ Preheat oven to 350°F. Butter an 8-by-12-inch baking pan and reserve.

◆ To prepare the squash, cut off the ends, cut the squash in half lengthwise, remove the seeds, then peel the halves from top to bottom with a sharp vegetable peeler or a small, sharp paring knife.

◆ Cut the halves lengthwise into ¼-inch-thick slices.

◆ Brush a baking sheet with the olive oil, arrange squash in a single layer on the baking sheet, and cook 30 to 35 minutes, or until soft.

◆ Make sauce by bringing whipping cream to a boil in a small saucepan. Reduce heat to simmer and cook 3 minutes, watching the cream carefully and stirring occasionally so it doesn't boil over. Add ½ cup of the crumbled blue cheese, along with salt, pepper, and nutmeg. Remove from heat, cover, and reserve.

◆ Bring a large pot of salted water to a boil and cook fresh pasta sheets 3 minutes or until al dente. If using dried lasagna noodles, cook according to package instructions. Remove pasta sheets, drain on paper towels, and reserve.

◆ Make filling by mixing the remaining 1 cup blue cheese, ricotta, and spinach. Season to taste with salt and pepper.

◆ To assemble lasagne, place one pasta sheet in bottom of reserved baking pan, cutting and arranging the pasta so entire bottom of pan is covered. Layer with one-third of filling, then one-third of squash. Repeat until all the ingredients are used, ending with a sheet of pasta.

◆ Pour sauce evenly over lasagne, arrange sage leaves on top, and sprinkle with hazelnuts.

Pinch of ground nutmeg

4 to 6 fresh pasta sheets or 8 dried lasagna noodles (about 7 ounces) (see Cook's Hint below)

1 cup whole-milk, part-skim, or fat-free ricotta cheese

8 ounces baby spinach leaves, blanched and coarsely chopped

12 fresh sage leaves

½ cup chopped hazelnuts

- Bake 35 to 40 minutes, or until golden brown on top and heated all the way through.

- To serve, cut into rectangles and divide among individual plates.

Serves 8

Cook's Hint: Fresh pasta sheets vary in size. You will need enough pasta to cover four 8-by-12-inch layers. If you inadvertently buy extra, it can be sliced to the thickness you desire, cooked, and tossed into soups or used as a base for Marinara Vegetable Sauce (page 181) or Crabmeat Tagliatelle in Creamy Lemon-Tomato Sauce (page 119).

*Outside of the Market Historic District.

THE PINK DOOR

Walk down Post Alley past the Glass Eye Gallery, past the courtyard with the haunted plum tree, past the colorful umbrellas in front of Kells. Look for the pink door on your left, the one between the faux Greek columns. If you get to Virginia Street, you've gone too far. Open the pink door to find . . . The Pink Door, the creation of Jackie Roberts, who playfully calls herself Jacquelina di Roberto, *La Padrona* (the owner). Here fun, funk, and carefully crafted Italian food have merrily mingled since 1981.

By night, candles glimmer, cherubs smile beatifically, and the fountain in the center of the room rumbles good-naturedly along with the animated crowd. A generous antipasto plate is made for sharing, organic produce from Market farmers plays a starring role on the menu, the signature dishes (such as fishermen's stew or any of the pastas) are reliably good, and the specials of the day can be stunning. The lively bar is a prime place to take dessert or an after-dinner drink, especially if the acrobats are performing.

A sunny summer day brings out locals and tourists alike. Then you can sit on one of Seattle's most beautiful rooftop terraces (complete with an herb garden) while you watch the ferryboats make their runs. It's like a garden party with 100 of your most attractive friends, when a leisurely lunch and a Bellini made with tree-ripened peach nectar seem just the thing. Life is good!

Penne Caprese

The Pink Door

Jackie Roberts, owner of the ever-popular Pink Door, gave me the recipe for this simple pasta for which you don't even have to peel or seed the tomatoes or cook the sauce! Jackie enjoys making the dish for her family in August or September, when local tomatoes are at their peak of flavor. I like to use a combination of red, yellow, and orange cherry and pear tomatoes for extra color and flavor.

- ◆ Bring a large pot of salted water to a boil and add pasta. Cook 8 to 10 minutes, or until al dente.

- ◆ While pasta is cooking, place tomatoes and oil in a large mixing bowl and stir to mix. Season to taste with salt and pepper and reserve.

- ◆ When pasta is finished cooking, strain and add to tomatoes while still hot. Add cheese and basil and toss gently. Season to taste with additional salt and pepper as needed.

- ◆ To serve, divide pasta among individual plates and garnish with basil leaves.

Serves 4

Cook's Hint: There is a marked difference between regular mozzarella, the mild, semisoft, elastic cheese that is widely used in cooking and for melting over pizza, and fresh, hand-pulled mozzarella, which can be made from cow's or buffalo's milk, and has a delicate, sweet flavor and softer texture. In this recipe, in addition to specifying fresh mozzarella (which is made fresh several days a week at DeLaurenti), Jackie Roberts insists on using tomatoes just plucked from the garden or purchased at the local farmers' market. Refrigerated tomatoes or those that have been shipped long distances don't taste very good, plus they lack the required amount of "liveliness and acidity" needed to balance the pasta in this dish, according to Jackie.

2 cups dry penne pasta

2 cups chopped heirloom tomatoes

⅓ cup extra virgin olive oil

Kosher salt

Freshly ground black pepper

1 cup cubed (½-inch) fresh mozzarella cheese (about ⅓ pound) (see Cook's Hint below)

¼ cup chopped fresh basil, plus extra basil leaves for garnish

Garbanzo Bean and Potato Patties with Apricot Sweet-and-Sour Sauce

Sabra

When served with a tossed green salad and whole-wheat pitas, these vegetarian patties form a delicious side dish or entrée that even avowed meat eaters will enjoy. For better taste and texture, it's worth going to the extra trouble of cooking your own chickpeas instead of using canned.

◆ Mix together chickpeas and potatoes, and mash well with a fork. (If you prefer a less smooth texture, allow some of the garbanzo beans to remain whole.) Add flour, 1 teaspoon of the pepper, ½ teaspoon of the salt, cumin, garlic, and parsley, and mix well. Taste and add the remaining salt and pepper if needed.

2 cups cooked chickpeas (about ⅔ cup dried), or 1 can (16 ounce) low-sodium garbanzo beans, rinsed and drained

3 medium white potatoes, peeled, boiled, and chopped

2 teaspoons all-purpose flour

1 to 1½ teaspoons freshly ground black pepper

½ to 1 teaspoon kosher salt

1 teaspoon ground cumin

1 teaspoon minced garlic, or ½ teaspoon granulated garlic

SABRA MEDITERRANEAN SANDWICH & JUICE SHOP

A place as old and historic as the Market is bound to spawn ghost stories. Tucked back in the Soames-Dunn Building (across the hall from Emmett Watson's) you'll find Sabra, which overlooks an atmospheric courtyard that contains the Market's famous haunted plum tree. Here the spirit of Princess Angeline, the daughter of Chief Seattle and a member of the Orcas Island tribe, supposedly plucks the ripe plums under cover of darkness. But woe to anyone who spots Angeline's fleeting form and blue eyes, since (unlike Casper), she is not considered a friendly ghost!

While ghost-busting at Sabra (which translates as "cactus" in Lebanese), you can enjoy Middle Eastern specialties including lentil soup and Mediterranean-inspired sandwiches, falafel, hummus (mashed chickpea sauce), *baba ghanoush* (purée of roasted eggplant), and tabbouleh, along with several combination platters. You order from the big board posted behind the counter, then eat your food indoors or outside in the haunted courtyard. If you dare.

◆ Heat olive oil in large skillet over medium-high heat. Form chickpea mixture into 2-inch patties, about ½ inch thick, and place in pan. Cook 3 minutes per side, or until light brown. If necessary, cook in two batches, adding more oil if necessary. Serve with Apricot Sweet-and-Sour Sauce or the condiment or sauce of your choice, such as chutney (see Red Raspberry Chutney, page 183), hot mustard, or cocktail sauce.

Makes 8 or 9 patties; serves 2 or 3 as an entrée, 4 as a side dish

Apricot Sweet-and-Sour Sauce

◆ Place all the ingredients in a small glass mixing bowl and whisk until smooth. Cover and refrigerate a few hours or (preferably) overnight to allow the flavors to meld.

Makes about ⅓ cup

Grand Central Strata

Grand Central Baking Company

Gwenyth Caldwell Bassetti, the founder of the venerable Grand Central Baking Company,* and her husband, Fred Bassetti, a Seattle architect, are longtime Market supporters. Gwen serves on the board of directors of the Market Foundation, and Fred was instrumental in saving the Market from the wrecking ball of "urban renewal" in the late 1960s. Grand Central Strata, a recipe from Gwen's groundbreaking book, cowritten with Jean Galton, *Cooking with Artisan Bread* (Sasquatch Books, 1998), is a savory bread pudding that is perfect for Sunday brunch. You can make it the night before company is coming, then simply slip it into the oven for final baking as guests arrive.

◆ Grease an 8½-by-11-inch or a 9-by-13-inch baking dish and reserve.

◆ Melt 1 tablespoon of the butter in a large skillet over medium-high heat. Add onion and mushrooms and cook 4 to 5 minutes, or until soft, stirring occasionally. Stir in spinach and basil and season with salt and pepper. Set aside to cool.

½ cup minced fresh flat-leaf parsley

1 tablespoon olive oil

Apricot Sweet-and-Sour Sauce (recipe follows)

Apricot Sweet-and-Sour Sauce

¼ cup apricot jam

1 tablespoon Dijon mustard

4 to 6 drops hot red pepper sauce

4 drops toasted sesame oil

¼ teaspoon soy sauce

◆

6 tablespoons (¾ stick) unsalted butter

½ cup chopped white or yellow onion

4 ounces button or cremini mushrooms, thinly sliced

2 bunches (about 2 pounds) spinach, stemmed, blanched, and coarsely chopped, or 1 package (10 ounces) frozen chopped spinach, thawed and squeezed dry

2 tablespoons chopped fresh basil, or 1 teaspoon dried basil

Kosher salt

Freshly ground black pepper

5 large eggs

- ◆ Whisk eggs in a large bowl until well mixed. Whisk in half-and-half and season with salt and pepper.

- ◆ Cut bread to cover bottom of prepared baking dish, with the pieces fitting snugly. Spread vegetable mixture over bread and top with mozzarella and Parmesan.

- ◆ Pour egg mixture over vegetables and cheese and top with remaining bread. (For a decorative effect, cut bread into triangles and arrange in a pattern.) Press bread lightly into egg mixture and dot with remaining butter. Cover and refrigerate at least 2 hours or (preferably) overnight.

- ◆ Preheat oven to 350°F. Place baking dish in a larger roasting pan and fill pan with hot water halfway up the sides of the baking dish. Bake until browned on top, about 50 to 60 minutes. Allow to stand 5 minutes before cutting and serving.

Serves 6

*Outside of the Market Historic District.

4 cups half-and-half, milk, or a combination

1 loaf sourdough or Grand Central Como bread (about a 2-pound loaf), crusts removed and thinly sliced

1 cup (4 ounces) shredded mozzarella cheese

½ cup (2 ounces) grated Parmesan cheese

Five-Spice Grilled Corn with Roasted Red Pepper Butter

icon Grill

8 ears white or yellow sweet corn, shucked

Roasted Red Pepper Butter (recipe follows)

Five-Spice Mix (recipe follows)

Downtown Seattle's icon Grill* is an atmospheric place where Dale Chihuly–inspired art-glass chandeliers dangle overhead and dozens of lamps create a warm glow over walls layered with an eclectic collection of artwork, bric-a-brac, and sculptures. In such a lively setting, it's only fitting that executive chef Nick Musser oversees a menu of "aroused Americana" favorites that include Fried Chicken with Buttermilk Mashed Potatoes and Cream Gravy, Molasses-Glazed Meatloaf, and Texas Fudge Funeral Cake. Nick prepared this all-American grilled corn at one of the Market's Sunset Suppers.

- ◆ Preheat grill or barbecue.

- ◆ Bring a large pot of salted water to a boil and cook corn 2 minutes. Pat dry and continue cooking over grill or barbecue 3 to

5 minutes, or until slightly charred. Brush with Roasted Red Pepper Butter several times during the grilling process.

◆ To serve, remove corn from grill and brush with pepper butter. Sprinkle with Five-Spice Mix and serve immediately.

Serves 8

Roasted Red Pepper Butter

◆ Place roasted peppers in a blender or food processor, pulse until smooth, pour into a small bowl, and reserve.

◆ In the same blender or food processor, pulse butter until smooth. Add reserved pepper purée, salt, white pepper, parsley, and pepper flakes and pulse until thoroughly mixed, scraping down work bowl as needed. Scoop into a small bowl and use immediately, or cover and refrigerate until ready to use.

Makes about 2 cups

Five-Spice Mix

◆ Heat a small dry skillet over medium heat and add Szechwan peppercorns, star anise, cloves, and coriander and fennel seeds. Cook 2 to 3 minutes, or until spices begin to give off their aroma, shaking pan back and forth frequently so spices don't burn. Remove from heat and allow to cool.

◆ Place spices in a coffee grinder or a mortar and pestle and grind to a fine powder. Pour into a small bowl, add salt, and mix well.

Makes about ½ cup

Cook's Hint: The Roasted Red Pepper Butter can easily be frozen. Simply spoon the softened butter onto a piece of plastic wrap and form it into a cylinder with a rubber spatula. Roll the plastic tightly around the cylinder, place in a heavy-duty freezer-safe bag, and use within six months, cutting off slices as needed. Besides melting over corn or steamed vegetables, the spiced butter is also excellent with grilled fish, chicken, or steak.

*Outside of the Market Historic District.

Roasted Red Pepper Butter

2 small roasted red bell peppers, coarsely chopped (see Techniques section)

1 cup (2 sticks) unsalted butter, room temperature, cut into chunks

1 tablespoon kosher salt

1 teaspoon white pepper

1 tablespoon chopped fresh parsley

2 teaspoons crushed red pepper flakes

Five-Spice Mix

1 tablespoon Szechwan peppercorns

2 whole star anise

12 whole cloves

1 tablespoon whole coriander seeds

1 tablespoon whole fennel seeds

¼ cup kosher salt

LE PANIER VERY FRENCH BAKERY

Le Panier, which means "the breadbasket," has been a fixture at the corner of Pike Place and Stewart Street since 1983. With its windows and doors thrown wide open, the shop releases rich aromas of baking bread and pastries that lure in tourists and locals alike.

Customers jockey for a cherished seat at the front counter, a seat that offers one of the best vantage points from which to watch the Market come to life in the early morning. While you munch a freshly baked croissant and sip a caffe mocha capped with whipped cream, the farmers begin setting up for the day, the artisans and craftspeople trundle their goods through the brick-cobbled streets, and the street musicians tune their instruments.

In addition to some of the best baguettes in the city, *pain aux oignons* (onion) and *pain noix* (walnut bread) are two specialty breads that Le Panier introduced to Seattle. *Pain aux oignons* is darkened by the sautéed Walla Walla onions baked into it. *Pain noix* is a large, round, rye-based loaf with a craggy top. Studded with fresh walnuts, it has a chewy consistency. The *pain aux graines* (eight-grain bread) is a healthful choice that incorporates poppy and flax seeds along with semolina, soy, and whole-wheat flour. A selection of seasonal breads that changes every two months might include herb *fougasse* (vegetable bread), *savoie* (baked with Emmentaler cheese), or focaccia bread.

For those with a sweet tooth, Thierry Mougin, the prototypical French baker, offers his specialty, the *amandine*—fresh, homemade almond paste inside a twice-baked croissant topped with fresh almond paste and sliced almonds. His chocolate almond meringue cookie was featured in *Bon Appétit* thanks to a customer's request. Come Christmas, Thierry makes *bûche de Noël,* a traditional French cake shaped and decorated to resemble a log. Available by special order only, it is one of the best desserts in the city and looks stunning on the holiday buffet table.

Thanksgiving Stuffing

Le Panier Very French Bakery

Unlike many turkey dressings, this simple, fruit-filled stuffing isn't terribly rich or fatty, a welcome relief during the calorie-laden holidays. In place of classic French bread, you can use additional onion bread for a stronger onion flavor, or more rye for a heartier stuffing.

◆ Preheat oven to 350°F. Lightly butter a large casserole or baking dish or spray with nonstick cooking spray.

◆ Bring stock to a boil in a medium saucepan and add apricots; remove from heat and reserve. Heat butter in a large skillet. Add onion and cook over low heat for 10 minutes, or until light golden brown in color. If a more moist stuffing is desired, cook 1 cup of the cubed onion bread during the last 5 minutes of cooking time.

◆ Add onion, broth and apricots, apples, thyme, sage, and pepper to a large mixing bowl. Gradually add bread cubes until all bread is moist. Add pecans (if used) and currants.

◆ Spread the stuffing evenly in the casserole dish and bake 20 to 25 minutes, or until lightly browned on top. If stuffing starts to brown too much, cover with aluminum foil during final minutes of baking. Alternatively, the stuffing can be cooked in the turkey cavity if precautions are taken. These include starting with stuffing that has already been heated through, placing the stuffing *loosely* in the cavity, and cooking the stuffing to a temperature of 160°F when a meat thermometer is inserted into the center of the cavity.

Makes 12 cups stuffing, enough for a 16-pound turkey

3½ cups homemade chicken stock, or 2 cups canned chicken broth plus 1½ cups water

1 cup chopped dried apricots

¼ cup (½ stick) unsalted butter

½ cup chopped white or yellow onion

2 medium Granny Smith apples, cored and cut into ½-inch cubes

1 tablespoon dried thyme

2 teaspoons dried rubbed sage

1 teaspoon freshly ground black pepper

3 cups bite-sized pain aux oignons (onion bread) cubes, dried overnight

3 cups bite-sized pain aux campagne (light rye bread) cubes, dried overnight

2 cups bite-sized classic French bread cubes, dried overnight

2 cups chopped pecans (optional)

1 cup dried currants, cherries, or cranberries, or a mixture

Chutney Hollow Squash

Canter-Berry Farms

This easy-to-make yet elegant side dish, which pairs the earthy flavor of winter squash with blueberry or fruit chutney, would be a beautiful and tasty addition to any holiday table.

◆ Preheat oven to 400°F.

◆ Place squash halves in baking dish, sprinkle with salt (if used), cover with aluminum foil, and cook 35 to 45 minutes, or until tender. Alternatively, place squash in a microwave-safe dish, cover with plastic wrap and vent, then cook on HIGH 10 to 12 minutes, turning halfway through, or until just tender. Remove from oven and let rest 2 minutes to finish cooking.

◆ Remove cooked squash from oven and place 1 tablespoon butter in each squash center. Add 1½ tablespoons chutney to each center and return squash to oven until heated through, about 1 minute for conventional ovens and 15 seconds on HIGH for microwave ovens. Garnish each squash half with an autumn-colored blueberry leaf or a mint leaf and serve immediately.

Serves 4

Cook's Hint: You can also use blueberry chutney as a delectable glaze or relish for the holiday bird, over cream cheese and crackers as an hors d'oeuvre, with a lamb or shrimp curry, or as a filling for baked apples.

2 small butternut or acorn squash, split and seeded

Kosher salt (optional)

4 tablespoons unsalted butter

6 tablespoons Canter-Berry Farms blueberry chutney or other fruit chutney

Fresh blueberry or mint leaves, for garnish

Italian Fonduta (Cheese Fondue)

DeLaurenti Specialty Food & Wine

Fondue (from the French *fondre*, which means "to melt") was popular back in the 1960s and '70s and has come back in vogue. This Italian version pushes the envelope thanks to the addition of Taleggio, a "stinky" cheese that ramps up the flavor along with the more mild Fontina d'Aosta and the slightly tart and very creamy Stracchino.

1 clove garlic, unpeeled

Pinch of kosher salt plus ½ teaspoon kosher salt

½ cup dry white wine, such as Orvieto Secco

2 tablespoons cornstarch

3 ounces Stracchino cheese, cut into 1-inch cubes

- In a small saucepan, boil garlic clove 5 minutes. Remove skin and discard. Place peeled garlic clove on a cutting board. With the back of a fork, crush the garlic with the pinch of kosher salt until it forms a paste.

- Place garlic mixture in a double boiler with wine and bring to a simmer over medium-high heat. In a medium mixing bowl, combine cornstarch with the cheeses.

- Reduce heat to medium and add cheese to top of double boiler, whisking constantly. When cheese is completely melted, add lemon juice and pepper, whisking well. Cook for another minute, stirring frequently, then taste and add the remaining ½ teaspoon salt, if desired. Transfer the cheese to a serving bowl or fondue pot.

- To serve, place a bread chunk on the end of a long serving fork and dunk in the hot cheese.

Makes 1½ cups; serves 2 to 3 as an entrée,
6 as an appetizer or cheese course

Spicy Vegetable Stew

Willie Green's Organic Farm

A fresh vegetable and bean stew redolent of garlic, cumin, chili powder, and cilantro really fits the bill for a hearty vegetarian feast, especially when served on a thick bed of organic fingerling or new potatoes.

- Heat olive oil in a large skillet (preferably nonstick) over medium heat. Add the garlic, onion, bell pepper, and carrot and cook 10 minutes, or until vegetables are tender-crisp, stirring often. If a nonstick skillet is unavailable, add more oil as needed.

- Add chili powder and cumin and stir well. Add tomatoes, stock, and beans and stir well. Reduce heat and simmer, covered, 20 minutes.

9 ounces Taleggio cheese, rind removed and cut into 1-inch cubes

4 ounces Fontina d'Aosta cheese, coarsely grated

½ teaspoon freshly squeezed lemon juice

½ teaspoon freshly ground white pepper

1 loaf rustic-style bread, cut into bite-sized chunks

1 tablespoon olive oil

1 clove garlic, minced

1 cup chopped white or yellow onion

½ cup chopped green bell pepper

½ cup diced carrot

1 tablespoon ground chili powder

1 teaspoon ground cumin

1 pound diced tomatoes

½ cup homemade vegetable stock, or ¼ cup canned vegetable broth plus ¼ cup water

1 can (15 ounce) black, kidney, or pinto beans, rinsed and drained

- About 15 to 20 minutes before serving, boil or steam potatoes until tender.

- Meanwhile, add zucchini and yellow squash to the skillet, cover, and simmer 5 minutes, or until squash is tender-crisp. Add the 2 tablespoons cilantro, stir well, and season to taste with salt and pepper.

- To serve, cut potatoes into bite-sized pieces, top with stew, and garnish with cilantro sprigs.

Serves 4 to 6

1½ pounds fingerling potatoes or whole tiny new potatoes, scrubbed

1 cup diced zucchini

1 cup diced yellow squash

2 tablespoons chopped cilantro, plus 4 to 6 extra sprigs, for garnish

Kosher salt

Freshly ground black pepper

WILLIE GREEN'S ORGANIC FARM

Jeff Miller, owner and operator of Willie Green's, has been farming since 1987, the past eight years spent on his picturesque spread in Monroe, Washington. This Pittsburgh native is a 1983 graduate of the Culinary Institute of America at Hyde Park, New York, the most prestigious school for professional chefs in the United States and perhaps the world. He worked his way around the country from New York to San Francisco before he decided to chuck his chef's whites for overalls.

Jeff started out with a quarter-acre of land, which has since grown to 24 acres that include 20 acres of salad greens and vegetables and 4 acres of raspberries. "I'm kind of anal to begin with," the thin, blond, intensely focused man admits. "The idea is to grow perfect beds of greens." It's something he does in abundance, to the delight of countless farmers' market customers and Community Supported Agriculture (CSA) subscribers.

In addition to baby spinach, mesclun salad mix, tender baby carrots, and fingerling potatoes, among the more unusual products you'll find on Jeff's table are *tatsoi* (an Asian green used fresh in salads or for stir-fried dishes), *zucchetta* (an heirloom variety of Italian squash with a long, curved neck), and braising mix (a mix of sturdy greens that stand up to slow cooking). Jeff and one of his farm helpers come to the Market every Wednesday in June through October while Organic Farmer Days are running, where they set up right along Pike Place on makeshift tables and under colorful awnings. "I love the atmosphere, vitality, activity, and the people at the Market," he says.

Pasqualina Verdi's Pesto Sauce

Whistling Train Farm

Decades ago, when the Market's Italian farmers first introduced pesto to the Scandinavian-descended population of Seattle, the fresh herb paste must have seemed strangely exotic. This rendition is even more "exotic" because it is cooked, although Shelley and Mike advise that it can easily be made in the food processor or blender by limiting the water and increasing the oil.

◆ Heat a large pot of water to boiling for pasta. Add pasta and boil 10 to 15 minutes, or until al dente. Drain pasta, then return to the pot and cover.

◆ Heat olive oil in a large skillet over medium heat. Add basil, garlic, and parsley and stir constantly for 2 to 3 minutes. Add water and simmer 10 to 15 minutes, stirring occasionally, until desired consistency is reached. Remove from heat and stir in half the cheese.

◆ Toss with cooked pasta. Add remaining cheese and toss again. Divide among individual plates and serve immediately.

Serves 4 to 6

Cook's Hint: Shelley and Mike suggest getting creative with your pesto by adding pine nuts, walnuts, or hazelnuts for richness and varying the herbs (such as summer savory or marjoram) according to your taste and what is in season.

1 pound dried pasta of your choice

2 tablespoons olive oil

2 bunches basil, finely chopped

2 or 3 cloves garlic, minced

5 or 6 sprigs flat-leaf parsley, minced (optional) (see Cook's Hint below)

1 cup water

½ cup grated Parmesan, Romano, or Pecorino Romano cheese (or a combination of all three)

WHISTLING TRAIN FARM

Everyone who knows the least bit about the Market either remembers or has heard stories about Pasqualina Verdi, a squat, ruddy-cheeked Italian immigrant with a kerchief over her hair who was dubbed the "queen of the Market."

The "queen" started at the Market in 1955. She was so passionate about her farm-fresh produce that she would often sneak unusual vegetables into the bags of unsuspecting customers in the hopes that they would try them. When her son Mike (who ran the farm) married Sue Verdi, Pasqualina acquired not only a daughter-in-law but also a soul sister. The two sold side by side for years at the Verdis' farm table across from Sosio's, offering recipes and life advice along with Mike's veggies and basil.

When Pasqualina died in 1991, a little bit of the old Market died with her. Sue fought a valiant battle with breast cancer and passed away in 1997. Mike went through tough times, but continued working the farm. Eventually, he started dating Shelley Pasco, a graphic designer by profession but a farmer at heart. It wasn't too long before wedding bells rang out for the pair in a wedding chapel in Las Vegas.

Shelley and Mike began farming in south King County at Whistling Train Farm, coming to the Market on Saturdays and setting up shop at Pasqualina and Sue's old space with Italian greens, fresh basil, and an assortment of vegetables. They added chickens and pigs to their growing list of farm-raised products, sold at area farmers' markets, and offered subscription sales to their customers.

Soon Shelley and Mike started selling at the Market on Organic Farmer Days, where Shelley is now a fixture on Wednesdays. In the summer of 2002, Shelley and Mike's greatest creation sprouted with the birth of baby Della. It's a joy to see the dark-haired babe peacefully sleeping while her mother sells her produce the old-fashioned way—customer by customer. To longtime Marketgoers, it's comforting to think that once again, there are two generations of Verdi women selling along Pike Place.

Raspberry Snap Peas

Alm Hill Gardens

This is a low-calorie treat—no butter or olive oil is added to mask the fresh taste of the snap peas and the raspberry wine vinegar. Feel free to adjust the amount of wine vinegar

½ pound snap peas, rinsed and ends with strings removed

3 to 5 tablespoons raspberry wine vinegar

2 to 4 tablespoons sesame seeds, toasted (see Techniques section)

ALM HILL GARDENS

For more than 25 years, the husband-and-wife team of Ben Craft and Gretchen Hoyt have been farming the land near the Washington-Canada border that Ben bought as a teenager. Starting out with just one acre of raspberries that produced fruit six weeks a year, Gretchen and Ben's farm—Alm Hill Gardens—has grown into a diversified fruit and vegetable business that produces 25 crops. It's a family affair. You can find Ben, Gretchen, son Joshua, daughter Katie, or a representative in the North Arcade of the Market just across from City Fish every day of the week year-round.

They begin the year bringing in colorful tulips from January to May; in mid-April the family continues with baby spinach, arugula, lettuce, and their famous "Spicy Salad Mix." May brings lilacs and peonies along with overwinter cauliflower. Raspberries begin coming in during June; then the peas—snap, shelling, and snow—make their appearance along with green onions and Imperial Star artichokes. July brings blueberries and beans of every description, including *haricots verts*, pole, purple, yellow wax, shelling, flageolet, black shell, and even good ol' green. Of course, come summer, a bumper crop of zucchini and other vegetables appears.

"Our greenhouse tomatoes ripened on the vine taste like vine-ripened tomatoes grown outdoors," Gretchen says. They go great with Alm Hill's big sprigs of basil, while the fresh dill pairs perfectly with the prodigious crop of pickling cucumbers. Corn comes in strong in September, along with blackberries and marionberries, lemon cucumbers and salad cukes. Fall broccoli, pumpkins, several varieties of potatoes, and winter squash herald the changing seasons, while the salad greens sometimes continue as late as November. December sees the family in the Market selling beautiful sprays of greenery and holly, as well as carefully constructed centerpieces and holiday wreaths.

"We get a lot of satisfaction and a lot of strokes when people tell us that they love the food we grow," explains Gretchen.

and sesame seeds, depending on the amount of acidity and crunch you prefer.

In a steamer or microwave oven, cook snap peas 3 to 5 minutes, or until tender/crisp. Toss peas with raspberry wine vinegar until they are evenly coated, then sprinkle with sesame seeds.

Serves 2 to 4

Stir-Fried Harvest Medley

Duffield Organic Farm

Foods from different nations, such as France, Italy, Japan, and China, join to create this eclectic and delicious entrée created by Judy Duff. Vegetables of your choice can be added or substituted in this recipe, for, according to Judy, "the key to farm cooking is creativity, *not* rigidity. Enjoy the harvest!"

◆ In a large skillet or wok, heat oil over medium-high heat until very hot. Add onion and stir-fry 2 minutes. Add broccoli, summer squashes, zucchini, haricots verts, mizuna, shungiku, and tah tsai and stir-fry 3 to 5 minutes, or until desired doneness. You can add the 1 to 2 tablespoons water while stir-frying if you like your vegetables cooked to a more tender stage.

◆ Divide vegetables among dinner plates, sprinkle with sesame seeds, and artistically arrange nasturtiums on top immediately before serving.

Serves 4

1 tablespoon safflower, soy, or canola oil

½ cup chopped white or yellow onion

¾ cup broccoli florets

1 Sun Drop summer squash, chopped into ½-by-1-inch pieces

1 Sunburst summer squash, chopped into ½-by-1-inch sections

2 small zucchini, chopped

1 cup haricots verts (French-style green beans), cut into 1-inch pieces

1 cup chopped mizuna (stems and leaves)

½ cup chopped shungiku (stems and leaves)

1 cup tah tsai or baby pak choi with whole leaves

1 to 2 tablespoons water (optional)

¼ cup sesame seeds, toasted (see Techniques section)

8 fresh edible nasturtiums

DUFFIELD ORGANIC FARM

F arming three plots of land in three separate cities and selling two days a week at the Pike Place Market during the growing season would seem like a full-time job to most mortals, but not to Judy Duff. But then, Judy and her family have never had an easy row to hoe.

When Judy, husband Dave, and daughter Deanna bought 3 acres of land adjacent to their home in Burien, Washington, they did not buy farmland. Instead, they pieced together acreage in a strictly residential area thickly populated with cottonwood and pussy willow trees, Scotch broom, and purple clover. They now refer to this piece of land as their "urban farm." In order to increase the quantity and variety of their crops, the Duffs leased 2 acres in Sumner, Washington. Most recently, they began leasing 10 acres in Kent, part of a 25-acre parcel that was once destined to become a Wal-Mart.

When they come to the Market on Fridays and Saturdays in June through October, the Duff family specializes in fresh, organic produce. Their farm table is always a delight to the eye as well as to the palate as they sell haricots verts; baby romaine, Oak Leaf, and French Brunia lettuces; fresh herbs; Japanese and Chinese greens; a wide variety of squashes; edible flowers; different varieties of vine-ripened tomatoes; and cornichons and Middle Eastern cucumbers .

"I believe farming has given my family the tenacity and patience to effect change," Judy says. "We follow generations before us and hope generations will follow us. Of late, we have lost far too many family members, but hold on to their spirits each time we plant a seed, for we know life continues to bloom in miraculous ways."

Potato Gratin

Maximilien-in-the-Market

T his creamy gratin, in which thinly sliced potatoes are cooked in milk, then baked in heavy cream flavored with garlic, is the most famous dish to come from the Dauphiné, a mountainous region near the French-Italian border. It is a mainstay side dish on Maximilien's menu, but at home I like to serve it during the wintertime as a hearty vegetarian entrée.

◆ Preheat oven to 400°F. Butter a 9-by-13-inch gratin dish or a 7½-by-12-inch glass baking dish and set aside.

◆ In a large saucepan, bring milk to a boil and add salt, nutmeg, and bouquet garni. Add potatoes to milk, bring milk back to a

6 cups whole milk

Pinch of kosher salt, plus extra for seasoning

Pinch of ground nutmeg

Bouquet garni (see Techniques section)

2½ pounds russet potatoes, peeled and cut into ⅛-inch slices

Freshly ground white pepper

⅔ cup whipping cream

MAXIMILIEN-IN-THE-MARKET

Tucked under the Market Clock and just past MarketSpice and Don & Joe's Meats, a neon-lit passageway leads to a hideaway restaurant. If not for the panoramic views of Elliott Bay, West Seattle, and the Olympic Mountains, you'd swear you were in the back streets of Paris. Welcome to Maximilien-in-the-Market, which is owned and operated by Axel Macé, who runs the front of the house, and Eric Francy, who serves as chef.

The two native Frenchmen bought the restaurant from original owners Francois and Julia Kissel, who opened the bistro in 1975. Macé and Francy worked for the couple until 1997, when they bought the place, perked up the dark green walls with a fresh paint job, and fine-tuned the menu to their liking.

Everybody looks beautiful in the soft pink light that bathes the room and plays off huge picture windows and gilt-framed mirrors. White tablecloths, votive candles, and sprays of flowers on the tables add a purely romantic touch.

Lunchtime highlights French bistro classics such as assorted charcuterie, mussels served five (count 'em!) ways, and Croque Monsieur. At dinner, appetizers including sautéed frog legs and escargots bathed in copious amounts of garlic-parsley butter entice. Among the entrée choices you'll find Sturgeon with Red Wine Sauce, Roasted Chicken Breast with Wild Mushroom Sauce, and Tournedos of Beef with Foie Gras. Don't miss the profiteroles, light cream-puff orbs filled with rich vanilla ice cream and drizzled with decadent chocolate sauce. *Vive la France*!

boil, reduce heat, and simmer 10 to 15 minutes. With a slotted spoon, stir potatoes occasionally to keep them from sticking to bottom of pan, but be careful not to break them up. Gently drain potatoes and discard milk.

2 cloves garlic, crushed

¼ pound Gruyère cheese, grated

◆ Layer potatoes in bottom of prepared dish so they overlap slightly and completely cover the bottom. Season with salt and pepper, arrange another layer of potatoes, season, and continue this process until all potatoes are layered.

◆ Bring whipping cream to a boil along with garlic. Remove garlic, then pour cream over potatoes, sprinkle with cheese, and bake 30 to 40 minutes, or until potatoes are tender.

◆ To serve, cut into wedges and serve piping hot.

Serves 4 to 6 as a vegetarian entrée, 8 to 10 as a side dish

Entrées

Chicken with Cherry-Wine Sauce
Pozole
Irish Stew
Zaire Chicken Curry
Braised Eggplant with Pork Spareribs
Northwest Chicken Stir-Fry
Chicken Masala
How to Roast a Beef
Korean Beef Barbecue (Bulgogi)
Cornish Game Hens with Raspberry Gravy
Rouladen
Chicken Adobo
Pancit Bihon
Chicken Gui with Stir-Fried Vegetables
Barbecued Short Ribs
Lamb Burgers with Balsamic Onions, Roasted Peppers, and Aïoli
Mechado
New Mexico Tamales

Chicken with Cherry-Wine Sauce

Chukar Cherry Company

This is a recipe I've made time and again not only because it's easy, healthy, and impressive enough for guests, but because it showcases two of our state's finest products—Washington wine and Bing cherries grown and processed in the Yakima Valley.

◆ Cook rice as directed on package. (Cook 1 or 2 cups depending on whether you want to serve ½-cup or 1-cup servings.)

◆ While rice is cooking, pour wine into a large nonreactive saucepan and add dried cherries. Bring to a boil, then turn down heat and simmer cherry-wine mixture about 15 minutes, or until the liquid is reduced by half and cherries lose their wrinkles and plump.

◆ While cherries and wine are simmering, sauté chicken pieces in a large skillet over medium to medium-high heat, using a minimum of olive oil. Chicken pieces should be white and completely cooked throughout, but still tender.

◆ When cherry-wine mixture is reduced by half, remove it from heat, add butter and sugar, and swirl until blended.

◆ To serve, place chicken pieces on top of cooked rice and pour cherry-wine sauce over the top. Vegetarians can enjoy this dish, too, if the sauce alone (no chicken) is served over the rice along with steamed or sautéed vegetables. Season to taste with salt, pepper, and rosemary (you can do this in the kitchen, or your family or guests can do it themselves at the table).

Serves 6 to 8

Cook's Hint: Pam Auld suggests that to vary the aroma and flavor, add a small amount of fresh rosemary (in place of dried) and white pepper (instead of black) to the finished dish.

1 to 2 cups white, brown, or wild rice

1 bottle (750 milliliter) good-quality red wine (Washington state Merlot or Cabernet Sauvignon recommended)

1 cup Chukar dried Bing cherries

6 boneless, skinless chicken breasts, cut into 1-inch chunks

1 to 2 teaspoons olive oil

1 tablespoon unsalted butter

Pinch of granulated sugar

Kosher salt

Freshly ground black pepper

Dried rosemary, crumbled

EL MERCADO LATINO

El Mercado Latino adds lots of spice, both literally and figuratively, to the Market. Colorful *ristras* (strings of fresh peppers, garlic buds, and dried flowers) dangle high above the entrance to this well-stocked cubbyhole grocery in the Sanitary Market Building. Just outside, you'll find boxes brimming with jewel-colored goat's horn, New Mexico floral gem, Bulgarian carrot, and Scotch Bonnet peppers, just a few of the 25-plus different varieties stocked during the summer season. You might also encounter *nopales* (cactus leaves), plantains (starchy bananas), tomatillos (small, green tomatoes), and chayotes (a gourdlike fruit). This is also a reliable place to find coconuts in the shell, fresh *galangal* (similar to gingerroot), and fresh lemongrass.

Inside the store, fresh and packaged Caribbean, South and Central American, Spanish, Creole, and even African foodstuffs crowd the shelves. Packets of spices ranging from fajita seasoning to *menudo* mix dangle from revolving racks. Frozen banana leaves (used like parchment paper for wrapping seafood and chicken before baking), *queso fresco* (a white, slightly salty fresh Mexican cheese), and *cajeta* (the caramel-like base for dessert sauces) are other interesting items for sale at this globally minded market.

Pozole

El Mercado Latino

Pozole is a mainstay of Mexican cuisine, a pork and hominy soup served with garnishes of lime wedges, crisp pork rinds, avocado pieces, onions, radishes, or whatever else strikes your fancy. And although there are almost as many versions of *pozole* as there are stewpots in Mexico, many include beans, ham, and pig's feet. Your kitchen will fill with the wonderful fragrance of corn as the *pozole* simmers and puffs into tender, flavorful buds. You can adjust the amount of heat and saltiness by the amounts of chile peppers and salt you add.

½ pound pozole (hominy)

3½ quarts (14 cups) water

½ to 1 teaspoon kosher salt

2 to 4 fresh New Mexico chile peppers or 2 to 4 dried mild red chile pods, chopped

1 pound pork or beef steak, cubed

⅛ teaspoon ground oregano

1 clove garlic, minced

◆ In a large stockpot, soak pozole in water overnight, then rinse with several changes of fresh, cold water. Bring the 3½ quarts water to a boil, and add pozole and salt. Cook over medium heat for 2 hours, stirring occasionally.

◆ Add chiles, pork, oregano, and garlic. Cover and simmer another hour, or until pozole is tender.

◆ To serve, ladle pozole into soup bowls. Place remaining ingredients in small bowls and encourage your family or guests to garnish their bowls of pozole.

Serves 6

Chopped onions, shredded cabbage, chopped radishes, salsa, sliced jalapeño peppers, diced avocado, crisp pork rinds, lime wedges, crumbled dried oregano, and tortilla chips, for garnish

KELLS IRISH RESTAURANT & PUB

Kells is named after the Book of Kells, the seventh-century illuminated manuscripts of the Gospels written in Latin and illustrated with Celtic art. Although never completed, the Book of Kells is a pivotal work wherein Christianity meets the Celtic culture.

Opened in 1983 by Ethna and Joe McAleese (who chose Seattle as their home when they emigrated from Belfast because the rain reminded them of Ireland), Kells serves traditional Irish dishes, Ethna's famous Irish soda bread, and fine Guinness Stout, Kells lager, and Grand Irish whiskey. With its 100-year-old bar imported from Ireland and the slogan *ceád maít failté*—a thousand welcomes—inscribed above the entryway, Kells truly feels like a wee bit o' Ireland as one of the McAleese clan escorts you to a table in the dark, intimate dining room or (weather permitting) the cheery outside patio with its colorful umbrellas.

1916 POST ALLEY

KELLS

ESTP 1983

Once seated, you will be tempted by hearty Irish fare such as steak and kidney pie, leg of lamb, shepherd's pie, and Dublin Coddle, a stew composed of potato, onion, browned sausage, and bacon. Golden-crusted "pasties," hand-held, stuffed pastries that Irish coal miners traditionally packed in their lunches when they went underground, come filled with chicken, seafood, corned beef, or vegetables.

There's live Irish music in the bar (through the door on the left) seven nights a week, and contented patrons often sing along while they raise a pint and share tales of the old country. As the McAleeses like to say, "If you can't go to Ireland, come to Kells."

Irish Stew

Kells Irish Restaurant & Pub

Sometimes the simplest things are the best—you'll love the way the lamb, vegetables, water, and spices cook down into a chunky stew that is best served with slabs of homemade Irish soda bread and pints of Guinness Stout.

◆ Season lamb chunks with salt and pepper. In a large skillet over medium heat, cook lamb pieces until browned, stirring occasionally. Add onions, carrots, potatoes, thyme, and additional salt and pepper, if desired. Stir well, then cover with water.

◆ Bring mixture to a boil, reduce heat to medium-low, and simmer, uncovered, approximately 1¼ hours. Add more water (or lamb or beef stock for extra flavor) if necessary. Ladle into soup bowls and serve.

Makes about 10 cups; serves 6 to 8

3 pounds lamb sirloin, cut into ½-inch chunks (Note: If your butcher will give you the lamb bone, add it to the stew for extra flavor)

Kosher salt

Freshly ground black pepper

1 pound white or yellow onions, cut into ¼-inch dice

1 pound carrots, cut into ¼-inch dice

2½ pounds large white potatoes, well scrubbed and cut into ¼-inch dice

½ teaspoon dried thyme, crumbled

KITCHEN BASICS

Located in the Sanitary Market Building in a space that once housed the American Pie Co., Kitchen Basics was established in 1984. The name says it all, for the store specializes in cookware, bakeware, and kitchen gadgets that are value-priced. Bargain hunters flock here for the assortment of baking pans, roasters, food storage sets, tea kettles, and coffee carafes, while gadget lovers are tempted by the old-fashioned meat grinders, spaetzle (German noodle and dumpling) makers, and cookie molds in all shapes and sizes.

Kitchen Basics is also the Northwest's largest dealer for Fiesta dinnerware, boasting the greatest selection of accessory pieces. These items aren't always available in department stores, and include gusto bowls, bouillon cups, fruit cups, oval servers, bread trays, and jumbo cups, saucers, and bowls. Current colors include such exotic offerings as cinnabar, persimmon, and seamist green.

Zaire Chicken Curry

Kitchen Basics

This curry is not the usual yellow, creamy type you might find at an Indian restaurant—instead, it's low-fat, hot, and sweet, swimming with currants and red and green peppers. A nice change and definitely worth a try!

◆ Heat olive oil in a large skillet over medium-high heat. Add chicken pieces and brown, turning down heat and cooking in two batches if necessary. Remove chicken pieces and pat dry with paper towels. Drain excess oil from pan and wipe out any remaining oil with a paper towel.

◆ To make stock, add water, salt, black pepper, curry powder, oregano, savory, garlic, and jalapeño to stockpot and simmer 5 minutes.

◆ To make stew, add chicken pieces to stock in stockpot, sprinkle with brown sugar, top with green and red bell peppers, onion, and currants, and simmer, covered, over very low heat for 45 minutes to 1½ hours, depending on how you like your chicken. Forty-five minutes gives you chicken of normal American-style tenderness; 1½ hours is the authentic African way, with the chicken literally falling off the bone.

◆ While chicken is simmering, prepare rice as package directs, timing it so that it will be ready at about the same time as the curry.

◆ Ladle chicken and vegetables into a large serving bowl. Place yogurt in a medium bowl and *slowly* add stock remaining in stockpot to yogurt, stirring to mix thoroughly. Place yogurt mixture back in the stockpot and heat *very* slowly, or the yogurt could curdle. Pour heated yogurt/stock mixture over chicken and vegetables.

◆ Ladle chicken pieces, vegetables, and yogurt sauce on top of rice, and serve with chutney.

Serves 6

---

2 tablespoons olive oil

1 chicken fryer (3½ pounds), skinned and cut into large pieces, or 6 chicken breasts with ribs, skin removed

1½ cups water

1 teaspoon kosher salt

1 teaspoon freshly ground black pepper

3 to 4 tablespoons curry powder

1 teaspoon dried oregano, crumbled

1 teaspoon dried summer savory, crumbled

1 clove garlic, minced

1 jalapeño pepper, whole (if you prefer your curry the authentic African way) or minced (if you like lots of extra heat), or a few drops of hot red pepper sauce

½ cup firmly packed brown sugar

1 green bell pepper, cut into thin strips

Half a red bell pepper, cut into thin strips

1 large white onion, cut into ⅛-inch slices

½ cup dried currants

1 cup uncooked brown rice

1 cup plain low-fat yogurt

Mango chutney or hot chutney

Braised Eggplant with Pork Spareribs

Saigon Restaurant

The tomatoes, eggplant, and fish sauce called for in this recipe simmer together to form a deep, rich, brown sauce—a perfect counterpoint to the meaty spareribs.

◆ Rinse spareribs in several changes of water until water runs clear. Place spareribs in 4-quart saucepan, add fish sauce and shallot, and mix well.

◆ Cook spareribs on medium to medium-high heat for 20 minutes, covered, stirring occasionally. Remove from heat, let spareribs rest a few minutes, then add the 6 cups water. (Before adding water, you can drain off any liquid fat that accumulates in the bottom of the pan for a lighter dish.) Bring mixture to a boil over high heat and skim off any foam that rises to the top. Add tomatoes, reduce heat to low, and simmer 40 minutes, uncovered.

◆ Meanwhile, in a large mixing bowl, dissolve salt in the 8 cups water, add eggplant, and soak. When spareribs are ready, drain salty water from eggplant and discard, rinse eggplant well, and add eggplant to the pan with the spareribs. Simmer another 20 minutes over low to medium heat, stirring occasionally.

◆ To serve, arrange spareribs and vegetables on a large platter and sprinkle with green onions.

Serves 4

2 pounds pork spareribs, trimmed of fat and cut into bite-sized pieces

¼ cup Vietnamese fish sauce (nuoc mam)

1 shallot, cut into ⅛-inch slices

6 cups water

1 pound ripe tomatoes, sliced

2 tablespoons kosher salt

8 cups (2 quarts) water

1 large Italian eggplant, or 4 Japanese eggplants, stems removed and discarded, remaining portion cut into bite-sized pieces

1 bunch green onion, root ends and top ¼ inch removed and discarded, remaining portion thinly sliced

S aigon, one of the first authentic Vietnamese restaurants to open in Seattle (circa 1977), has always been a family affair. Original owner Lucy Pham Nguyen was first drawn to the Market because working there reminded her of the open-air markets in her native Vietnam. When Lucy decided it was time to retire, she kept the small business "all in the family" by turning the reins over to her sister Vinh Thi Pham. Vinh is the type of woman who greets her regular customers by name and keeps track of their favorite dishes.

You can rub elbows with everyone from Seattle cops to briefcase-toting businesspeople at the counter here, or choose one of the small tables set against the wall. Local chefs like it, too. In his book *Tom Douglas' Seattle Kitchen*, Chef Tom Douglas (owner of nearby Etta's Seafood) says, "To this day, my favorite lunch is the impeccably pure and delicious *pho*—beef noodle soup—made at the tiny Saigon Restaurant in Pike Place Market."

With nearly 100 dishes to choose from, you might opt for a Saigon salad—beef, chicken, or prawns sautéed with onions and tomatoes, served on a bed of rice noodles, shredded lettuce, bean sprouts, and cucumber. The salad is tossed with Saigon sweet-and-sour sauce and garnished with shredded carrots and roasted peanuts. Saigon also serves a steaming bowl of chicken soup that becomes even more authoritative when spiced with a couple of squirts of *Sriracha* hot chile sauce (a traditional Vietnamese condiment). If the pepper sauce doesn't cure you of a stuffy head cold, the warm noodles and broth will at least make you feel a whole lot more content.

Northwest Chicken Stir-Fry

Chicken Valley

T his tasty, easy-to-prepare, colorful main dish substitutes Northwest ingredients in a traditional Asian stir-fry. The dried cherries are available in the Pike Place Market at Chukar Cherry Company (page 175), the hazelnuts from Holmquist Hazelnut Orchards (page 156).

◆ Heat peanut and sesame oils in large skillet or wok over medium-high heat. Add chicken and stir-fry 3 to 4 minutes, or until chicken turns white and is completely cooked through. Remove from wok and reserve.

1 tablespoon peanut oil

3 drops toasted sesame oil

¾ pound boneless chicken breasts, skin removed and cut into bite-sized pieces

2 cloves garlic, minced

1 small yellow onion, cut into ¼-inch slices

¼ cup dried Bing or tart cherries, plumped (see Techniques section)

CHICKEN VALLEY

The fried chicken from Chicken Valley is a deep-fried pleasure so perfect that it puts Colonel Sanders to shame. Juicy thighs, plump drumsticks, and tender breasts are dunked in Chicken Valley's light, perfectly seasoned batter (don't even bother asking for the top-secret formula) and deep-fried to crispy perfection. At least one local celebrity chef can't come to the Market without picking up half a pound of the luscious fried livers and gizzards to munch during his shopping forays.

Chicken Valley started life as Sunny Valley in the 1940s, and its sign, which reads "Chicken Valley Farm Stores," is a nostalgic blast from the past. Present owner Sam Lee acquired the business in 1985, and in addition to the fried goodies he also offers fresh raw poultry to cook at home. Choose from among chicken parts and chicken stock, ducks, whole capons, Cornish game hens, pheasants, turkeys, quail, squab, partridges, geese, and rabbit.

◆ Add garlic and onion and stir-fry 2 to 3 minutes, or until onions just start to wilt. Add plumped cherries and hazelnuts and stir-fry 30 seconds. Add spinach leaves and stir-fry, turning leaves gently from top of the skillet to bottom. When spinach turns bright green and just begins to wilt, remove from heat. Return reserved chicken pieces to wok and stir well.

◆ Mix balsamic vinegar with brown sugar and arrowroot and add to skillet. Stir well, cover skillet, and shake back and forth a few times to blend.

◆ Serve family style on a platter or in a large pasta bowl over soba noodles or angel hair pasta.

Serves 4

¼ cup toasted, chopped hazelnuts, with skins removed (see Techniques section)

1 pound fresh spinach leaves, rinsed, drained, and spun dry

1½ teaspoons balsamic vinegar

¼ teaspoon brown sugar

½ teaspoon arrowroot

Soba noodles or angel hair pasta, cooked according to instructions on package

Chicken Masala

MarketSpice

Garam is the Indian word for "warm" or "hot," and *garam masala* is a blend of up to 12 dry-roasted, ground spices that originated in northern India. The blend might include dried chiles, fennel, mace, cinnamon, cloves, coriander, cumin, cardamom, and nutmeg and is as individual as the person mixing it. Buy it at specialty markets, gourmet shops, spice shops, or Indian markets.

◆ Heat oil in a large skillet over medium heat, add onions, and cook 8 to 10 minutes, or until lightly browned, stirring occasionally. Combine granulated garlic, salt, garam masala, ginger, and cayenne, and add to onion, stirring to blend.

◆ Arrange chicken breasts or legs in the pan with onions. Cook 2 to 3 minutes, or until slightly browned, turning once. Add water and cover, bring to a simmer, and cook 8 to 10 minutes, or until chicken is just tender. Add more water if needed, but *do not overcook.*

◆ Remove chicken to a plate and pour remaining onions and pan juices into a blender. Allow to cool slightly and purée until smooth. (If desired, the dish can be made ahead up to this point and reheated.)

◆ Return purée to pan, add yogurt, and stir well. Add chicken and cook a few minutes more, or until heated through. If the sauce is too thick, thin with stock; if too thin, remove chicken and cook sauce over higher heat, stirring constantly. Do not bring to a boil, or the sauce could curdle. Serve over rice.

Serves 4

2 to 3 tablespoons canola, corn, or soy oil or clarified butter or ghee (see Techniques section)

2 large white or yellow onions, cut into 1/8-inch slices

1 teaspoon granulated garlic

1 teaspoon kosher salt

2 teaspoons ground garam masala

1/2 teaspoon ground ginger

1/2 teaspoon ground cayenne pepper, or to taste

2 pounds boneless, skinless chicken breasts, cut into quarters, or chicken thighs

1 cup water or homemade chicken stock, or 1/2 cup canned chicken broth plus 1/2 cup water

1/3 cup plain yogurt

2 to 3 cups cooked white or brown rice

How to Roast a Beef

Crystal Meats

Roasting meat has been variously described as an inherited trait, a science, and an art. In the hope that roasting beef is a skill that all of us can learn, here are some tips from Delores and Michael Greenblat, owners of Crystal Meats.

Start with a tender roast. This is most important since roasting cooks by dry heat and will not break down tough meat fibers. A standing rib roast or similar cut will hold its shape better during roasting and will have a richer flavor if cooked on the bone. Bring the roast to room temperature before you put it in the oven, so that the meat will cook evenly.

Despite what many people think, putting salt and pepper on the meat prior to cooking will not toughen it. Be sure to season just before the roast goes into the hot oven, however. Insert a meat thermometer into the thickest part of the roast, making sure it doesn't touch fat or bone, which would falsify the reading.

The perfect roasting pan should be just one inch larger than the roast itself; a larger pan can burn the pan juices and a smaller one can steam the meat. A rack works well, because it creates a nicely browned exterior, promotes even cooking, and prevents stewing or steaming. Bone-in roasts have their own built-in rack—simply cook bone side down.

Searing the meat, rather than cooking at one low temperature throughout, produces the best results. To sear a roast, preheat

CRYSTAL MEATS

Delores and Michael Greenblat, owners of Crystal Meats, like to say that they "trim the meat, not the customer," and the Greenblat family has been doing just that since 1947, when Michael's father bought the business for $5,000. The Greenblats specialize in a variety of quality meats, including poultry, beef, pork, deli, and smoked meats. You'll find them in the Corner Market Building near Oriental Kitchenette and Patti Summers.

the oven and an empty roasting pan to 500°F. Add the meat and sear for 15 minutes. Turn heat down to 350°F and roast until the meat reaches the desired doneness. Your roast will be cooked rare at 120°F; medium-rare at 125°F; medium at 135°F; and well-done at 150°F.

Allow the roast to rest about 15 minutes so that its juices will redistribute and the slices will attain a nice uniform red or pink color throughout. Carve and enjoy with freshly grated horseradish and your favorite side dishes, such as Yorkshire pudding and vegetables.

Korean Beef Barbecue (Bulgogi)

Deluxe Bar-B-Que

Bulgogi, which is often referred to as the national meat dish of Korea, is easy to make and delicious, full of gingerroot and green onions. It's also versatile—if you aren't a beef fan, you can substitute chicken. The spicy beef pairs well with Stir-Fried Harvest Medley (page 74).

◆ In a bowl large enough to hold the beef, mix sugar, soy sauce, green onion, garlic, gingerroot, and pepper. Add beef, cover bowl, and marinate meat in refrigerator at least 1 hour or (preferably) overnight to allow the flavors to meld.

◆ Preheat broiler and arrange beef slices on a large broiler pan. When broiler is hot, place the pan in oven and broil 6 to 10 minutes, or until beef reaches the desired doneness, turning once. Serve immediately over rice.

Serves 4

Cook's Hint: To make a complete meal, double the proportions of ingredients for the marinade, divide marinade into two separate containers, and marinate sliced vegetables such as red bell peppers, cherry tomatoes, mushrooms, and carrots in the refrigerator for a few hours. Skewer vegetables and broil along with meat.

2 tablespoons granulated sugar

¼ cup soy sauce

¼ cup minced green onion

2 teaspoons minced garlic

1 teaspoon minced gingerroot

Dash of freshly ground black pepper

1 pound rump roast of beef, thinly sliced

Cooked short-grain white or brown rice

DELUXE BAR-B-QUE

The Economy Market was originally the stable for farmers' horses, and got its name because in the early days it was also the section of the Market that sold day-old produce at discount prices. During the 1920s this area was home to the Economy Dance Hall, and during the 1940s the LaSalle Hotel just upstairs housed an upscale bordello run by business-savvy madam Nelly Curtis, a.k.a. Zelda Nightingale.

Today the nefarious elements are gone from the Economy Market, and you'll find Deluxe Bar-B-Que serving take-away fried, roasted, and teriyaki chicken along with jo-jo potatoes, steamed and fried rice, and salads. The teriyaki chicken and pineapple skewers make a great portable snack. This is a good place to stop to get a quick lunch, chicken parts for the picnic basket, or take-out when you simply don't feel like making dinner.

Cornish Game Hens with Raspberry Gravy

Alm Hill Gardens

This is an easy yet lusty presentation of Cornish game hen, fancy enough to serve guests. The skin becomes burnished with the color and flavor of raspberries, the succulent meat subtly flavored, the gravy a pale pink. For an elegant meal, serve it with Raspberry Snap Peas (page 72) and jasmine or brown basmati rice.

◆ Preheat oven to 400°F. Prepare a large roasting pan with a rack by oiling rack or spraying with nonstick cooking spray.

◆ With a whisk, blend raspberry vinegar and olive oil in a small mixing bowl until combined.

◆ Rinse Cornish game hens in cold water, then blot inside and out with paper towels and remove any excess fat from cavities. Pack inside of cavities with frozen raspberries. Tie legs together and arrange hens on rack, breast side up.

¼ cup Alm Hill Gardens raspberry vinegar or other fruit-flavored vinegar

½ cup extra virgin olive oil

3 Cornish game hens, about 1½ pounds each (thawed if frozen)

2 cups frozen raspberries

2 tablespoons all-purpose flour

Kosher salt

Freshly ground black pepper

- Brush about half the vinaigrette evenly over hens. Place in oven and cook 10 minutes. Remove hens from the oven and brush with remaining vinaigrette. Reduce heat to 350°F, and cook hens 40 to 50 minutes more, or until skin is crisp and juices run clear when thigh is pierced with a skewer. Every 10 minutes, brush or baste hens with pan juices. Remove hens from rack and set aside.

- To make gravy, separate the fat and the raspberry juice left over in the roasting pan. Reserve raspberry juice for later use. Combine 2 tablespoons of the fat with flour, stirring until mixture is no longer lumpy. Place fat/flour mixture in a medium skillet over medium heat.

- When mixture is heated, slowly add reserved raspberry juice, stirring constantly so that no lumps form. Continue to add raspberry juice (or water if you run out of the juice) until gravy reaches desired consistency. Add salt and pepper to taste, cover skillet, and remove from heat.

- To serve, cut hens in half and arrange half a bird on each dinner plate. Pour the gravy into a small pitcher or gravy boat and serve at the table.

Serves 6

Rouladen

Bavarian Meat Delicatessen

Rouladen is meat cut from the top or bottom round of beef. It is sold at Bavarian Meats trimmed, pounded thin, and all ready to stuff and roll for this traditional German recipe. Serve with Braised Red Cabbage with Apples (page 56) and German spaetzle (tiny dumplings or noodles) or roasted potatoes.

- Lay out one slice of meat on a piece of waxed paper. Sprinkle with salt and pepper, then spread thinly with mustard. Place one bacon slice lengthwise over meat, then sprinkle one-quarter of the onions and one-quarter of the pickles over

4 beef rouladen

Kosher salt

Freshly ground black pepper

Prepared German mustard (German Lion or Hengstenberg brands recommended)

4 thin slices bacon, uncooked

2 tablespoons diced onion

2 tablespoons diced dill pickles

BAVARIAN MEAT DELICATESSEN

Thirty-something identical twins Lyla and Lynn Hofstatter represent the third generation of gourmet sausage makers at Bavarian Meat Delicatessen, a little slice of Germany in the Soames-Dunn Building, just past Seattle Cutlery. Grandfather Max Hofstatter came to America from Munich in 1933 at the age of 19, worked as a sausage maker, and started his quality frankfurter business in the Market in 1961. During the 1970s, the twins' father Jerry and uncle Bob Hofstatter took over.

Now Lyla and Lynn and partner Manny Dupper oversee operations at the company plant about a mile north of the Pike Place shop. Every day, fresh products from the plant are delivered to the Pike Place store, where a rush of spicy, refrigerated air from the meat cases washes over you as you walk through the double doors. Slabs of bacon, coils of smoked links, and mottled blood-and-tongue loaf perch behind glass. Regular customers converse with the clerks in crisp German, as they fill their shopping bags with *braunschweiger* (the most famous of the liverwursts), Westphalian smoked ham, and head cheese. Of course, Polish sausage, wieners, pork sausage links, and all the wursts—brat, bock, and knock—are in ample supply.

One of the Hofstatter twins' innovations, Smokin' Hot Cheese Sausage (bratwurst blended with jalapeño peppers, cayenne pepper, white pepper, and cheddar cheese, then alder-smoked), is a bit of a departure from what Grandpa Hofstatter would have made. "We're not sure if he'd like a cheese sausage with his warm Lowenbrau," Lyla admits. "Nonetheless, we think he would be really proud that my sister and I have decided to run the family business."

meat. Roll meat tightly, like a jelly roll, and secure with toothpicks or rouladen rings (available at Bavarian Meats and other German markets). Repeat procedure with remaining three pieces of meat.

◆ Heat 1 tablespoon of the butter in a large skillet with a lid and brown all four rolls, adding the remaining 1 tablespoon butter if the meat starts to stick. Add enough water to cover the rouladen, cover skillet, turn down heat, and simmer 45 minutes. Add more water if needed to keep rouladen covered while they cook.

◆ Remove rouladen and, if desired, make a gravy from pan drippings by adding flour mixed with a little red wine.

◆ Place rouladen on dinner plates and serve.

Serves 4

1 to 2 tablespoons unsalted butter

All-purpose flour or arrowroot

Red wine or beef stock

Chicken Adobo

Oriental Kitchenette, Oriental Mart, and the House of Woks & Bowls

This recipe's for garlic aficionados—the fried garlic sprinkled on top makes a crunchy counterpoint to the rich, brown, garlicky, slightly salty sauce. You'll unabashedly soak up every drop! Accompany with Pancit Bihon (page 94) and steamed rice, as they do at Oriental Kitchenette, if desired.

½ cup Philippine coconut vinegar or distilled white vinegar

½ cup Philippine soy sauce or Japanese soy sauce

½ teaspoon garlic salt

3 bay leaves

½ teaspoon finely ground black pepper

Kosher salt to taste

ORIENTAL KITCHENETTE

Paper dragon snakes (a.k.a. "Seattle slugs") skitter between the feet of unsuspecting passersby, woks steam with stir-fried food, and smiling faces greet you in the southwest corner of the Corner Market Building, where the Apostol family has been encsconced since emigrating from the Philippines in 1973. Parents Mila and Manny, daughters Leila and Joy, and sons Edward and Lem operate three synergistic businesses here seven days a week. Their businesses have always been a family affair; the "kids" have kids of their own, so the third generation is now learning the ins and outs of life in the Market.

Lunch at Oriental Kitchenette, the family's demonstration kitchen and eatery, is as much a cooking class as a meal, as Mila Apostol and her family encourage customers to pull up a stool, sit at the counter, and watch the cooks prepare homestyle Filipino food. Choose among chicken or pork *adobo* (the Philippine national dish), *pancit bihon* (a traditional Filipino dish made of noodles, vegetables, and seafood or meat), and vegetarian noodles, plus daily specials from other parts of the Pacific Rim.

In addition to Oriental Kitchenette, the Apostols own Oriental Mart and the House of Woks & Bowls. The House of Woks & Bowls features Asian kitchenware, shoes, kimonos, straw bags, and other novelties. The Oriental Mart is like a visit to the gourmet emporiums of the Pacific Rim, all condensed into one small space. This specialty grocery stocks a staggering number of sauces and condiments, varieties of rice and noodles, and other staple ingredients of Filipino, Chinese, Japanese, Thai, Korean, and Indonesian cuisines. One basic ingredient is coconut vinegar, the Apostol family's secret ingredient for an authentic chicken *adobo*.

- In a large bowl or resealable plastic bag combine vinegar, soy sauce, garlic salt, bay leaves, pepper, salt, and the 3 or 4 crushed garlic cloves. Add chicken parts and marinate in refrigerator several hours or (preferably) overnight.

- Heat a large skillet over medium-high heat and add 1 tablespoon of the oil. When hot, add the 2 or 3 tablespoons minced garlic and stir-fry until lightly browned. Remove fried garlic and reserve.

- Add the remaining 1 or 2 tablespoons of oil to skillet over medium heat. Remove chicken parts from marinade and pat dry, reserving marinade. Add chicken parts to the skillet and cook 10 to 20 minutes, or until well browned on all sides and completely cooked through. The final cooking time will depend on the type of chicken parts you choose. (If using large chicken breasts, you can cover the pan to speed the cooking process.) Remove chicken parts to a clean platter and set aside.

- Slowly add reserved marinade to pan drippings to make gravy, stirring constantly and scraping up the bits on bottom of pan. Once all the marinade has been added, reduce sauce to the desired consistency. Add chicken to gravy, stir thoroughly, and heat through.

- To serve, divide chicken and gravy among dinner plates, then garnish with fried garlic.

Serves 4 to 6 as an entrée, 6 to 8 as a side dish

3 or 4 cloves garlic, crushed, plus 2 to 3 tablespoons minced garlic

2 pounds chicken parts (legs, thighs, or breasts with ribs)

2 to 3 tablespoons peanut or corn oil

Pancit Bihon

Oriental Kitchenette, Oriental Mart, and the House of Woks & Bowls

Based on *bihon* noodles (rice noodles made of rice, corn flour, and water), this steamy stir-fry, chock full of crisp vegetables, silky noodles, and garlic, is Oriental Kitchenette's most popular dish. You'll need an extra-large skillet, wok, or stockpot, or try stir-frying in two batches. Leftovers are delicious reheated for the next day's meal, and you can experiment with this basic recipe by adding your own favorite meats, vegetables, or seasonings, such as gingerroot, five-spice powder, or hot chile peppers.

◆ Soak bihon noodles in warm water for 3 to 4 minutes. Do not oversoak. Drain in a colander and reserve.

◆ Heat oil in a large skillet, wok, or stockpot. Add garlic and cook until lightly browned. Add onion and stir-fry 2 minutes. Add meat and stir-fry until done. Add carrots, cabbage, green onions, and snow peas (if used); mix thoroughly.

◆ Sprinkle mixture with salt, pepper, and soy sauce to taste. Stir-fry until vegetables are tender/crisp in texture. Place ½ cup of the chicken stock in a bowl, add drained noodles, and stir. Add noodles to meat and vegetable mixture and mix thoroughly.

◆ Add remaining stock and cook entire mixture a few minutes more. For drier noodles, add less stock. Serve as a main or side dish, garnished with green onions and lemon wedges.

Serves 4 as a main dish, 8 as a side dish

*(Note: If preparing as a main dish, increase meat to 3 to 4 cups)

**(Note: Oriental Kitchenette uses Philippine soy sauce, which gives the Pancit Bihon a rich brown color, but Chinese or Japanese soy sauce works equally well)

---

1 package (8 ounce) Philippine bihon noodles

3 tablespoons peanut or corn oil

6 cloves garlic, minced

1 white or yellow onion, cut into ¼-inch slices

1½ to 2 cups meat, such as chicken, turkey, or beef strips; peeled and deveined shrimp; or Chinese sausage*

2 carrots, cut into matchstick-sized strips

Half a head of cabbage, cut into large squares

Half a bunch of green onions, roots and top ¼ inch removed and discarded, remaining portion thinly chopped

½ cup snow peas (optional)

1 teaspoon kosher salt

1 teaspoon freshly ground black pepper

1 to 3 tablespoons soy sauce**

1½ to 2 cups homemade chicken stock, or 1 cup canned chicken broth plus 1 cup water

Diced green onions, for garnish

Lemon wedges, for garnish

GARLIC TREE RESTAURANT

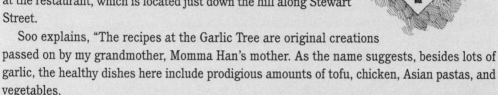

The Garlic Tree is a friendly family business run by Hong Ja Han (just call her "Mom"), daughter Soo, and son Jack. Mom has owned a variety of restaurants in the United States and Korea since 1967, and opened her Market location in the early 1990s. Homestyle Korean food made with cherished family recipes passed down through the generations is the draw at the restaurant, which is located just down the hill along Stewart Street.

Soo explains, "The recipes at the Garlic Tree are original creations passed on by my grandmother, Momma Han's mother. As the name suggests, besides lots of garlic, the healthy dishes here include prodigious amounts of tofu, chicken, Asian pastas, and vegetables.

"Some of our special dishes are garlic wings, garlic chicken, and crab rangoons," Soo continues. "Usually from one teaspoon to one tablespoon of garlic is added per dish, but more or less can be specified, as can the amount of dried red chile peppers. And no, not everything on the menu has garlic in it!"

Chicken Gui with Stir-Fried Vegetables

Garlic Tree Restaurant

You'll prepare this versatile dish time and again because of the many different vegetables you can use and the exquisite flavor of the chicken. Make it in the summer when you have an abundance of green bell peppers, Walla Walla onions, and zucchini in the garden.

◆ Combine water, soy sauce, honey, garlic, gingerroot, black pepper, and the ½ cup green onion in a small mixing bowl and reserve.

◆ Split each chicken breast by making a horizontal cut almost all the way through each one. Fold out so that each breast makes one large, thin piece of chicken. Divide reserved sauce and place half in a bowl or resealable plastic bag large enough to hold the chicken breasts without crowding. Add chicken

⅓ cup water

⅓ cup soy sauce (Kikkoman brand recommended)

1½ teaspoons honey

1 teaspoon minced garlic

½ teaspoon minced gingerroot

¼ teaspoon freshly ground black pepper

½ cup chopped green onion

1 pound boneless, skinless chicken breasts

1 tablespoon light vegetable oil, such as peanut, corn, or canola

breasts, cover, refrigerate, and marinate for at least 1 hour. Reserve remaining sauce for vegetables.

◆ Pan-fry, broil, or grill chicken 3 to 6 minutes, or until cooked through. Keep chicken warm while cooking vegetables.

◆ Heat oil in a large skillet or wok over medium-high heat until almost smoking. Add broccoli (if used) and stir-fry 2 to 3 minutes, then add remaining vegetables and marinade (approximately ⅓ cup) and stir-fry until vegetables are tender/crisp. In a small glass dish, stir cornstarch and water until completely dissolved, and add to vegetables. Stir thoroughly to blend with vegetables, and cook 1 minute, or just until sauce thickens. Add sesame oil and stir again.

◆ To serve, arrange a bed of vegetables and rice on a dinner plate, then top with sliced chicken breast.

Serves 2 to 3

6 cups of an assortment of any or all of the following vegetables, cut into bite-sized pieces: broccoli, napa cabbage, bean sprouts, white or yellow onions (Walla Walla when in season), green onions, carrots, mushrooms, and green bell peppers

½ teaspoon cornstarch

2 teaspoons water

Several drops of toasted sesame oil

2 cups cooked white or brown rice

Barbecued Short Ribs

Don & Joe's Meats

Barbecued short ribs are as all-American as the Fourth of July, yet this variation takes on a bit of an Asian overtone when the dark, sweet sauce is served over steamed white or brown rice. Don's wife, Diana, likes this recipe because it's "quick, easy, and delicious!" Versatile, too, since it can be cooked either on top of the stove or in the oven.

◆ Preheat oven to 350°F.

◆ Heat fat in a large skillet over medium-high heat, then add short ribs and brown on all sides. Add onion and celery to skillet and cook until vegetables are tender.

◆ Combine tomato sauce, vinegar, sugar, water, Worcestershire sauce, mustard, and salt in a small mixing bowl. Pour over ribs and vegetables. Cover and simmer meat about 1½ to 2 hours or until tender (the bones should come off easily). If sauce becomes too thick during cooking, add a little water.

2 tablespoons beef fat or light vegetable oil, such as corn, soy, or canola

3 pounds beef short ribs, cut into portion-sized pieces, if necessary

1 white or yellow onion, chopped

½ cup chopped celery

1 can (8 ounce) tomato sauce

⅓ cup distilled white vinegar

⅔ cup granulated sugar

½ cup water

3 tablespoons Worcestershire sauce

DON & JOE'S MEATS

The Market is known as a place that nurtures small, family-owned businesses, and one of the most endearing family business stories is the tale of Don & Joe's. The original Don and Joe were Don Kuzaro, Sr., and his brother-in-law, Joe Darby, who worked together at Dan's Meat Market while harboring that all-American dream of owning the business. When Dan's left the Market in 1969 to go wholesale, Don and Joe were given the first shot at buying the retail store, and Don & Joe's Meats was born.

Present owner Don Kuzaro, Jr., started working for his dad and uncle at age 17 as a self-described "clean-up kid." Other than a four-year stint in the Navy, Don, Jr., worked in the shop as a meat cutter until he bought the business from his father in the mid-1980s.

"I had a great opportunity to work with my father until he retired," Don, a boyish-looking man with a crewcut, white cap, and apron, reminisces. "He was working so hard when I was growing up that I hardly knew him. Working together brought our family together."

Working together also led Don to find his wife, Diana, daughter of longtime Market farmer Curly Hanada. While the two were helping out their dads at the Market on Saturdays, Diana and Don met, fell in love, later married, and had two daughters. To this day, Diana still helps out on Saturdays at the store, where she, Don, and the friendly crew offer a full selection of fresh meat including choice and prime beef, American lamb, pork, veal, poultry, and specialty items.

Don and his staff make all the sausages sold at the store and the smoked hams, fresh turkeys, and lamb chops are longtime favorites. He takes pride in offering the less traditional "cuts," such as brains, sweetbreads, and Rocky Mountain oysters.

After more than 30 years in the meat business, Don still enjoys the Market. "I like being able to walk out of our shop and see the bay and the ships and feel the wind in my face," he says.

Alternatively, you can cook ribs in the oven by transferring ribs, vegetables, and sauce to a large baking dish with a cover or a Dutch oven and cooking 1½ to 2 hours, or until tender.

◆ Remove bones and any excess fat that is floating on top of meat, and serve with hot rice and horseradish.

Serves 4

1 teaspoon prepared mustard

Dash of kosher salt

Cooked white or brown rice

Fresh or prepared horseradish

Lamb Burgers with Balsamic Onions, Roasted Peppers, and Aïoli

Café Campagne

The Market's own Don & Joe's Meats (page 97) custom-grinds the lamb shoulder that Café Campagne uses in its lamb burgers to produce a blend that is about 80 percent lean. If you don't live near the Market, you can ask your favorite butcher to do the same. The burgers are served at the café along with classic *frites*, or thinly cut French fries sprinkled with kosher salt.

◆ Place the lamb, garlic, rosemary, pepper flakes, and black pepper in a large stainless-steel bowl, and gently mix with your hands or a large spoon. Do not overmix, or burgers will develop a sausagelike consistency and could be tough.

◆ Divide ground meat into four equal portions and form into balls, then flatten slightly.

◆ Preheat grill or broiler and cook burgers to desired doneness.

◆ To serve, place burgers on buns, layer with onions and roasted pepper slices, then drizzle with Aïoli.

Serves 4

Balsamic Onions

◆ Preheat oven to 400°F.

◆ In a medium skillet with an ovenproof handle, heat olive oil over medium-high heat and add onion slices without crowding. Cook 1 minute, then turn onion slices and cook 1 minute more. Season with salt and pepper, then add enough balsamic vinegar to just reach the tops of the onions. Remove from heat, cover skillet with an ovenproof lid or aluminum foil, and bake 8 to 10 minutes. Turn onions and bake another 8 to 10 minutes, or until tender. Be extremely careful when moving

---

1½ pounds lean ground lamb

2 teaspoons chopped garlic

½ teaspoon dried rosemary, crumbled

½ teaspoon crushed red pepper flakes

½ teaspoon freshly ground black pepper

4 good-quality hamburger rolls, such as Grand Central Bolo or Pallone, split horizontally

Balsamic Onions (recipe follows)

1 roasted red bell pepper (see Techniques section), seeds and membranes removed, cut into ⅛-inch slices

Aïoli (page 35)

Balsamic Onions

1 tablespoon olive oil

1 large red onion, peeled and cut into four ¾-inch slices

Kosher salt

Freshly ground black pepper

1 to 1½ cups balsamic vinegar

the skillet in and out of the oven, since the balsamic vinegar is very hot, emits a very strong aroma, and sloshes easily.

◆ Remove onions from oven and cool to room temperature in the vinegar. Use immediately or transfer to a nonreactive bowl, cover, and refrigerate until about 30 minutes before serving.

CAMPAGNE AND CAFÉ CAMPAGNE

Even on a dark winter's night, the mood is bright at Campagne. The popular bar hums with activity, while the hot orange neon of the Public Market sign glows brilliantly through the large picture windows in the main dining room. French art posters and floor-to-ceiling wine racks line the walls, and the honey-kissed walls glow as warmly as the oak-planked floors. Although many consider this a special-event place, there's not a stuffy note in the room.

The menu, which highlights the country-style food of southern France, changes with the seasons. Foie gras, sweetbreads, butter, and cream are star players here, but the portions are sensible and the pace is leisurely. Desserts are a must, and include a sophisticated Twice-Baked Chocolate Gateau and the classic crème brûlée. They're as rich and decadent as anyone could desire, rather like an evening at Campagne, which first opened in the Capitol Hill neighborhood in 1985 and has resided in the Market since 1987.

Just down the hill along Pine Street, Café Campagne offers a more casual and affordable dining experience. The inviting space is reminiscent of a bustling French bistro, with cherry-wood paneling, large mirrors, and a lengthy marble-topped bar. Half a dozen tables for two offer outside seating along Post Alley.

For a weekday lunch or weekend brunch, a perfectly prepared omelet or classic salade Niçoise might fit the bill. By dinnertime, Lamb *Crepinettes* (savory lamb sausages) form a hearty main dish; lighter appetites might opt for grilled salmon served on a bed of cucumbers, white beans, and *haricots verts*.

Whichever Campagne dining experience you choose, you'll find yourself in the very capable hands of founder Peter Lewis; Executive Chef Daisley Gordon, a native of Jamaica and a graduate of the renowned Culinary Institute of America who has traveled throughout France to perfect his skills; and wine director, Shawn Mead, who chooses wines from small French producers that partner perfectly with the country-French fare.

Mechado

Lina's Produce

Cooks in some parts of the Philippines use 7-Up as a marinade ingredient for meats, much as American cooks use wine. An easy-to-make, economical, flavorful stew with an appealing interplay of colors and textures, *mechado* is full of garlic and black pepper, like many Filipino main dishes. Serve it in large soup bowls over cooked rice or accompanied by crusty bread.

◆ Combine 7-Up, vinegar, the 1 tablespoon garlic, black pepper, bay leaves, soy sauce, and brown sugar in a large stockpot, and bring to a boil over medium-high heat. Add beef, potatoes, and red bell pepper. Stir well and cook 3 minutes, or until beef browns on the outside, stirring constantly. Cover pan, reduce heat to low, and simmer 20 to 25 minutes, or until meat and potatoes are tender, stirring occasionally. Set aside.

¾ cup 7-Up

2½ tablespoons distilled white vinegar

1 tablespoon plus 1½ teaspoons minced garlic

½ to 1 tablespoon freshly ground black pepper, depending on heat level desired

2 bay leaves

1½ tablespoons soy sauce

3½ teaspoons firmly packed brown sugar

2 pounds boneless chuck roast, cut into bite-sized cubes

LINA'S PRODUCE

Lina's Produce offers some of the Asian fruits and vegetables that can be a bit difficult to find at other highstalls in the Market. Here you'll find bitter melon; Chinese long beans; mustard, collard, and turnip greens; yams and sweet potatoes; Japanese and Thai eggplant; local squashes; and a good selection of fresh herbs and peppers.

Lina Fronda, the woman behind the name, is a real Market veteran. In 1963, when she came to Seattle from Luzon (the chief island in the Philippines), she went straight to work in the Market with her husband Domingo Constantino. Domingo had owned the spot at Arcade 7 since 1958. When he died in 1980, Lina took over the highstall produce stand and eventually married a man she met in her homeland. Ever since, Lina and hubby Edmundo have been working side by side in the Market's Main Arcade.

◆ After meat is done, add oil to a large skillet and heat over medium-high heat. Add the remaining 1½ teaspoons garlic and stir-fry until lightly browned, then reduce heat to medium, add green bell pepper, and cook 3 minutes more, stirring constantly. Add the garlic/bell pepper mixture to meat and its sauce in stockpot and stir well. Bring to a boil, add tomato sauce, and stir constantly until mixture is warmed through. Serve immediately.

Serves 4 to 6

2 medium potatoes, cut into bite-sized cubes

1 red bell pepper, cut into bite-sized squares

¼ cup light vegetable oil, such as peanut, corn, or canola

Half a green bell pepper, cut into bite-sized cubes

4 ounces (half an 8-ounce can) tomato sauce

THE MEXICAN GROCERY

This small storefront on Pike Place entices you with a display of *pan dulces* (sweet rolls) that glisten in pastel colors on a tray just inside the front window. Once inside, shelves lined with Ibarra chocolate (cinnamon-flavored chocolate, great for brewing spicy hot chocolate or eating out of hand), *chipotle* peppers (canned or dried), and even Mexican prayer candles (we can all use a little help from above sometimes!) tempt.

In the refrigerated case you'll discover red, green, and *pico de gallo* salsas made fresh in the store every morning. There are also three kinds of tamales delivered daily; an assortment of tempting tacos, tostadas, and burritos; and a trio of Mexican cheeses including *queso fresco*, a white, slightly salty, fresh cheese. Along with a supply of crunchy tortilla chips, fresh tortillas, and a couple of colorful piñatas, you could put together a dinner party for 6 or 60 at a moment's notice and have lots of fun in the process.

New Mexico Tamales

The Mexican Grocery

Masa, the traditional dough used to make corn tortillas and tamales, formed the foundation of ancient Mexican cuisine and is still the heart of that country's cooking today. Yet making tamales is a lot of work. Even in Mexico they're considered party or fiesta food because they're so time-consuming to prepare, so they are often reserved for birthdays, christenings, or New Year celebrations. Tamales can be filled with everything from beef to seafood to beans, or even left unfilled, but pork is the most traditional filling. Serve the tamales with refried beans and rice. If you have any pork filling left over, spoon it into tortillas or tacos and serve with rice and beans.

◆ To prepare the ojas: Remove corn whiskers from ojas. While preparing the rest of recipe, soak ojas in cold water until they become soft and begin to separate.

◆ To make the pork filling: Heat enough water in a stockpot to cover pork. Bring water, onion, the 2 cloves garlic, and cumin seeds to a boil; add pork. Reduce heat, cover pot, and simmer 3 to 4 hours, or until the meat pulls apart easily with a fork. Remove meat from stockpot, strain broth, and reserve. With your fingers or two forks, shred pork into a large bowl, discarding any fat, and place it in refrigerator until ready to use.

◆ To make the sauce: Boil chile pods in the water for 20 minutes. Let cool, then pulse pods and liquid in a blender on high. Pour mixture through a fine-mesh sieve placed over a glass or stainless-steel dish.

◆ In a skillet heat the 1 tablespoon lard and sauté the 2 to 4 cloves garlic. Add flour and mix thoroughly, then add chile sauce and stir until well blended. Remove from heat and add to cooked pork. Stir thoroughly, then return pork mixture to refrigerator.

◆ To prepare the masa: Put masa into a large bowl, add the 2 cups lard, and mix with your hands until the fat is thoroughly incorporated into masa. Add salt (if used) and slowly add the

About 40 ojas (corn husks for rolling tamales)

Shredded Pork Filling

1 yellow onion, quartered

2 cloves garlic, sliced

1 teaspoon whole cumin seeds

4 pounds pork butt roast

Sauce for Pork Filling

24 New Mexico, ancho, or pasilla chile pods

4 cups water

1 tablespoon lard or bacon fat

2 to 4 cloves garlic, minced

1 tablespoon flour

Masa Mix

6 cups fresh masa (Note: Fresh masa is available at The Mexican Grocery)

2 cups lard or bacon grease

2 teaspoons kosher salt (optional)

About 2 cups reserved pork broth

2 cups pork broth, mixing well after each addition of broth. You may not have to use all of the broth, depending on moisture content of masa. Knead masa until it is light and fluffy.

◆ To assemble the tamales: Remove ojas from the soaking water and remove any additional corn silk whiskers that have appeared. Place ojas on a kitchen towel to keep them moist. Lay out one oja until smooth. Spoon about ¼ cup of masa into center of oja, then spread it over the corn husk with the back of a spoon, leaving about 1 inch at sides and 2 inches at top and bottom of oja. Spoon a couple of tablespoons of pork mixture over the oja and use the back of a spoon to spread it out. Fold the oja so that the edges of masa come together, then wrap plain part (side border) of oja around outside of the tamale. Fold bottom end of husk over body of tamale, then fold in the tip. Alternatively, you can roll tamales and tie at either end with torn strips of the ojas.

◆ To cook the tamales: Boil 2 cups of water in a steamer, then place several ojas over bottom of steamer. Arrange tamales over ojas, then cover tops of the tamales with additional ojas. Place a kitchen towel over top of ojas to catch any condensation that might form, then cover steamer.

◆ Steam 1 hour. If steamer boils dry, add an additional cup of *hot* water. Tamales are done when they pull apart easily from the ojas. The dough should be spongy and compact and not cling to the husk.

◆ Remove tamales from steamer and arrange on a large platter or divide among dinner plates.

Makes about 32 tamales; serves 8 to 10

Seafood Entrées

Black Cod Miso Yaki
Zuppa del Frutti di Mare (Seafood Soup)
Cataplana Clams
Prawns Aglio
Roast King Salmon with Pinot Noir Mustard Sauce
Halibut Cheeks en Papillote
Tahitian Poisson Cru (Fresh Fish)
Green Tea Shellfish Risotto
Crabmeat Tagliatelle in Creamy Lemon-Tomato Sauce
Crab-Stuffed Halibut with Crawfish Cream Sauce
Creamed Dungeness Crabmeat Omelet
Crispy Skin Salmon with Citrus Sauce and Black Rice Cakes
Grilled Halibut with Lemon Herb Splash
Grilled Salmon with Roasted Hazelnut Butter
Trout à la Grecque
Mushroom Salmon Pie with Gruyère Cheese
Barbecued Salmon

Black Cod Miso Yaki

Pure Food Fish Market

Sal Beppu, a personable young fishmonger of Filipino/Japanese descent, gave me this recipe devised by his grandmother, Teru Beppu. It was printed in the Beppu family cookbook, which is compiled for the annual family reunion. If black cod, a.k.a. sablefish (in the Northwest) or butterfish (in Hawaii), is unavailable, Sal suggests substituting salmon steaks. I've also had tasty results using halibut steaks.

◆ Place miso, sake, garlic, gingerroot, green onion, sugar, and vinegar in a large nonreactive bowl with a cover or a large resealable plastic bag and mix until sugar is dissolved and a thick paste forms. Add black cod steaks, turn a few times to coat completely with marinade, then cover and refrigerate at least 2 hours or (preferably) overnight, turning occasionally.

◆ Ten minutes before you are ready to cook, set one oven rack 3 to 4 inches from broiler and a second rack in the center of the oven, then preheat the broiler. Lightly oil a broiler pan with a rack or spray with nonstick cooking spray. Place black cod steaks on broiler pan rack and cook 2 minutes. Move broiler pan to center oven rack and decrease oven temperature to 375°F. Cook fish 12 to 17 minutes, depending on thickness of the steaks and doneness desired.

◆ To serve, divide black cod steaks among individual plates (remove outside skin and center bones, if desired), garnish with lemon wedges, and serve with rice.

Serves 4

Cook's Hint: Miso, or fermented soybean paste, is a basic flavoring in Japanese cooking. It is available at Asian grocers such as Oriental Mart in the Pike Place Market, upscale grocery stores, and health food stores. It imparts a rich, slightly yeasty flavor to the velvety black cod.

⅔ cup shiro (white or mild) miso

2 tablespoons sake or dry white wine

1 clove garlic, crushed

1 teaspoon grated gingerroot

1 green onion, roots and top ¼ inch removed and discarded, remaining portion minced

2 tablespoons granulated sugar

1 tablespoon distilled white vinegar

Four 6-ounce black cod steaks, rinsed, drained, and patted dry

Lemon wedges, for garnish

2 to 3 cups cooked white or brown rice

PURE FOOD FISH MARKET

Pure Food Fish was one of the original fish stores in the Market, circa 1917. And present owner Sol Amon's family has an even longer history of working along Pike Place. His father, Jack Amon, emigrated from Turkey to Seattle and worked and owned fish stalls in the Market beginning in 1911. Jack acquired Pure Food Fish in 1956, and Sol and his brother Irving took over in 1959.

Today Pure Food Fish's specialties include fresh Pacific Northwest salmon, Dungeness crab, Red King crab, and fresh halibut. Their alder-smoked, garlic/Cajun-spiced, hard-smoked, and Nova-style smoked salmon are very popular. (Ask for a nibble before you buy!) Canned seafood (salmon and Dungeness crab) and seafood gift boxes (smoked trout, oysters, and salmon) make easy-to-transport, nonperishable gifts.

The advent of fast commercial air travel and the company's easy-to-use website have given people everywhere the chance to buy from Pure Food Fish even if they can't check the blackboard for the catch of the day or place their orders at the single long counter at the Market in person. The company ships fresh seafood all over the world in their reusable insulated coolers with reusable gel-ice cold-packs. As the company motto says, "Let us do the fishing for you!"

Sol and his tireless crew, including Harry, Walt, David, Chris, and Richard, are quick to offer a smile and a menu suggestion. They know their fish, although Richard loves to tell the tale of one customer who didn't. "This woman called me long distance to tell me that the fish I had shipped her was bad. I asked her what was wrong and she said it was all blue. I realized she had cooked the cold-packs we ship the fish in to keep it fresh and cold!" Whether Richard is telling a fish tale or not, there's no doubt that Jack Amon must be smiling from above at the growth and evolution of Pure Food Fish.

Zuppa del Frutti di Mare (Seafood Soup)

DeLaurenti Specialty Food & Wine

Seafood soups and stews can sometimes be difficult to make, but this one defies the odds with only eight easy-to-find ingredients. The addition of saffron gives the soup an intriguing musky flavor and pleasing orange-red color that belies its humble beginnings and allows the goodness of the seafood to shine through.

◆ Heat butter and olive oil in a large saucepan over medium-high heat. Add shallot and cook 1 to 2 minutes, or until softened but not browned, stirring frequently. Add wine and cook 1 to 2 minutes, or until reduced slightly, stirring constantly.

◆ Add tomatoes and their juice, crushing the tomatoes with your hands or the back of a large spoon. Add chicken stock and saffron, stir well, and bring stock to a simmer.

◆ Add seafood to pan, cover, and simmer 5 to 7 minutes, or until fish is done and shellfish opens. Remove any mussels or clams that do not open. Season to taste with salt and pepper.

◆ To serve, divide the seafood and broth among individual bowls. Top with baguette slices that have been rubbed with the garlic clove.

Serves 4

1 tablespoon unsalted butter

1 tablespoon extra virgin olive oil

1 shallot, minced

½ cup dry white wine

1 can (12 ounce) whole Italian tomatoes

1½ cups homemade chicken stock, or ¾ cup canned chicken broth plus ¾ cup water

Pinch of saffron

2 pounds mussels (scrubbed and debearded just before cooking) or clams (scrubbed), or 1 pound shrimp (rinsed, shells cut down the back with kitchen shears, and deveined) or scallops (rinsed and patted dry)

1 pound seafood fillets, such as halibut or salmon fillets, rinsed, skinned, patted dry, and cut into ¼-pound pieces

Kosher salt

Freshly ground black pepper

Four ½-inch baguette or rustic bread slices, grilled or broiled

1 clove garlic, peeled and halved

DELAURENTI SPECIALTY FOOD & WINE

Stepping into DeLaurenti is a feast for all the senses. Against a background of pristine white walls and tiled floors, handsome cherry-wood shelves rise like monoliths. With their gilded labels and jewel-like colors, the myriad bottles of olive oil and balsamic vinegar, cans of tomatoes, and bottled mustards and olives that line the shelves look like miniature works of art.

At the downstairs cafe, the espresso machine whooshes into action while large, stainless-steel ovens crank out thin-crusted pizza, available in the cafe or at the convenient pizza window. Sleek displays of panini, salads, bottled Italian waters and sodas, and bakery items from Macrina and Le Panier tempt.

In the lengthy, well-lit deli case, you'll find Spanish chorizo, dried Italian salami, smoked prosciutto and pâtés, and 22 types of olives. Cheese is another top priority, with 220 varieties available, and the store also sells rustic breads from Seattle's top bakeries.

Upstairs, in the bulk-foods section, you can choose just about any shape or size of pasta imaginable, along with rice, beans, and dried herbs and spices. Chunks of Guittard and Callebaut chocolate, candied violets and rose petals, dried Royal Anne cherries, and Sultana raisins make this the ideal place to come when the holiday baking season rolls around. The wine department boasts 1,800 bottles, including (as you might expect) a strong Italian contingent along with prized Northwest wines.

The story of the venerable DeLaurenti family reaches back to 1928, when Angelina Mustello, an Italian immigrant, opened a small store on the Market's Mezzanine Level that catered to the Italian, Greek, and Sephardic Jewish immigrants who sought out hard-to-find products from their homelands. In 1930, Angelina's daughter, Mamie, met and married Peter DeLaurenti, a bakery deliveryman. The same year, Angelina's store closed due to the Depression, but when the space became available again in 1948, Mamie and Pete bought it and opened Pete's Italian Grocery.

In 1973 one of Mamie and Pete's sons, Louie, bought the business, changed the name to DeLaurenti, and moved it up to First and Pike. Louie, his wife Pat, and daughter Vicki continued to run the store until early 2001, when the siren song of retirement called to the elder generation.

After 54 years, the store's patriarch passed the baton to Patrick McCarthy, a serious young man who runs the Market's flagship gourmet grocery in the same caring, hands-on way as his predecessors. He's opened DeLaurenti on Sundays, offers Saturday afternoon wine tastings, sends out a weekly e-mail newsletter, and completely renovated and updated the venerable store in early 2003—innovations that have helped this one-of-a-kind Italian grocery move into the 21st century with grace and style.

Cataplana Clams

Brasa

At her popular restaurant in Belltown, James Beard Award–winning chef Tamara Murphy uses smoked paprika to highlight the flavor of steamed clams cooked in a *cataplana*, a traditional copper cooking vessel from Portugal. Experimenting with unusual spices and cooking techniques to create robust foods from the earth and hearth is a touchstone of Tamara's culinary style at Brasa,* which translates as "live coals" in Portuguese. Chef Tamara says, "I love the Market! I have worked downtown for the past 10 years, use the Market on a consistent basis, and know it like the back of my hand. I have my favorite spots for greens and flowers, tomatoes and mushrooms, meat and dairy. I use the butcher, baker, and the candlestick maker. I go to the Market just to get ideas. I appreciate the farmers so much. Thank you—from a Market chef!"

◆ Preheat oven to 500°F. Remove leaves and stems from tarragon and parsley and reserve. Remove root ends of chives and discard, then cut remaining portions into ½-inch pieces.

◆ Place herb leaves and stems, shallots, garlic, lemon juice, paprika, wine, and butter in a medium (11-inch) cataplana and stir well. Add clams, toss with liquid, and close lid. Put cataplana on center rack in oven and cook 12 to 15 minutes, or until clams open. Discard any clams that do not open. (Note: If a cataplana is not available, place herb and liquid mixture in a large saucepan and bring to a boil. Reduce the heat to a simmer, add clams, cover, and cook 5 to 7 minutes, or until clams open.)

◆ To serve, open cataplana and toss clams and juice to mix evenly; then garnish with additional herbs, if desired. Use empty side of cataplana as a bowl for shells and serve immediately.

Serves 1 as an entrée, 2 as an appetizer

---

2 sprigs tarragon, plus extra for garnish (optional)

2 sprigs flat-leaf parsley, plus extra for garnish (optional)

6 fresh chives, plus extra for garnish (optional)

3 shallots, thinly sliced

1 teaspoon minced garlic

Juice of 2 lemons

¼ teaspoon smoked bittersweet or spicy paprika (pimentón)

¼ cup dry white wine

2 tablespoons unsalted butter

2 pounds Manila or native littleneck clams, shells scrubbed

Cook's Hint: A *cataplana* is a domed copper or aluminum clam cooker that originated in the Algarve region in southern Portugal. The *cataplana* resembles two clamshells, and is traditionally used to cook clams in their own juices, although the versatile cooking vessel can also be used to cook mussels, squid, cod, small fowl, and roast meat. When cooking clams or mussels, the bivalves are put in half the vessel for cooking, then the top is folded over and secured with a metal pin. The *cataplana* goes in the oven until the shellfish open, then it is opened at the table and the unfilled half is used to dispose of the clam and mussel shells. *Cataplanas* are available at The Spanish Table (page 194), as is smoked paprika. When asked about this trendy ingredient, Chef Tamara says, "I treat smoked paprika like fresh pepper. A little goes a long way."

*Outside of the Market Historic District.

IL BISTRO

Tucked under the Market Theatre sign on a narrow, cobbled street that could easily have been plucked from the back alleys of Florence, Il Bistro is one of those intriguing, romantic places that keeps calling you back. A wall of windows draws light into the cavelike, subterranean space with its vaulted ceilings, well-worn Oriental rugs, and dark furniture. Muted jazz plays in the background.

By night, when an expensive automobile (or three) is invariably parked outside, couples cuddle and votives flicker at the handful of tables set up just outside the doorway. Inside, patrons celebrate special occasions with classic Italian specialties such as Carpaccio (sliced beef tenderloin with shaved Parmesan, arugula, and truffle oil), *Cesare* (Caesar salad), Gnocchi (potato dumplings in tomato-cream sauce), *Scaloppine di Vitello alla Marsala* (veal Marsala), *Caretto d'Agnello* (rack of lamb with Sangiovese wine sauce), and Cioppino (seafood stew).

Order the *Torta al Mascarpone*, Italian cheesecake with a thick almond crust and lemon glaze. Even if you don't think you have room for dessert, you'll finish every velvety forkful. The ever-lively bar is worth trying in and of itself, for it's as atmospheric as the dining room, and offers a wide selection of coffee drinks, single-malt Scotches, brandies, and Cognacs.

Prawns Aglio

Il Bistro

Aglio means "garlic" in Italian, and this prawn dish is full of the healthful bulb, along with tomatoes, basil, oregano, and olive oil. Be sure to assemble all the ingredients before cooking, as it comes together very quickly.

◆ Heat oil in a large skillet over medium-high heat until oil is smoking. Add shrimp, garlic, basil, oregano, tomatoes, and salt and pepper to taste. Cook 1 to 2 minutes, or until shrimp and garlic are lightly browned.

◆ Add lemon juice and vermouth to skillet, and cook 1 to 2 minutes, or until prawns turn white inside. Remove prawns from skillet and place on four appetizer plates or one dinner plate.

◆ Add butter to pan and cook 1 to 2 minutes, then pour over prawns. Garnish with lemon slices and parsley.

Serves 1 as an entrée, 4 as an appetizer

Cook's Hint: Cooking shrimp in their shell, instead of shelling completely or leaving just the tails on, adds more flavor to the dish and keeps the shellfish from getting tough.

1 tablespoon olive oil

12 medium shrimp, rinsed and cut up the back of the shell to devein, but with complete shells left on

1 tablespoon minced garlic

1 tablespoon minced fresh basil

1 tablespoon minced fresh oregano, or 1 teaspoon dried oregano, crumbled

2 plum tomatoes, cored and sliced through the center into ⅛-inch rounds

Kosher salt

Freshly ground black pepper

Juice of half a lemon

¼ cup dry white vermouth (Boissiere brand recommended)

1 tablespoon unsalted butter

Lemon slices and parsley, for garnish

Roast King Salmon with Pinot Noir Mustard Sauce

Sapphire Kitchen and Bar

This creative dish comes from Leonard Ruiz Rede, former chef at the now-departed and still-lamented Café Sophie in the Market Historic District along First Avenue. Lenny has gone on to star as chef/proprietor of his own restaurant atop Queen Anne Hill—the atmospheric, Mediterranean-inspired Sapphire Kitchen and Bar.* This light and healthy recipe, a favorite of mine from the first edition of this book, has definitely stood the test of time, using Northwest ingredients (king salmon and Pinot Noir) to their best advantage. Mustard seeds are available in the Pike Place Market at The Souk and at MarketSpice.

◆ Place wine in a small nonreactive saucepan over high heat and boil until reduced by half. Remove from heat, add honey, and stir until honey dissolves.

◆ In a small, dry skillet, heat mustard seeds until they begin to pop and release their aroma. Remove from heat and add to wine/honey mixture. Add red wine vinegar, shallot, tarragon, salt, and pepper. Pour into a jar with a lid, shake well to blend, and refrigerate at least 8 hours, or overnight. (The mustard sauce can be made ahead to this point and refrigerated for up to 1 week. Shake well before using.)

◆ Preheat oven to 450°F. Place salmon steaks or fillets in a greased baking pan and season with salt and pepper. Brush with olive oil, place in oven, and cook 5 to 7 minutes, or until they reach desired doneness.

◆ Divide the arugula among six dinner plates, then drizzle each plate with 2 tablespoons of mustard sauce. Arrange the cooked salmon over the arugula, sprinkle with bell pepper, and serve immediately.

Serves 6

*Outside of the Market Historic District.

1 cup Pinot Noir or other good-quality red wine

¼ cup honey

¼ cup black or brown mustard seeds

½ cup red wine vinegar

1 teaspoon chopped shallot

2 teaspoons chopped fresh tarragon

½ teaspoon kosher salt, plus extra for seasoning

Freshly ground black pepper, plus extra for seasoning

2 pounds king salmon steaks or fillets (about 6 ounces per serving)

2 tablespoons olive oil or melted unsalted butter

1 bunch arugula, rinsed, drained, and spun dry

1 red bell pepper, diced

LOWELL'S RESTAURANT

One of the Market's oldest eating establishments, Mannings Coffee House (the present-day Lowell's) opened for business in 1908 when Edward and William Manning spent $1,900 to try their hand at running a coffee cafe. Back then, a cup of java sold for two cents, a pound of coffee for 30 cents, and the Manning brothers parlayed their initial investment into a chain of 46 restaurants and bakeries that spanned the West Coast. Mannings Coffee House in the Market was sold in 1957, then resold about six months later to one of its managers, Reid Lowell, who renamed the space Lowell's Cafeteria.

Owned by Bill Chatalas since 1980, Lowell's Restaurant anchors the Main Arcade with killer views of Elliott Bay and the Olympic Mountains to the west. Each of its three levels boasts a different dining experience. With a cafeteria line, checkered linoleum floor, and leather-and-chrome stools, the ground level has the feel of a 1950s diner tucked into the lower levels of a cruise ship.

Many Market workers and locals ascend to the second floor, where they jockey for a seat at one of the wooden booths that project over the Main Arcade like the crow's nest of a ship. This prime people-watching spot is a good place to nurse a beer and observe the farmers and artisans selling their goods, fishmongers hawking their wares, and tourists and locals elbowing their way through the Market.

If you make the journey up to Lowell's third level, you'll be rewarded with floor-to-ceiling views of the ferryboats, mountains, and container barges plying Puget Sound.

But no matter which dining experience you choose, you'll enjoy classic American fare and friendly service at reasonable prices. Breakfasts are huge and popular; fresh salmon, halibut, oysters, and steamed clams and mussels are on the menu seasonally; and everything is cooked to order.

Halibut Cheeks en Papillote

Lowell's Restaurant

In this elegant dish, choice halibut cheeks are cooked with fresh vegetables and dill butter in the French method called *en papillote* ("in paper") which keeps the fish tender and creates a rich sauce.

◆ Preheat oven to 375°F. Cut six 12-by-12-inch squares of parchment paper. Fold squares in half, then cut into half-hearts. Open and reserve. Reserve two baking sheets for later use.

- In a medium mixing bowl, toss together the carrot, onion, celery, and bell pepper until well mixed. Reserve.

- To make dill butter, place 1 cup (½ pound) of the butter in a small mixing bowl. Add 3 tablespoons of the minced dill to butter. Mix thoroughly, then refrigerate.

- To make drawn butter, melt the remaining ¼ cup butter in a small skillet over low heat. As white foam rises to the top, skim and discard. When only heavy yellow butter remains, add the wine, lemon juice, and the remaining 1 tablespoon of minced dill. Stir well and reserve.

- On a level work surface, spread out one of the parchment-paper hearts until it is fully open. Using a pastry brush, coat the inside with drawn butter, place about 6 ounces (or ⅙) of the halibut cheeks on one-half of the heart along the fold, and top with a tablespoon or two of the reserved vegetable mixture. Dot with 1 tablespoon of the dill butter and sprinkle with salt and pepper. Do not overstuff parchment, as it needs room to expand during baking.

- Fold the other half of the parchment over fish and vegetables, then fold over and roll the edges of parchment to seal tightly. It is very important that you form a tight seal all around, or the parchment could pop open during baking and the fish and vegetables will not cook properly. Repeat with remaining pieces of parchment, fish, and vegetables. (You may have both leftover vegetables and fish—if so, make an extra parchment packet for tomorrow's lunch!)

- Place parchment packets on baking sheets and bake 15 to 20 minutes, or until slightly puffed. As they heat and if your seals are tight, the parchment packets will fill with hot air, puff, and make a buttery dill sauce for the fish.

- To serve, place parchment packets on dinner plates and, with a sharp knife or kitchen shears, cut open the packets in an X-shaped pattern. Garnish with lemon wedges and dill sprigs, and serve with rice.

Serves 6

---

1 carrot, cut into matchstick-sized strips

1 medium red onion, cut into ¹⁄₁₆-inch slices and pulled apart into rings

2 ribs celery, cut into matchstick-sized strips

1 red bell pepper, cut into matchstick-sized strips

1¼ cups unsalted butter, softened

4 tablespoons minced fresh dill plus extra dill sprigs, for garnish

¼ cup dry white wine

Juice of 1 lemon wedge (one-sixth of a lemon) plus extra lemon wedges, for garnish

2¼ pounds halibut cheeks (about 6 ounces per serving), rinsed, drained, and patted dry

Kosher salt

Freshly ground black pepper

3 cups long-grain white or brown rice, prepared as the package directs

Tahitian Poisson Cru (Fresh Fish)

Poisson cru is the Tahitian take on the better-known Latin dish called ceviche. In both iterations, citrus juice "cooks" raw fish or shellfish, which is then mixed with fresh vegetables, chile peppers, and cilantro or other fresh herbs, all at the cook's whim. This version comes from Sharron and Robert Shinbo, longtime Market residents and supporters. (Sharron has volunteered her time of the Pike Place Market Preservation and Development Authority [PDA] Council for many years.) These two savvy cooks first experienced the dish while sailing in Tahiti, but, closer to home, they often find exotic ingredients (such as fresh coconut) at the Market's highstalls and specialty shops, including Lina's Produce, Mai Choy, and El Mercado Latino. The Shinbos suggest serving the dish with long-grain rice or buttered baguettes, the latter idea inspired by the small French bakeries they visited in the Tahitian islands.

◆ To prepare cucumber, rinse outer skin and pat dry. Cut off ends, then, with a vegetable peeler, peel three or four strips down length of cucumber at equal distances. Cut cucumber in half lengthwise and remove seeds. Cut the cucumber into quarters, then cut quarters into bite-sized pieces and reserve.

◆ In a nonreactive mixing bowl, stir together rice vinegar, white vinegar, sugar, lime juice, and Coconut Water until sugar is dissolved. Taste and add salt as needed.

◆ Place one-third of marinade in a small nonreactive mixing bowl and add cucumber, carrot, and onion. Stir well, cover, and refrigerate at least 4 hours or (preferably) overnight to allow the flavors to meld.

◆ Place one-third of the marinade in a small nonreactive mixing bowl, add tomatoes, and stir. Cover and refrigerate at least 4 hours or (preferably) overnight to allow the flavors to meld.

◆ Place the remaining marinade in a small nonreactive mixing bowl, add tuna, and stir. Cover and refrigerate 1 to 2 hours (no longer) to allow the flavors to meld.

1 English (hothouse) cucumber

¼ cup unseasoned rice vinegar

¼ cup distilled white vinegar

¼ cup granulated sugar

Juice of 2 limes

1 cup Coconut Water (recipe follows)

Kosher salt

1 carrot, cut into matchstick-sized strips

1 small red or Walla Walla onion, cut into ¹⁄₁₆-inch slices and pulled apart into rings, small center pieces discarded

4 plum tomatoes, peeled, seeded, and cut into bite-sized pieces

1 pound sushi-grade ahi or albacore tuna or swordfish, cut into bite-sized pieces

1 head butter lettuce, rinsed, drained, and spun dry, cut into bite-sized pieces

1 ripe avocado, cut into bite-sized pieces

Fresh Shredded Coconut, for garnish (recipe follows)

◆ To serve, carefully toss lettuce, cucumbers (and marinade), tuna (and marinade), and tomatoes (and marinade) in a large nonreactive serving bowl. Be careful not to break up fish or vegetables. Arrange avocado on top, sprinkle with Fresh Shredded Coconut, and serve family-style.

Serves 4 to 6

Coconut Water and Fresh Shredded Coconut

◆ Preheat oven to 450°F.

◆ To open coconut, use a corkscrew, ice pick, or screwdriver to make holes through two of the three eyes, then drain water through a fine-mesh strainer set over a bowl. Reserve coconut water, which should measure about ½ cup.

◆ To prepare meat, bake coconut 18 to 20 minutes, then remove from oven. When cool enough to handle, place coconut on a hard surface and crack it with a hammer to break shell into large chunks. Carefully pry meat from shell with a screwdriver or knife. Using a vegetable peeler, remove thin brown skin from outside of coconut pieces. Grate remaining white portion with the fine side of a grater, and reserve.

Makes about 1 cup of Coconut Water

Green Tea Shellfish Risotto

The Perennial Tea Room

In addition to drinking tea, the staff at The Perennial Tea Room enjoys cooking with their favorite beverage. Here they pair Japanese *sencha* (a bright green tea with an aroma like sweet, fresh-mown grass) and Northwest shellfish for a Pacific Rim twist on the Italian classic—risotto. They suggest serving the risotto with *crostini* and a crisp Soave (or other dry white wine) or a cup of *sencha*.

Coconut Water and Fresh Shredded Coconut

2 fresh coconuts (Note: To choose a fresh coconut, pick it up. It should feel heavy for its size. Then shake it; you should hear the milk sloshing around inside.)

4 cups cold water

1 tablespoon plus 1 teaspoon loose-leaf Japanese sencha (green) tea, plus extra for garnish

3 tablespoons unsalted butter

1 pound bay scallops, rinsed and patted dry, or 1 pound Alaskan spot prawns or large shrimp, peeled, deveined, cut in half lengthwise, and patted dry

- Heat water to no more than 180°F, then pour over tea leaves and steep 2 minutes. Strain tea into a medium saucepan and keep it warm over low heat, but do not boil or reduce liquid.

- Melt 1 tablespoon of the butter in a medium skillet over medium-high heat and cook scallops, prawns, or shrimp 2 to 3 minutes, or until scallops just turn opaque or prawn or shrimp tails just curl, stirring occasionally. Add zucchini and cook 1 to 2 minutes more, stirring occasionally. Remove from heat and reserve.

- Melt the remaining 2 tablespoons butter in a large saucepan over medium-high heat. Add leeks and cook 1 minute, or until bright green and slightly softened, stirring constantly. Add rice and cook 2 to 3 minutes, or until rice is completely coated with butter and slightly toasted, stirring constantly. Add wine and cook until it is almost totally absorbed, stirring often, about 1 to 2 minutes.

- Stir in 1 cup of the warm tea. Reduce heat to medium-low and simmer, stirring often, about 5 to 6 minutes, or until liquid is almost totally absorbed, stirring occasionally.

- Continue adding tea in ½-cup increments, cooking about 3 minutes per each addition of liquid, and stirring frequently until tea broth is almost absorbed. Continue this process until rice reaches a creamy consistency and is cooked al dente (still slightly firm in the middle), and all the tea broth is used.

- Remove risotto from heat and add seafood and zucchini mixture, plus any juices that have accumulated, stirring gently so as not to break up the seafood or vegetables. Add salt and pepper, taste, and add additional seasoning as needed.

- To serve, divide risotto among individual bowls and sprinkle with tea leaves that have been crushed in a mortar or pestle or a spice grinder. Serve immediately.

Serves 4

1 cup (about 5 ounces) diced zucchini

1 cup cleaned, chopped leeks, white and light green part only

1½ cups uncooked arborio rice

1 cup dry white wine (Italian Soave recommended)

½ teaspoon kosher salt

¼ teaspoon freshly ground white pepper

Crabmeat Tagliatelle in Creamy Lemon-Tomato Sauce

Vivanda Ristorante

This is my favorite kind of recipe—easy to prepare, yet yielding extraordinary results. The lemon really perks up the tomato-cream sauce (spiked with vodka), while still allowing the taste and texture of the crabmeat to shine through. Just be sure to cook the pasta and assemble all the ingredients before starting, since it goes together so quickly. Also note that I've specified a serving size for two rather than six people, since this very romantic entrée would be a special treat for that certain someone on an anniversary or Valentine's Day.

◆ Bring a large pot of salted water to a boil, add the pasta, and cook 10 to 15 minutes, or until al dente. Drain and keep warm until ready to use.

◆ Melt the butter and olive oil in a large skillet over medium-high heat. Add the garlic and cook 1 to 2 minutes, or until garlic is soft but not browned, stirring often. Add the crabmeat and stir well, then add the vodka, salt, pepper, and lemon zest and stir well.

◆ Add the tomato sauce and stir well, then add 1 tablespoon of the cream and cook 1 to 2 minutes or until reduced slightly, stirring often. Season to taste with salt, pepper, and pepper flakes, if desired.

◆ Add the remaining 1 tablespoon of cream if needed for a thinner consistency, then add the tagliatelle, toss with the sauce, and divide among individual plates. Serve immediately.

Serves 2 as an entrée, 4 as an appetizer

6 ounces tagliatelle pasta

1 tablespoon unsalted butter

1 tablespoon olive oil

2 teaspoons minced garlic

6 ounces Dungeness crabmeat, picked over for shells and cartilage

2 tablespoons vodka

Pinch of kosher salt, plus extra for seasoning

Pinch of freshly ground black pepper, plus extra for seasoning

1 teaspoon grated fresh lemon zest

1½ cups plain homemade or store-bought tomato sauce (see Marinara Vegetable Sauce, page 181)

1 to 2 tablespoons whipping cream

Crushed red pepper flakes (optional)

VIVANDA RISTORANTE

A sophisticated, sunny-bright, fine-dining space that opened at 95 Pine Street the first day of summer in 2002, Vivanda Ristorante combines "Mediterranean seafood with an Italian soul," according to owner Kamyar Khoshdel, an intense man with a long history in the restaurant business. "Our menu utilizes the freshest of Pacific Northwest ingredients, since we have the top products from Washington farmers right at our doorstep."

When they dine at Vivanda, guests find an emphasis on Italian flavors, with influences of Greece, France, Spain, and Morocco thrown in for good measure. Memorable dishes created by Chef Peter Levine include the Lobster Club Sandwich, Moroccan Lamb Stew, Olive-Crusted Halibut, and Lobster and Crab Ravioli.

Panna Cotta with Passionfruit Sauce or Warm Banana Bread Pudding end the meal on a sweet note. Of course, just sitting at the granite-topped bar or on the sunny patio with a cocktail in hand and the unbeatable views of Puget Sound, the Olympics, and the Market is another sweet way to conclude the evening. Sunsets in summer are an especially happy time to come to Vivanda, which is open for lunch and dinner daily.

Crab-Stuffed Halibut with Crawfish Cream Sauce

Sotto Voce and From The Bayou

This is one of the most popular dishes served at From The Bayou, Sotto Voce owner Kevin Roy's authentic Cajun restaurant near Tacoma. The sauce is a creamy, pale-pink concoction made extra-special by the addition of roasted red bell peppers and crawfish tails, while the stuffed halibut is full of down-home goodness.

◆ Preheat oven to 375°F. Lightly oil a baking sheet or spray with nonstick cooking spray and set aside.

◆ Prepare halibut fillet by making a horizontal cut from one side of each fillet to the other, but not all the way through, so that the fillet can be folded out like the pages of a book. Cover fish, refrigerate, and reserve.

◆ Heat olive oil in a large skillet over medium heat and add onion, garlic, and bell pepper and stir well to mix. Add black pepper,

1½ pounds halibut fillet, about 1 inch thick, skin and bones removed, rinsed and patted dry and cut into four 6-ounce pieces

¼ cup Sotto Voce Olio Santo or garlic-flavored olive oil

1 cup chopped white or yellow onion

1 teaspoon minced garlic

½ cup chopped green bell pepper

Pinch of freshly ground black pepper, plus extra for seasoning

Pinch of garlic powder, plus extra for seasoning

SOTTO VOCE

Y ou'll discover a bit of the bayou at Sotto Voce, an alluring storefront on the east side of Pike Place where candles burn, jewel-like bottles of olive oil and flavored vinegars line the dark-paneled shelves, and the products are available for sampling.

Owner and proprietor Kevin Roy started out on the Market's farm tables in 1991 selling specially blended herbed, spiced olive oil. He learned the secret formula from his mother while growing up on a farm in Opelousas, Louisiana, the heart of Cajun country.

Kevin's original product, Olio Santo, is a heady blend of rosemary, thyme, bay leaf, peppercorns, and mild chile pepper that marinates in a beautiful glass bottle along with garlic-infused olive oil. Kevin created Olio Basilico, infused with sweet basil and white peppercorns, for basil lovers. There are also oils flavored with lemon, mushrooms, sun-dried tomatoes, bell peppers, and habanero peppers.

Premium-quality spiced and herbed wine vinegars are another draw here, and there are 11 from which to choose. Aceto Ligurese is an authoritative blend of tart cranberries, baby dill, garden sage, lemon thyme, and mustard seeds. Aceto Oriental, infused with lime slices, wild ginger, chile peppers, and cilantro, takes a cue from the Far East.

Not content with the success of his olive oils and vinegars alone, Kevin and some childhood friends opened From The Bayou in Parkland, Washington. This soulful Cajun restaurant may be the only place in Puget Sound that serves fried alligator. And no, it does not taste like chicken!

garlic powder, and cayenne and cook 5 to 7 minutes, or until the vegetables are softened but not browned, stirring often.

◆ While onions are cooking, lightly beat egg in a medium mixing bowl, then gently mix in cheese, bread crumbs, and crabmeat, being careful not to break up crab. When onions are finished cooking, add them to crab mixture, stirring gently to mix. Season to taste with salt, pepper, garlic powder, and cayenne.

◆ Open halibut fillets and divide stuffing over one side of each piece of fish. Fold over top portion and squeeze gently to bring both sides together. Arrange fillets on prepared baking sheet without crowding and cook 12 to 15 minutes, or until the halibut flakes.

◆ To serve, divide halibut fillets among individual plates and cover generously with Crawfish Cream Sauce.

Serves 4

Pinch of cayenne pepper, plus extra for seasoning

1 large egg

½ cup grated sharp Cheddar cheese

⅓ cup unseasoned dry bread crumbs (see Techniques section)

½ pound Dungeness crabmeat, picked over for shells and cartilage

Kosher salt

Crawfish Cream Sauce (recipe follows)

Crawfish Cream Sauce

◆ Heat olive oil in a large skillet over medium heat and add onions, garlic, green bell pepper, and roasted red bell pepper and stir well. Add salt, black pepper, garlic powder, and cayenne, stir well, and cook 5 to 8 minutes, or until vegetables are softened but not colored, stirring often.

◆ Reduce heat to low, add crawfish, and cook 3 to 5 minutes, or until crawfish turns opaque, stirring occasionally. Add half-and-half, bring to a simmer, and cook 5 to 10 minutes, or until slightly reduced. Add cheese, stir well, and cook just until it has melted into the sauce. Season to taste with salt, pepper, garlic powder, and cayenne.

Makes about 3 cups

Cook's Hint: Although crawfish meat is much more readily available in Louisiana than in Seattle, Exotic Meats is a good local source (see Mail-order Information). Substituting peeled and deveined shrimp gives the sauce a bit different, but equally delicious, taste.

Crawfish Cream Sauce

2 tablespoons Sotto Voce Olio Basilico or garlic-flavored olive oil

1 cup chopped white or yellow onion

1 teaspoon minced garlic

½ cup chopped green bell pepper

⅓ cup chopped roasted red bell pepper (see Techniques section)

Pinch of kosher salt, plus extra for seasoning

Pinch of freshly ground black pepper, plus extra for seasoning

Pinch of garlic powder, plus extra for seasoning

Pinch of cayenne pepper, plus extra for seasoning

½ pound crawfish meat or shrimp, peeled and deveined

2 cups half-and-half

½ cup shredded Parmesan cheese

Creamed Dungeness Crabmeat Omelet

Athenian Inn

This omelet is like a blast from the past, a warm, nostalgic reminder of the type of breakfast we all used to enjoy before oat bran and Pilates came into vogue. If you feel like a splurge, forget the cholesterol and calories and revel in every bite.

◆ Whisk eggs and water until light and foamy. Heat butter in a large skillet over medium to medium-high heat and add egg mixture. Allow eggs to set around edges; then, with a spatula, pull up edges so the uncooked egg can make contact with the heat. Continue this process until the omelet is cooked about halfway through, then turn omelet over and cook the other side.

◆ Just before serving, mix crabmeat with Sherry Cream Sauce. To serve, pour sauce into middle of omelet, fold over, then cut omelet into two equal portions. Drizzle with additional cream sauce, if desired.

Serves 2

Sherry Cream Sauce

◆ In a large skillet over medium heat, melt the ¼ cup butter, whisk in flour until thoroughly blended, then add half-and-half a little at a time until thoroughly incorporated, whisking constantly. Add mustard, paprika, and salt, whisk well, and turn down heat to low.

◆ In a medium skillet over low heat, melt the remaining 1½ teaspoons butter and cook onion 1 to 2 minutes, stirring often. Add mushrooms and cook 2 to 3 minutes, stirring often, just until they begin to lose their juice. Remove from heat and add sherry. Add mushroom/sherry mixture to cream sauce, stir until thoroughly blended, and keep warm until ready to use.

Makes about 2 cups

4 or 5 large eggs

1 tablespoon water or milk

1 tablespoon unsalted butter

¼ cup Dungeness crabmeat, picked over for shells and cartilage

Sherry Cream Sauce (recipe follows)

Sherry Cream Sauce

¼ cup plus 1½ teaspoons unsalted butter or margarine

¼ cup all-purpose flour

2 cups half-and-half

½ teaspoon dry mustard

¼ teaspoon sweet paprika

¼ teaspoon kosher salt

1 teaspoon grated onion

1 cup fresh sliced button mushrooms

1½ teaspoons dry sherry

Three Greek brothers started the Athenian Inn in 1909 as a bakery, luncheonette, and candy shop, with sweets made on the premises. With its central location in the Main Arcade, the popular Athenian Inn quickly grew from a small restaurant into a restaurant and tavern, and was one of the first establishments in Seattle to be granted a liquor license (for beer and wine) in 1933. Bob and Louise Cromwell bought the place in 1966, and Louise is still a fixture at the entrance, acting as hostess and den mother several days a week.

Under her watchful eye, the Athenian Inn boasts an overflowing menu of ethnically diverse items, such as Scotch Eggs, Dungeness Crab Louie, *Sinigang* (the Athenian kettle of fish), and Athenian Greek Salad. Cocktails and beer are important here, with 20 brews on tap and 200 beers by the bottle.

You can come as you are. Everyone from businesspeople to tourists to First Avenue street people stops by the well-worn premises for breakfast, lunch, early dinner, a snack, or a drink from 6:30 A.M. to 6:30 P.M. Monday through Saturday. You might want to time your visit to coincide with the rising or setting of the sun, since the waterfront views are outstanding here. Be sure to notice the bright neon sign outside the Athenian Inn; it's the original one placed there by those three Greek brothers in 1933.

Crispy Skin Salmon with Citrus Sauce and Black Rice Cakes

Flying Fish

Christine Keff has traveled the globe to find inspiration for her two popular restaurants in the Seattle neighborhood of Belltown. Flying Fish,* her Asian-leaning "seafood bistro," opened in 1995, and the Latin-inspired Fandango* opened in 2000. The year 1999 was a magical one for Chris; she was named Best Northwest Chef by the James Beard Foundation, and Flying Fish received an extremely rare four-star rating from the *Seattle Post-Intelligencer*. Even after her many successes and travels, Chris says, "The Pacific Northwest is a great place to cook because of its cultural diversity and the availability of so many fresh food products. And the Market is such a good resource for chefs. My favorite time to visit is early in the morning. It's

2 teaspoons canola or vegetable oil

2 tablespoons minced gingerroot

2 tablespoons minced green onion

2 tablespoons minced garlic

3 tablespoons unseasoned rice vinegar

4 tablespoons hoisin sauce

1 tablespoon sambal oelek (see Cook's Hint)

2 tablespoons black vinegar

great to be part of the bustle as the vendors unload and set up, to walk down Pike Place with a cup of coffee in the misty early light."

◆ Heat a small nonstick saucepan over medium heat. When pan is hot, add 1 teaspoon of the canola oil and cook gingerroot, green onion, and garlic 1 to 2 minutes, stirring constantly. Add rice vinegar, hoisin, sambal oelek, and black vinegar, stir well, and bring to a simmer. Add chicken stock, stir well, and bring to a simmer. Remove from heat and allow glaze to cool, then season to taste with salt and pepper. The recipe makes ¾ cup glaze, which can be used immediately or stored in the refrigerator up to 5 days.

◆ Ten minutes before cooking, preheat the grill. Just before cooking, oil grill, brush flesh side of salmon with glaze, and place skin side down on grill. Cook 3 to 4 minutes, or until skin is crisp, then turn and continue cooking 2 to 3 minutes more, or until salmon is just opaque, about 10 minutes per inch of thickness.

◆ While salmon is cooking, gently toss watercress leaves with orange sections and reserve.

◆ Just before you are ready to serve salmon, heat a large nonstick skillet over medium heat. When pan is hot, add the remaining 1 teaspoon of canola oil and the rice cakes. Cook 3 to 4 minutes, turning once, or until rice cakes are heated through.

◆ To serve, place a rice cake and a salmon fillet in the center of each plate, ladle Citrus Sauce around fish and rice, and arrange a handful of reserved watercress/orange salad over the top.

Serves 4

Black Rice Cakes

◆ Rinse rice in a colander under cold running water until water runs clear, then drain well and set aside.

◆ Mix curry paste and water in a blender and pulse until well blended. Place curry mixture in a medium saucepan and bring

¼ cup homemade chicken stock, or 2 tablespoons canned chicken broth plus 2 tablespoons water

Kosher salt

Freshly ground black pepper

Four 6-ounce salmon fillets, bones removed, rinsed, drained, and patted dry

2 bunches watercress, rinsed, drained, and spun dry

4 navel, Valencia, or juice oranges, skin and membranes removed, cut into sections

4 Black Rice Cakes (recipe follows)

Citrus Sauce (recipe follows)

Black Rice Cakes

1 cup glutinous Thai black rice

1 tablespoon Thai yellow curry paste

2¼ cups water

to a boil. Add rice and stir well. Turn down heat to a simmer, cover saucepan, and cook 35 to 40 minutes, or until rice is tender and creamy. Pour rice onto a rimmed baking sheet and pat down to a ¾-inch thickness. Place in refrigerator until cool, then cut into rounds with a 3-inch cookie cutter or clean drinking glass.

Makes 4 cakes

Citrus Sauce

◆ Pour orange, lemon, and lime juices into a small saucepan, bring to a boil, and cook 6 to 8 minutes, or until liquid becomes thick and syrupy and about 2 tablespoons remain. Watch pot carefully during final 2 minutes of cooking time to be sure syrup doesn't boil away. Cool syrup, place it in a blender and, with the motor running, slowly add olive oil in a thin, steady stream. When oil is incorporated and sauce is thick and opaque, transfer it to a small mixing bowl and season to taste with salt and pepper. Use immediately, or cover and refrigerate up to 5 days. If refrigerated, allow sauce to come to room temperature before serving.

Makes about ½ cup

Cook's Hint: Some of the more esoteric ingredients in this recipe, such as *sambal oelek* (a popular sauce in Indonesia, Malaysia, and southern India made of chiles, brown sugar, and salt), *hoisin* (a thick, reddish-brown Chinese sauce made of soybeans, garlic, chile peppers, and spices), unseasoned rice vinegar, Chinese black vinegar, glutinous Thai black rice, and Thai yellow curry paste are available in the Market at Oriental Mart and El Mercado Latino. Cost Plus Imports (just north of the Market) has an interesting collection of imported specialty foods, and Uwajimaya in Seattle's International District is the region's most reliable source for difficult-to-find Asian ingredients. Outside Seattle, Asian markets and some upscale grocery stores are good sources.

*Outside of the Market Historic District.

Citrus Sauce

½ cup freshly squeezed orange juice

2 tablespoons freshly squeezed lemon juice

2 tablespoons freshly squeezed lime juice

⅓ cup extra virgin olive oil

Kosher salt

Freshly ground black pepper

Grilled Halibut with Lemon Herb Splash

DISH D' LISH

Seafood and citrus form a classic pairing, but the flavor of each is enhanced in this boldly flavored, zestful "splash" (similar to a vinaigrette for seafood) devised by Kathy Casey. Chef Kathy advises that if fresh halibut is not available, try sea scallops or peeled, deveined shrimp threaded on rosemary sprigs or wooden skewers. If using skewers, be sure to soak them in water for about half an hour before grilling.

◆ Preheat grill or broiler. Lightly rub halibut on each side with a little oil and season with salt and pepper.

◆ Cook fish for approximately 2 to 3 minutes per side, depending on thickness and doneness desired.

◆ To serve, place halibut on individual plates and drizzle each piece of fish with 1 tablespoon or more of Lemon Herb Splash. Pass remaining "Splash" on the side.

Serves 4

Lemon Herb Splash

◆ In a small bowl or glass jar with a tight-fitting lid, mix together all the ingredients until well blended. Use immediately, or cover and refrigerate until ready to use.

Makes ½ cup sauce, enough to top 4 to 6 pieces of fish.

Cook's Hint: To add a nice, light smoke flavor, soak a few wood chips in water and throw them on the coals just before placing the fish on the grill.

1½ pounds fresh halibut steaks or fillets, rinsed, drained, patted dry, and cut into four 6-ounce pieces

Vegetable oil as needed

Kosher salt

Freshly ground black pepper

Lemon Herb Splash (recipe follows)

Lemon Herb Splash

6 tablespoons extra virgin olive oil

2 tablespoons freshly squeezed lemon juice

2 teaspoons minced fresh lemon zest

1½ teaspoons minced fresh rosemary

1½ teaspoons minced fresh basil

1 tablespoon minced fresh flat-leaf parsley

⅛ teaspoon crushed red pepper flakes

½ teaspoon minced garlic

¼ teaspoon kosher salt

DISH D' LISH

In a prime marquee location under the Market clock, just north of Rachel the Pig and all the flying-fish hoopla at Pike Place Fish, sits DISH D' LISH, created by the husband-and-wife team of Kathy and John Casey and opened in the fall of 2002. In the elegant space with dark-wood cabinetry and inviting display cases, you'll find prepared gourmet foods to go (Food T' GoGo), such as a seasonal variety of salad dressings, sauces, entrées, baked goods, salads, and complete meals. Don't miss the Ultimate 4-Cheese Mac, the Sake Teriyaki Chicken or Beef Tenderloin Stix, or the Nine-Layer Chocolate Cake. There's also Kathy's line of specialty food products and cookbooks, and Northwest gift bundles, many of which include Northwest wines and microbrews.

Style is one of the characteristics that Kathy Casey, hailed as "Seattle's Cocktail and Culinary Diva," possesses in spades. She came to prominence at the tender age of 23 while executive chef at the Seattle restaurant Fullers, then went on to become a restaurant-industry consultant, appear on television shows including her own PBS special, and author award-winning cookbooks. She also pens the monthly "Dishing" column for the *Seattle Times*.

It seems most fitting that in her latest incarnation Kathy has opened a business in the Pike Place Market, a dream she nurtured for 15 years. She reminisces, "The Market has always been dear to my heart. I started taking the bus there when I was 14. I loved to look at the beautiful produce and watch the interesting characters. My most vivid memory was stopping at Pasqualina Verdi's stand (page 71). She would turn to me and stick out her hand, full of apricots, and say in a loud voice, 'Eat this!'

"I obeyed, and they were delicious! After that I always visited her whenever I went to the Market and bought little bags of the season's bounty to nibble on while riding the bus home. I suppose you could say that Pasqualina was a big influence on my drive and desire to always try new things and search for new flavors. To this day, I still love to see what new inspiration the Market will bring to me."

Grilled Salmon with Roasted Hazelnut Butter

Cutters Bayhouse

A simple and luscious preparation of the Northwest's favorite fish, using the Northwest's favorite nut, this dish is especially decadent if made when Alaskan Copper River king salmon are running in late May and early June. Copper River is the "filet mignon" of salmon, a rich, full-flavored variety, with a red-orange color and superior, moist taste.

◆ To prepare the butter, pulse toasted nuts in a food processor until finely ground (almost powder consistency) and set aside. Using whisk or electric mixer, whip butter until light and fluffy and fold in nuts by hand. If desired, add herbs, shallots and/or lemon zest.

◆ To grill fish, preheat charcoal grill to 600°F. Be sure grill has been well cleaned with a wire brush to prevent fish fillets from sticking. Cover flesh side of each fillet with 1 tablespoon of hazelnut butter and place on grill with buttered side down.

◆ Cover top of each fillet with an additional 1 tablespoon of the hazelnut butter and season with ¼ teaspoon of the seasoning salt. Cook approximately 2 minutes.

◆ Using a long spatula, turn fish approximately 45 degrees with flesh side still down, and cook an additional 2 minutes to form diamond-shaped grill marks. Turn fillets over with spatula so that skin side of fish is now down. Cook approximately 1 to 2 more minutes, or until internal temperature reaches 140°F.

◆ Just before removing fillets from the grill, top each filet with an additional 1 tablespoon of the hazelnut butter and ¼ teaspoon of the seasoning salt. Serve flesh side up and garnish with lemon slices.

Serves 4

Cook's Hint: The prepared hazelnut butter may be made ahead and refrigerated for up to 1 week, or well wrapped and frozen for up to 3 months, but should be returned to room temperature before using.

½ cup (2 ounces) raw hazelnuts, toasted (see Techniques section)

½ cup unsalted butter, softened

Minced shallots or minced fresh herbs (optional)

Minced fresh lemon zest (optional)

1½ pounds salmon fillet, bones removed, rinsed, drained, patted dry, and cut into four 6-ounce pieces

2 teaspoons seasoning salt or kosher salt and freshly ground black pepper

Lemon slices, for garnish

CUTTERS BAYHOUSE

I n its prime spot overlooking the Seattle waterfront, Cutters Bayhouse* has been a fixture along Western Avenue since 1983. The dining room offers one of the most impressive views in the city as wraparound expanses of glass showcase the freighters, ferries, and sailboats that ply the Sound, while the Olympic Mountains rise majestically in the background.

The atmosphere here is casual and warm, with neutral walls, dark-maroon leather booths, and chalkboards that announce the day's catch. Meals begin with a breadbasket of Cutters' freshly baked-on-the-premises Italian herb bread. After perusing the expansive and far-ranging menu, those with lighter appetites might opt for a selection of treats from the Sea Bar, which includes sushi and raw options.

Heartier types might choose the Stir-Fried Dungeness Crab, Cedar-Planked King Crab Legs, or Fried Pacific Razor Clams. The restaurant's House-Smoked Salmon Chowder or Crab-cakes with Sweet-and-Sour Plum Sauce are other reliable options.

Save room for dessert, but beware, since portions are gargantuan. You can't go wrong with Key Lime Pie or the ooey-gooey Chocolate Volcano Cake, a flourless chocolate cake with a warm ganache center, drizzled with caramel sauce and topped with a cloud of whipped cream.

*Just outside of the Market Historic District.

Trout à la Grecque

Mr. D's Greek Delicacies

M r. D had successful restaurants throughout downtown Seattle before opening his eponymous Market eatery in 1980. Trout à la Grecque, with its garlic- and thyme-infused marinade, is an adaptation for home cooks of one of his former restaurants' signature dishes. "D" suggests serving it with a Greek salad (ripe tomatoes, Greek olives, and feta cheese), rice pilaf or French fries, and fresh green vegetables that have been lightly steamed.

◆ Preheat broiler. Mix olive oil, lemon juice, thyme, garlic, salt, and pepper in a small glass mixing bowl. Place fish skin side down in a large skillet with an ovenproof handle (or wrap handle in aluminum foil to protect it from heat). Spread fish out so that both halves are open and lie flat in a butterflied position.

¼ cup olive oil

Juice of 1 lemon

1 teaspoon dried thyme

4 garlic cloves, minced

Kosher salt

Freshly ground black pepper

4 whole trout (about 8 ounces each), filleted, and with heads and tails removed

½ cup dry white wine

MR. D'S GREEK DELICACIES

A s you walk through the Market, you'll often see hungry pedestrians hastily munching away at a goopy yellow *gyros* cone before the ingredients all drop on the ground. You'll chuckle inwardly because you know they've just paid a visit to Mr. D's Greek Delicacies, where *gyros,* the street snack of Greece, is one of the specialties.

With his work-hardened hands and easy smile, Demetrios Moraitis is the namesake behind Mr. D's. At the south end of the Triangle Building, you'll often find the Market's own "Zorba the Greek" entertaining customers and passersby with his bouzouki (Greek mandolin) playing, singing, and dancing. Sometimes he even carves the spinning hunk of compressed *gyros* meat into likenesses of U.S. presidents or the Venus de Milo. The busts are stored in Mr. D's meat locker deep below Pike Place, and are brought out each Halloween for the Market's annual ghost tours.

"The Market is a great place to express yourself. It has a power, drawing people together," Mr. D says in his thick Greek accent. "I enjoy working in an atmosphere of smiles and laughter, of song and dance. Who wouldn't?"

◆ Drizzle half the olive oil mixture evenly over fish and place under broiler. Cook about 3 minutes, or until fish is opaque but not done.

◆ Remove skillet from oven and place on stovetop over medium heat. Mix wine with the remaining half of the olive oil mixture. When pan is hot, add wine/olive oil mixture to pan and cook, spooning liquid over fish. Continue cooking and spooning liquid over fish 3 minutes more, or until it is tender and just begins to flake.

◆ Remove trout to dinner plates and serve immediately.

Serves 4

Mushroom Salmon Pie with Gruyère Cheese

Quality Cheese

Gruyère, a cow's-milk cheese from Switzerland, has a rich, nutty flavor and a pale yellow color. It forms a mellow backdrop in this soul-satisfying quiche, the perfect choice for an elegant brunch, luncheon, or light dinner when served with a mixed green or fresh fruit salad.

◆ Preheat oven to 350°F. Spread cheese evenly over bottom of pie shell.

◆ Melt butter in a large skillet over medium heat. Add salmon and mushrooms and cook 3 minutes, turning salmon strips once. Remove from heat, cut salmon into 1-inch pieces, then arrange salmon and mushrooms evenly over pie shell.

◆ Beat eggs with half-and-half, oregano, thyme, salt, and pepper and pour over salmon and mushrooms. Bake 45 to 50 minutes, or until center is set and top is golden. If edges of pie start to brown too much, cover pie loosely with aluminum foil during the last 10 to 15 minutes of baking time.

◆ Remove pie from oven and let rest 5 minutes. If desired, garnish pie with sautéed mushrooms and a sprinkling of oregano. Slice and serve while still warm.

Serves 6

1 cup finely grated Gruyère cheese

Pastry for a 9-inch single pie shell, unbaked

1 tablespoon unsalted butter

¾ pound salmon fillet, skin and bones removed, rinsed, drained, patted dry, and cut into 1-inch strips

1 cup sliced fresh button or cremini mushrooms plus extra whole, sautéed mushrooms, for garnish (optional)

3 large eggs

1½ cups half-and-half

Pinch of dried oregano plus extra, crumbled, for garnish (optional)

Pinch of dried thyme, crumbled

¼ teaspoon kosher salt

Pinch of freshly ground black pepper

QUALITY CHEESE

There's been a cheese shop in the Corner Market Building since before World War II, and as she bustles behind the white-enamel display case, owner Pearl Linteau describes the present-day shop as "a mecca for dairy lovers." It's easy to see why, for Quality Cheese offers more than 130 cheeses from the Northwest, the United States, and around the world.

About one-third of the cheeses are domestic and two-thirds imported. They include Appenzeller (the granddaddy of Swiss cheeses), Parmigiano-Reggiano (the heartthrob from Italy), and fresh mozzarella balls flown in from California (the key ingredient in *Caprese*—the classic Italian summer salad composed of fresh mozzarella, ripe tomatoes, and fresh basil leaves). Northwest cheeses include Sally Jackson's handcrafted cheeses from eastern Washington (the sun-dried tomato, basil, and oregano is a customer favorite) and Tillamook cheeses from Oregon.

Barbecued Salmon

Pike Place Fish

This is a simple recipe devised by Dick Yokoyama, manager of Pike Place Fish and owner Johnny's brother, who advises that it is always better to undercook, rather than overcook, your salmon. He notes that "a fish that has been book-filleted, butterflied, or split is one that has been split open and boned out or not, producing two sides of the fish joined by the belly skin or the back so that the halves lie flat."

◆ Preheat barbecue or grill to 350°F.

◆ Mix garlic powder, pepper, and salt (if used) in small bowl. Sprinkle spice mixture evenly over flesh side of fish. Arrange onion and lemon slices evenly over seasonings on flesh side of fish.

◆ Place salmon skin side down on grill, cover, and cook 15 to 20 minutes, depending on thickness of fish and the way you like it cooked. Dick suggests cooking until salmon just flakes.

◆ You can also bake the fish instead of grilling it. To bake fish, place it skin side down in a shallow baking pan that has been lightly greased or sprayed with nonstick cooking spray. Prepare as above and bake at 350°F 10 to 15 minutes without turning, depending on thickness of fish.

Serves 8

1 teaspoon garlic powder

1 teaspoon freshly ground black pepper

1 teaspoon kosher salt (optional)

5 pounds salmon, cut into book fillets

1 medium white or yellow onion, cut into ¼-inch slices

2 lemons, cut into ⅛-inch slices

PIKE PLACE FISH

There's always a festive air at Pike Place Fish, located at the hub of the Market, under the neon clock and behind Rachel the Pig. While musician Jonny Hahn bangs away at his piano in one of the prime musician's spots, the Pike Place fishmongers chant customers' orders in unison and pop open shopping bags like rifle shots.

In gravelly voices they urge passersby to stop, stop, stop and buy, buy, buy. While the tourists' videocameras whir, the clerks out front hoist a salmon or a halibut from the icy pile and toss it skyward. Somehow, their cohorts behind the counter (almost) always manage to catch the cold, slippery charges—with a *whap!*—like baseballs in a catcher's mitt.

Meanwhile, a gaggle of schoolchildren stops in its tracks as a fishmonger holds up a yellow-eyed rockfish and fans its tail as though it were "swimming" through the air. Even locals pause for a stolen moment to gaze at the unsightly monkfish that gapes over ice, its jaws propped open, the better to see jagged rows of teeth; the geoduck with its elephant-trunk neck; and the barnacle-encrusted oysters piled six inches high.

Pike Place Fish was started by two partners in 1930. Present owner Johnny Yokoyama began working at his parents' highstall, Roy's Fruits and Vegetables, at the age of eight and

grew up in the Market. In 1965 he bought Pike Place Fish for $3,500, $1,200 less than he spent for the Buick Riviera he bought the same year. Ironically, the highstall produce stand where Johnny grew up was right next to the present-day Pike Place Fish market.

In recent years, the Market's most famous (or infamous!) fish stall has become known as "the home of the low-flying fish." Thanks to its seafood-throwing shenanigans and obvious esprit de corps, Pike Place Fish has been featured in countless television programs and in a national advertising campaign. There's a best-selling book and training video entitled *Fish!*, and Johnny Yokoyama tours the country giving motivational speeches. And it all started back in 1986 when a couple of fishmongers started calling out customers' orders as a way to add a little excitement to their workday.

Desserts

Chocolate Pot de Crème
Hazelnut Cherry Pie
Peach Grunt
Lemon Sponge Pudding
Chocolate Espresso Cheesecake
Bananas Foster à la Woodring
Chilled Strawberry Soup
Royal Chocolate Truffles
German Apple Cake
Raspberry Shortcake with Rose Geranium Cream
Wild Urban Blackberry Pie
Lemon Ice
Blackberry Mousse with Lemon Madeleines
Raspberries with Honey-Almond Cream
Hazelnut Chocolate Chip Cookies
Sour Cream Cranberry Pie

Chocolate Pot de Crème

Place Pigalle

Fresh mint leaves (optional) appears in sidebar

½ *pound good-quality bittersweet chocolate, coarsely chopped*

3 cups whipping cream

6 large egg yolks

Fresh mint leaves (optional)

Pot de crème translates from the French as "pot of cream," but I simply refer to this intensely chocolatey dessert as a "pot of pleasure." Bill Frank, the longtime owner of Place Pigalle, says his restaurant's best-selling dessert (tied with crème brûlée), is so popular that businesspeople have been known to run their fingers around the rim of the *pot* (a small white ramekin) to get every last lick.

◆ Melt the chocolate in a double boiler or a stainless-steel or glass bowl placed over a saucepan filled with simmering (not boiling!) water, stirring occasionally. Be careful not to get any water into the chocolate or it could seize (clump and harden) and become unusable. Slowly add 2 cups of the whipping cream, whisking until chocolate and cream are well mixed, and bring just to a boil, whisking occasionally and being careful not to scorch the cream.

◆ Remove the chocolate/cream mixture from the heat. In a medium mixing bowl, whisk the egg yolks until light and fluffy. Whisking constantly, slowly pour the chocolate mixture into the yolks until thoroughly combined.

◆ Divide the chocolate mixture evenly among six ramekins or custard cups (6-ounce capacity), then refrigerate 1½ to 2 hours, or until the chocolate sets and chills. After the chocolate chills completely, cover the ramekins with plastic wrap. The desserts can be refrigerated for up to one week or, alternatively, the ramekins can be well wrapped and frozen, then thawed overnight in the refrigerator before serving.

◆ Just before serving, whip the remaining 1 cup cream until stiff peaks form. Remove the ramekins from the refrigerator, add a dollop of whipped cream to each, and garnish with fresh mint leaves, if desired.

Serves 6

PLACE PIGALLE

I t's well worth braving bronze pigs and flying fish to make your way toward Place Pigalle restaurant (tucked under the Market clock) for its nonstop Elliott Bay views, authentic French feel, and Market-inspired, sometimes eclectic, always thoughtfully prepared food and outstanding wine list.

Once you're safely inside, a periwinkle blue ceiling hovers above, white and black tiles checker the floor, and sophisticated paintings grace the walls. The kitchen is just past the small raised bar (half a dozen seats!) that dispenses a wide array of French and Swiss eaux-de-vie, Armagnac, and other premium and unusual spirits.

For lunch, nothing beats Pigalle's classic Salade Niçoise. A bed of baby greens is anchored by a perfectly seared chunk of albacore tuna and surrounded by baby new potatoes, oil-cured olives, roasted red bell peppers, and hard-boiled eggs arranged just so. A sprinkling of fresh tarragon and balsamic vinaigrette completes the dish. If salad doesn't grab you, then a whole Dungeness crab served with freshly made mayonnaise is another option. Or perhaps a bowl of some of the creamiest oyster stew in town, served with sourdough rolls and unsalted butter.

Dinner might begin with Onion Soup Gratinée or a Belgian endive salad, and progress to Rabbit Roulade stuffed with apple, chestnuts, spinach, and blue cheese. Or Duck with Quince Chutney. Or any of the daily salmon, pasta, and seafood specials. But no matter what you order, do not skip dessert. Top-selling desserts here include the crème brûlée and the chocolate pot de crème. After one bite of either, it's easy to see why.

Cook's Hint: Bittersweet chocolate varies widely in flavor and sugar levels (some can be very dark and almost bitter). So for this recipe that contains only three ingredients and no added sugar, be sure to choose a bittersweet chocolate you like to eat out of hand since its flavor forms the foundation for the dessert.

Hazelnut Cherry Pie

Pike Place Nuts

Mid-June to early August is the time to get your fresh red cherries to make this light, easy-to-prepare summertime treat. Choose fruit that is plump, firm, smooth, and vibrant in color, with fresh green stems, for the best flavor and texture.

◆ Preheat oven to 375°F. Lightly grease a 9-inch pie plate or spray with nonstick cooking spray.

◆ Place hazelnuts, graham cracker crumbs, coconut, and brown sugar in a medium mixing bowl and mix well, making sure there are no lumps in the brown sugar.

◆ Beat egg white with electric mixer until stiff but not dry. Fold into nut mixture, blending well. Pat crust into bottom of pie plate and up onto sides if enough remains. Bake pie crust 5 to 7 minutes, or until lightly browned around edges. Remove crust from oven and cool on wire rack.

◆ When crust is cool, arrange cherries in an even layer over crust. Prepare pudding according to package instructions for pie filling, pour over cherries in crust, and refrigerate. When pudding is thick and creamy, slice pie and garnish each slice with a dollop of whipped cream and additional hazelnuts and/or cherries, if desired.

Serves 6 to 8

½ cup hazelnuts, toasted, skinned, and finely crushed (see Techniques section)

½ cup graham cracker crumbs

½ cup flaked coconut

2 tablespoons firmly packed brown sugar

1 egg white

2 cups fresh sweet red cherries, pitted

1 package (3.4 ounce) vanilla or chocolate pudding and pie filling

Whipped cream or whipped topping (optional)

Additional crushed hazelnuts and/or cherries (optional)

PIKE PLACE NUTS

The buttery aroma of freshly roasted cashews hangs in the air as you approach the tiny space occupied by Pike Place Nuts on Economy Row, tucked between Danny's Wonder Freeze and Art Stall Gallery. Much as at a circus or carnival, the nuts are offered in red-and-white-striped paper bags. They have become so popular that the nut shop started the Pike Place Cashew Club. Now loyal customers can enjoy two pounds of just-roasted jumbo cashews (or peanuts, or a combination) delivered to their homes or businesses every month. Whatever type of nut you choose, remember that Pike Place Nuts is "for people crazy about nuts."

Peach Grunt

Sazerac, Hotel Monaco

Jan Birnbaum is chef/partner and "the Big Dawg" at two restaurants he created—Catahoula Restaurant & Saloon in Calistoga, California, and Sazerac* in downtown Seattle's Hotel Monaco, which offers "American food with a Southern twist." He finds the Market "a place of inspiration," but don't ask him about his run-in with the monkfish at Pike Place Fish (page 134). Jan explains that grunts are usually stewed fruits topped with biscuits or dumplings and simmered on the stovetop. But in his version, wine-poached peaches are baked with a cookie-crumb topping, then served over ice cream drizzled with caramel sauce. As Jan, who was raised in New Orleans, might exclaim, "*Laissez les bon temps roulez!*" (Let the good times roll!).

◆ Preheat oven to 350°F. Lightly oil an 8-by-8-inch baking pan or spray with nonstick cooking spray and reserve.

◆ Stir sugar and water in a large, heavy-bottomed, nonreactive saucepan over low heat 2 minutes, or until sugar dissolves. Increase heat to medium-high and boil 8 minutes without stirring, or until syrup turns a deep amber color. Occasionally, swirl pan to mix sugar and brush down any sugar crystals that form on sides of pan with a wet pastry brush.

◆ Remove pan from heat and, wearing oven mitts to protect your hands from splatters, gradually stir in wine, which will bubble vigorously. Return pan to medium-high heat, bring to a boil, and cook 2 to 3 minutes, or until reduced to ½ cup.

◆ Add peaches and scrape vanilla bean seeds into syrup with the back of a small, sharp knife. Stir in salt, then simmer peaches 5 to 8 minutes, or until tender, stirring occasionally.

◆ Place peaches in prepared baking pan and sprinkle with Grunt Topping. Bake 25 to 35 minutes, or until peaches are bubbly around the edges and the top is golden brown.

◆ To serve, spoon into individual bowls, top with ice cream, and drizzle with caramel sauce.

Serves 6 to 8

½ cup granulated sugar

¼ cup water

½ cup Muscat or other sweet dessert wine

6 cups peeled, sliced, firm peaches (about 2 to 2½ pounds)

¼ vanilla bean, split lengthwise

Pinch of kosher salt

Grunt Topping (recipe follows)

1 quart good-quality vanilla ice cream

Good-quality caramel sauce

Grunt Topping

½ cup all-purpose flour

¼ cup (½ stick) unsalted butter, room temperature and cut into chunks

2½ tablespoons firmly packed light brown sugar

1½ teaspoons granulated sugar

½ cup whole almonds, coarsely chopped

½ cup whole pecans, coarsely chopped, or ½ cup pecan pieces

½ teaspoon ground ginger

½ cup coarsely crushed gingersnap cookies

Grunt Topping

◆ Preheat oven to 350°F. Lightly oil an 8-by-8-inch baking pan or spray lightly with nonstick cooking spray.

◆ In a medium mixing bowl, stir together flour, butter, brown sugar, granulated sugar, almonds, pecans, and ginger until moist clumps form. Mix in gingersnaps. Pour the topping into the baking pan and press it out to the corners. Cook 15 to 18 minutes, or until it firms slightly and gives off a strong nutty aroma. Cool on a wire rack, then crumble into bite-sized pieces.

*Outside of the Market Historic District.

Lemon Sponge Pudding

Snoqualmie Valley Honey Farm

This dessert conjures up memories of childhood—comfort, sweetness, and satisfaction. The pudding forms two layers as it bakes, and when you turn it out onto a plate, a rich lemony pudding covers the warm, spongy cake.

◆ Preheat oven to 350°F. Generously butter four custard cups. Get out a baking pan that will comfortably hold all of the custard cups, and reserve.

◆ Blend honey, flour, and salt in a large bowl. Add melted butter and stir well. Add lemon juice and zest and blend well. Combine beaten egg yolks and milk and stir into honey mixture.

◆ Fold in egg whites, leaving a few lumps. Ladle pudding into custard cups, then place custard cups in reserved baking pan. Pour hot water around custard cups until it is halfway up sides, being careful not to splash any water into custard.

◆ Cook pudding 35 to 40 minutes, or until it turns light brown on top and a toothpick inserted in the middle comes out clean. To serve, cut around edges, turn pudding out onto dessert plates, and garnish with fresh berries and a dollop of whipped cream, if desired.

Serves 4

½ cup mild-flavored honey, such as fireweed, apple, or lemon cream

¼ cup all-purpose flour

½ teaspoon kosher salt

2 tablespoons unsalted butter, melted

2½ tablespoons freshly squeezed lemon juice

Grated zest of 1 lemon

3 egg yolks, beaten

½ cup whole milk

3 egg whites, beaten until stiff

Fresh berries (optional)

Whipped cream (optional)

SNOQUALMIE VALLEY HONEY FARM

One summer, Nancy Hutto learned how to say "honey" in 12 different languages at her stand in the Main Arcade. "Honey is such a universally known and appreciated product that people often ask for 'plain honey,'" Nancy explains. "They're amazed at all the flavors created from different flower-nectar sources and the variety of products available. So we educate people about honey."

Among the products Nancy gathers from the 300 colonies of bees she keeps at her honey farm in North Bend, Washington, are 10 liquid honeys, including clover, buckwheat, and the popular Mount Rainier fireweed. Cream honeys (honeys with fruit or spices added) are her specialty, and she counts spiced apple, ginger lemon, and espresso (for coffee lovers who just can't get enough!) among the 20 enticing flavors she produces.

Pure hand-rolled or solid-molded beeswax candles, bee pollen, honeycomb, a honey cookbook, and Royal Jelly Balm for the lips or skin are other options on her colorful farm table. The balm comes in various scents and flavors and is made with beeswax, royal jelly, fine oils, herbs, and propolis, a natural antibiotic gathered by the bees.

Nancy comes from a long line of beekeepers, and waxes poetic when asked about her family's legacy. "Honey is a neat product because bees take something that wouldn't otherwise be used—nectar—and turn it into a gift of the gods," she says. "And no other plant or animal is killed to make it." You'll find Nancy or a representative of Snoqualmie Valley Honey Farm ready to introduce you to the world of honey (and how to say it in 12 languages) with free samples seven days a week, year-round.

Chocolate Espresso Cheesecake

The Pike Place Market Creamery

Dense cheesecake fortified with espresso and chocolate and paired with a chocolate cookie-crumb crust is a sensuous experience to make and a celestial experience to eat.

◆ Preheat oven to 350°F. Lightly grease a 9-inch springform pan.

◆ Melt chocolate chips in a microwave or a double boiler (see Cook's Hint below), being careful not to scorch the chocolate or let it contact the water. Pour into a bowl and reserve.

12 ounces semisweet chocolate chips

26 chocolate wafer cookies, crushed

2 tablespoons plus 1 cup granulated sugar

1 tablespoon finely ground espresso coffee (do not use liquid espresso or instant espresso powder)

¼ cup unsalted butter, melted

- To make crust, place cookies, the 2 tablespoons sugar, ground coffee, and butter in a medium mixing bowl. Blend thoroughly and pour into the prepared springform pan. Pat crumb mixture on bottom of pan and up sides if enough remains. Refrigerate while you prepare the filling.

- To make filling, place softened cream cheese in a large mixing bowl and beat with an electric mixer at low to medium speed until creamy. Add the 1 cup sugar to cream cheese and beat on medium speed until fluffy. Sprinkle flour over cream cheese mixture and blend thoroughly. Add eggs and egg yolks, one at a time, being sure each is thoroughly incorporated. Beat in reserved melted chocolate, hot espresso, and whipping cream at low speed.

- Pour batter over crust and bake 1 hour. Turn off heat and leave cake in oven an additional 40 minutes without opening door. Place cheesecake on wire rack and cool completely, then garnish edges of cheesecake with chocolate-covered espresso beans, if desired.

- Refrigerate at least overnight or (preferably) for 1 or 2 days to let the flavors meld. Slice and serve with whipped cream, if desired.

Serves 8 to 12

Cook's Hint: To melt chocolate, first chop it into small pieces. Pour water into the bottom pot of a double boiler, bring barely to a simmer (do not boil!), then put the chocolate in the top of the double boiler and place it over the warm water. Slowly melt the chocolate while stirring constantly. Make sure that no steam or condensation from the spoon comes in contact with the chocolate at any point. If the natural starch in chocolate combines with water, the mass will thicken, or "seize," making it lumpy and unusable. When the chocolate is about halfway melted, remove the top pot and continue stirring until the chocolate is completely melted. Alternatively, to melt chocolate in a microwave, put it into a microwave-safe dish and microwave on LOW 30 seconds, then stir. Microwave on LOW another 30 seconds and stir again. If big lumps of chocolate still remain, microwave another 30 seconds. Continue this process until only small lumps remain, then stir to finish melting.

3 packages (8 ounce) cream cheese, softened

3 tablespoons all-purpose flour

3 large eggs

2 large egg yolks

¼ cup hot espresso or extra-strength coffee

1 cup whipping cream

36 dark chocolate–covered espresso beans (optional)

Whipped cream (optional)

THE PIKE PLACE MARKET CREAMERY

Small-business owners—those people who tend their shops day in and day out, really know their product, and care about their customers—provide their clientele a different, and entirely more pleasant, experience than the sterile megamall or hypermart on the freeway. And perhaps nobody in the Market exemplifies the good qualities of the small-business owner better than Nancy Nipples, the proprietress and self-described "head milkmaid" of The Pike Place Market Creamery. Tucked back in the Sanitary Market, the Creamery is a place where regular customers can count on a smile, a kind word, a hug, and a backrub from Nancy, who has been on the job since 1977.

The head milkmaid is one of the healthiest-looking and fittest people in the Market, living testament to her philosophy that "eating good food helps you feel good. At the Creamery we also believe in eating food that tastes good."

Among Nancy's good-food offerings, you'll find brown and white eggs from free-running hens and *aracauna* eggs from a species of South American chicken (some call them Martha Stewart eggs because of their pale-pastel shells). There are also giant ostrich and emu eggs, tiny spotted quail eggs, duck eggs (with their chubby yolks), goose eggs, and turkey eggs.

The milk case highlights cow's milk in glass bottles, thick Devonshire cream imported from England, and mascarpone, a sweet Italian cream cheese. Cow-themed greeting cards and other knickknacks round out the theme here, but the star of the show is really Nancy, recipient of the Mayor's Small Business Award in 2000.

WOODRING ORCHARDS

The new owner of Woodring Orchards, Dale Nelson, has taken a successful business and made it his own. The original owners, the Rankin family, started coming to the Market in 1985, selling gallons of fresh cider on the farm tables. Over the years they expanded the scope of Woodring Orchards to include processed ciders; cider syrup, glazes, and chutney, as well as low-sugar jams, jellies, and apple butter.

With a background as a chocolatier and as an expert in developing and creating specialty food products, Dale was attracted to Woodring Orchards because of the unique items it already produced, because of its 5,000-square-foot processing plant (he was tired of testing and putting up products in his mother's kitchen!), and because he is a champion of small family farmers. He had seen many of the orchards in eastern Washington torn out due to stiff competition from overseas products and to make way for development. He hoped that by buying the fruit for his specialty items from small operations, he might help some family farmers stay in business.

Dale bought Woodring Orchards in 2001, and today he and his wife Robin, and his parents operate the processing facility in Cashmere, Washington. From local farmers, Dale selects tree-ripened fruit at its peak of ripeness. Then the family processes the fruit in small batches for the highest quality and flavor, turning out apple ciders and juice blends, fruit spreads and butters, chutneys, and seasonal specialties.

You'll find Woodring's complete product line (including Dale's latest creations) at their permanent space in the Main Arcade, where you're invited to taste before you buy.

Bananas Foster à la Woodring

Woodring Orchards

This dessert is Woodring Orchards' easy-to-prepare answer to the New Orleans classic Bananas Foster, in which sliced bananas are sautéed in a sauce composed of brown sugar, rum, and banana liqueur. I like to make it during the winter holidays, when the air is chilly, eggnog is in ample supply, and I'm dreaming of a vacation in a warm clime.

◆ Warm caramel sauce in a small skillet over low heat for 1 to 2 minutes, stirring constantly until it melts and glistens. Add eggnog and stir well. Add bananas, stir well, and simmer 3

1 jar (8 ounce) Woodring Orchards caramel sauce or other high-quality caramel sauce

¼ cup eggnog (Note: If eggnog is unavailable, substitute ¼ cup half-and-half plus ¼ teaspoon freshly ground nutmeg or to taste)

2 ripe bananas, cut into ½-inch slices

¼ cup brandy

minutes, or until tender, stirring often. Add brandy and lemon juice, and stir until blended and heated through.

◆ To serve, scoop ice cream into individual bowls and ladle banana sauce over ice cream.

Serves 4

1 tablespoon freshly squeezed lemon juice

4 cups high-quality vanilla ice cream

Chilled Strawberry Soup

For years, my colleague and friend Sharon Kramis has been singing the praises of home cooks who use local, seasonal produce in their daily meals. Sharon was a student of the late James Beard, and spread his (and her) philosophy through her popular cooking classes and cookbooks such as *Northwest Bounty* (Sasquatch Books, 1999). For several years, she and her husband Larry kept a condominium just north of the Market so they could partake of the farmers' bounty right at the source. Nowadays, Sharon is a consultant with the Anthony's Homeport restaurants, where she continues to champion the use of the freshest seafood and farm-grown produce. This "best-of-the-season" strawberry soup is one of her creations, served when local strawberries are at their sweet peak of perfection.

◆ In a food processor or blender, pulse strawberries, banana, orange juice, sour cream, and raspberry liqueur until smooth.

◆ Add ice cubes and swirl briefly to chill the liquid, removing ice cubes before they melt completely. (Warning: Do not crush the ice!)

◆ To serve, divide soup among small, chilled bowls. Garnish with mint sprigs and serve immediately.

Serves 4 to 6

Cook's Hint: Sharon suggests serving the soup with pound cake "croutons." To make the croutons, cut a pound cake into ½-inch cubes until you have about 1½ cups. Preheat the broiler, then toast the cubes, turning once to brown on two sides. Float the croutons on top of the bowls of soup before serving.

4 cups fresh strawberries, stems removed and sliced

1 fresh banana, peeled and cut into 4 pieces

1 cup freshly squeezed orange or canned pineapple juice

1 cup light sour cream

1 tablespoon raspberry liqueur or raspberry syrup

2 ice cubes

6 mint sprigs, for garnish

The Dilettante chocolate boutique on First Avenue is an elegant space whose windows are populated in various seasons by chocolate Santa Clauses, Easter bunnies, and Northwest trophy salmon. Specialties include European-style truffles, toffees, marzipan, buttercreams, caramels, dragées, chocolate bars, sauces, and toppings. The miniature chocolate chips and the chocolate couverture are perfect for baking and candymaking.

Dilettante's signature piece of chocolate, the Ephemere Truffle, boasts a creamy dark chocolate center enriched with butter, flavored with vanilla, and then dipped in either dark or milk chocolate. The Champagne Truffle Romanov, a semisweet chocolate center flavored with the essence of Champagne and strawberries, is a best-seller.

Dilettante Chocolates traces its roots back to the courts of Europe at the turn of the 20th century, when Julius Rudolph Franzen created pastries for Franz Josef, emperor of Austria, king of Hungary. While serving the emperor, Julius obtained the closely guarded formulas of the chocolate confectionery and later served as master candymaker for Czar Nicholas II at the Imperial Court of Russia in St. Petersburg. When he immigrated to the United States

around 1914, Julius shared his secret candy-making formulas with his brother-in-law, Earl Davenport. Today Earl's grandson, Dana Davenport, a master confectioner, continues the family tradition with Dilettante Chocolates.

Royal Chocolate Truffles

Dilettante Chocolates

This is the truffle for chocoholics who like their vice of choice pure and unadulterated. Nothing beats the deep, dense taste and texture of this classic truffle, which is as easy to make as it is scrumptious to eat.

◆ Pour whipping cream into a 3-quart saucepan and bring just to the boil. Remove from heat at once and cool to 120°F. Melt chocolate in a double boiler until it reaches 120°F.

⅔ cup whipping cream

1 pound semisweet chocolate (couverture chocolate recommended), chopped fine

¾ cup cocoa powder (natural process), for coating (for dense truffles)

◆ Add chocolate to cooled cream (not cream to chocolate), and stir until mixture is smooth. Scrape mixture onto a baking sheet, spreading evenly. Refrigerate 30 minutes to 1 hour, or until firm.

◆ To make truffles with a dense texture, proceed to the next step. If you prefer a light, fluffy texture, take mixture out of refrigerator just before it is set, scrape it into the chilled bowl of an electric mixer, and whip it with a rotary beater until it is fully aerated. Chill thoroughly and it will retain the air you whipped into it. When ready to form it into ball-shaped pieces, work a small portion at a time, keeping the remainder refrigerated. Don't roll in cocoa. When entire batch is finished, freeze until solid, then dip in melted chocolate (in white chocolate if the flavor contrast appeals to you) to keep the air trapped inside filling. Do not let the truffle come back to room temperature until it has been dipped and securely protected by a solid shell of coating. Arrange on a serving plate and keep refrigerated until 15 minutes before serving.

◆ For truffles with a dense texture, remove mixture from refrigerator and form into small balls with a melon-ball scoop. Put balls on a sheet of waxed paper. After you have formed six balls, roll in cocoa powder. Arrange on a serving plate and return to refrigerator. If truffle paste gets too warm to hold its shape, refrigerate briefly until it becomes firm enough to work with.

◆ When entire batch is finished and artistically arranged on a serving plate, keep refrigerated until 15 minutes before serving.

Makes 5 dozen truffles

Cook's Hint: This is a very versatile recipe that can be adapted to your personal tastes. Add as much as ¼ cup of your favorite liqueur after stirring together chocolate and cooled cream, then finish as in master recipe. Use any flavoring extract or oil that appeals to you; vanilla, almond, and peppermint go well with dark chocolate. Add flavorings a little at a time, tasting carefully as you go.

½ pound white chocolate (couverture chocolate recommended), chopped fine and melted (see Cook's Hint, page 142), for coating (for fluffy truffles)

German Apple Cake

The recipe for this dense, moist cake, chock-full of grated apples and walnuts, appeared in the first edition of this book and was given to me by Pat and Jim Rankin, the original owners of Woodring Orchards. It is best made at the height of apple season with new-crop apples, although it's so tasty, you'll want to make and eat it year-round.

◆ Preheat oven to 350°F. Lightly grease a 9-by-13-inch baking pan or spray with nonstick cooking spray.

◆ Beat eggs and oil in a large mixing bowl until pale yellow and creamy, then add sugar, flour, cinnamon, baking soda, salt, and vanilla. Stir until well blended, then add apples that have been drained of any juice that accumulates during grating. Mix well and add walnuts.

◆ Pour dough into prepared baking pan and cook 35 to 45 minutes, or until cake shrinks from sides of pan and a toothpick inserted in the middle comes out clean. Cool cake on wire rack. When completely cool, ice cake with Cream Cheese Icing, cut into slices, and enjoy.

Serves 12

Cream Cheese Icing

◆ Beat cream cheese, butter, and vanilla with a wire whisk or electric mixer until smooth and fluffy. Add confectioners' sugar a little at a time, until it is incorporated and icing is smooth.

2 large eggs

½ cup vegetable or canola oil

2 cups granulated sugar

2 cups all-purpose flour

2 teaspoons ground cinnamon

1 teaspoon baking soda

½ teaspoon kosher salt

1 teaspoon pure vanilla extract

4 cups grated apples, medium grate (about 3 large, firm apples, such as Fuji or Granny Smith)

½ cup chopped walnuts

Cream Cheese Icing (recipe follows)

Cream Cheese Icing

2 packages (3 ounces each) cream cheese, softened

1 tablespoon unsalted butter, melted

1 teaspoon pure vanilla extract

1½ cups sifted confectioners' sugar

Raspberry Shortcake with Rose Geranium Cream

The Herbfarm

Chef Jerry Traunfeld has been interested in cooking and gardening since he was a child. So it was no surprise that after attending culinary school and working in restaurants in San Francisco and Seattle, he quickly accepted a job offer at The Herbfarm* in 1990. There, along with owners Ron Zimmerman and Carrie Van Dyck, Jerry creates the restaurant's legendary nine-course, prix-fixe dinners centered around regional, seasonal ingredients and a bounty of fresh herbs from the restaurant's massive kitchen garden. In 2000 Jerry won the James Beard Award for Best Northwest Chef, and in 2001 his book *The Herbfarm Cookbook* was chosen Best Cookbook from a Restaurant or Chef by the International Association of Culinary Professionals. As Jerry says, "I've been personally shopping at the Pike Place Market since I first moved to Seattle in 1978. It's a tremendous gift to have such a great resource of local fresh produce, fish, meats, cheeses, and ethnic ingredients in one place. Plus, it's always been the best place in Seattle for fresh-cut herbs."

◆ Preheat oven to 425°F. Line a baking sheet with parchment paper and reserve.

◆ Combine flour, baking powder, baking soda, the ¼ cup sugar, and salt in a medium mixing bowl. Cut in butter with a pastry blender or two crisscrossed knives until mixture resembles coarse meal. Stir in sour cream and milk.

◆ Drop dough in eight mounds onto prepared baking sheet. Sprinkle with the remaining 2 tablespoons sugar. Bake 15 minutes, or until lightly browned. Transfer biscuits to a wire rack to cool slightly before splitting.

◆ To serve, cut biscuits in half horizontally. Put bottom halves on dessert plates and spoon large dollops of Rose Geranium Cream over each. Cover with berries, letting them spill out at the sides, and replace biscuit tops. Serve immediately.

Serves 8

2 cups all-purpose flour

1½ teaspoons baking powder

½ teaspoon baking soda

¼ cup plus 2 tablespoons granulated sugar

¼ teaspoon kosher salt

¼ cup (½ stick) unsalted butter, chilled and cut into four pieces

1 cup sour cream

½ cup whole milk

Rose Geranium Cream (recipe follows)

4 cups (2 pints) fresh raspberries

Rose Geranium Cream

◆ Bring cream to a boil in a small saucepan. Add rose geranium leaves, cover, remove from heat, and allow to sit at room temperature for 30 minutes. Strain into a small mixing bowl, pressing solids with a wooden spoon to force out as much cream as possible. Discard rose geranium, cover cream, and refrigerate until completely chilled.

◆ Just before ready to serve, whip chilled cream to medium-soft peaks.

Cook's Hint: To measure flour in this recipe, Jerry recommends spooning the flour into the measuring cup, then leveling it off with a straight edge (such as a kitchen knife). To be even more precise, measure your flour using a kitchen scale; it should weigh 9 ounces.

Makes about 3 cups

*Outside of the Market Historic District.

Wild Urban Blackberry Pie

One dreary mid-March day, about a week after I'd had some minor surgery and was sticking close to home, my friend Paul Dunn showed up at my doorstep with a freshly baked blackberry pie still warm from the oven. For years, this Market resident and self-described "casual home cook" has been on a quest to find the "perfect" pie crust. And for years I've had the good fortune to sample the results. Although Paul used frozen berries when he made my wintertime pie, he uses "wild urban blackberries" during the summer. He picks these wild berries on hillsides or railroad cuts in the Puget Sound region.

◆ Preheat oven to 350°F.

◆ Roll out one of the pie crust balls on a lightly floured surface until it is slightly larger than a 9-inch circle. If the dough sticks, add additional flour as needed. Fold dough in half and transfer to a 9-inch pie plate, and unfold it so it covers pie pan evenly. Press dough into pan. Prick bottom of crust with tines

Rose Geranium Cream

1½ cups whipping cream

12 large fresh rose geranium leaves

"Perfect" Pie Crust for a 2-crust, 9-inch pie (recipe follows)

All-purpose flour

4 cups fresh blackberries, gently rinsed and patted dry

1 cup granulated sugar, plus extra for sprinkling on top of pie

1 tablespoon freshly squeezed lemon juice

3 tablespoons quick-cooking tapioca

1 tablespoon unsalted butter

of a fork a few times, and place prepared pie crust in the refrigerator while preparing the filling.

◆ In a mixing bowl, gently stir together the berries, sugar, lemon juice, and tapioca. Let stand 15 minutes.

◆ Remove prepared pie crust and the remaining dough ball from the refrigerator. Pour berries into crust, then dot fruit with small pieces of butter.

◆ Roll out remaining ball of dough on a lightly floured surface (adding more flour if needed) and position it evenly over pie tin, allowing an overlay of ¾ to 1 inch and cutting off any excess dough. Flute the edges, making sure they are securely sealed. Brush top of crust with water, then sprinkle with granulated sugar. Cut several vents in pie crust to allow steam to escape, or see Cook's Hint below.

◆ Bake 35 to 40 minutes, or until golden brown. Serve while still warm, or cool on a wire rack.

Serves 6 to 8

"Perfect" Pie Crust

◆ In a medium mixing bowl, combine flour, sugar, and salt. Divide the vegetable shortening into several pieces, then, using a pastry blender or two crisscrossed knives, cut it into the flour mixture until pea-sized crumbs form.

◆ In a small mixing bowl, combine egg, water, and vinegar. Add to flour mixture a tablespoon at a time, stirring in with a fork until the dough forms a ball. Flour your hands, divide the dough into two balls, and flatten slightly.

◆ Wrap each dough ball in plastic wrap, and refrigerate at least 2 hours and up to 3 days. Alternatively, wrap the dough in aluminum foil, seal in a heavy-duty freezer-safe bag, and freeze up to 1 month.

Makes enough pastry for two 9-inch pie crusts

Cook's Hint: Paul suggests using uncooked penne noodles as vent holes. Just take five noodles and twist them into the top crust and fruit at equidistant spots about 1½ inches from the edges of the pie tin. Remove before slicing the pie.

"Perfect" Pie Crust

2 cups all-purpose flour, plus extra for dusting hands

1 teaspoon granulated sugar

¼ teaspoon kosher salt

½ cup vegetable shortening, chilled

1 large egg, beaten

3 tablespoons cold water

1 tablespoon distilled white vinegar

PROCOPIO GELATERIA

Procopio Gelateria* (Italian ice cream parlor) was inspired by Francesco Procopio dei Coltelli, who is credited with popularizing ice cream in Florence, Italy, back in the 1600s. This master *gelatiere* (ice cream maker) moved to Paris in 1670 and opened the first Parisian cafe, Café Procope. Until that time, ice cream had been reserved for royalty only, but Procopio introduced *gelato* to the public and counted Benjamin Franklin, Voltaire, Rousseau, and Napoleon among his customers.

The term *gelato* refers to a wide variety of frozen desserts, including fresh fruit ices, cream ices, and *semifreddi*. These frozen desserts are made with pure, fresh ingredients such as fruits, nut pastes, cocoa, real liqueurs, milk, and cream. The types and flavors of gelati that Procopio Gelateria, located on the Pike Place Hillclimb just below the Market, makes depend upon the season and availability of fresh ingredients and the whim of longtime owner Brian Garrity.

*Just outside of the Market Historic District.

Lemon Ice

Procopio Gelateria

You'll enjoy this tart, refreshing ice, as puckery and flavorful as a lemon drop, especially on hot summer days. It's reputed to have been Napoleon's favorite flavor.

◆ In a small saucepan, combine water and sugar and heat over medium heat 2 to 3 minutes, or until sugar is dissolved, stirring occasionally. Do not allow to come to a boil. Remove from heat and allow to cool.

◆ Add lemon juice, lemon zest, and citric acid to sugar mixture and stir well to combine. Place in an ice cream maker and freeze according to manufacturer's instructions, or place in a glass or metal pan and freeze 2 to 3 hours, or until mushy. Stir well and allow to freeze until mushy again, then stir well again. Scrape lemon ice into an airtight plastic freezer container with a lid, cover, and freeze completely. Before serving, allow ice to thaw at room temperature about 5 minutes, or until desired consistency.

Serves 4

2 cups water

¾ cup granulated sugar

¾ cup freshly squeezed lemon juice

2 teaspoons grated fresh lemon zest

2 teaspoons citric acid (available in health food stores under the name C-Crystals or 100 percent pure crystalline vitamin C)

Towering arched windows, twinkling votives, the lights of faraway boats sparkling in Elliott Bay, and a sophisticated crowd create the atmosphere for a romantic, leisurely rendezvous at Chez Shea. The 30-seat restaurant, located in the historic Corner Market Building (built in 1912), offers three- and four-course prix-fixe dinners. Dessert is à la carte (don't miss the Lavender Crème Brûlée or the Chocolate Ganache Torte), and the thoughtfully chosen wine list includes bottles from France, California, Washington, and Oregon.

Sandy Shea, chef/owner of Chez Shea (which loosely translates as "Shea's Place"), felt fated to claim the unusual space from the moment she moved into an apartment building directly across the street. When the space became available in 1983, she bought it. Sandy labels her style of cooking "contemporary regional": It's based on French tradition, but it draws influences from Mediterranean, Mexican, Asian, and American cuisines. Sandy and her staff value seasonality, selecting the choicest produce from the Market and changing the menu six times a year.

Right next door, Shea's Lounge is a chic, narrow, New Yorkish sort of place for a leisurely glass of wine, port, or grappa; a round of appetizers; or a more substantial meal pre- or post-theater or late into the night. Some of the lavish dishes served at Chez Shea find their way onto the Shea's Lounge menu, along with a handful of more casual, ethnic-inspired offerings.

Blackberry Mousse with Lemon Madeleines

Chez Shea

While many of the other desserts in this book are decidedly "homey," this dessert from one of the Market's top restaurants is unquestionably elegant yet surprisingly easy to make. The madeleines are dense, lemony little cakes that pair nicely with the mousse or shine alone with tea or coffee.

◆ In a large, heavy saucepan, cook berries and the ½ cup sugar over medium heat 15 minutes, or until mixture is juicy, stirring occasionally. Transfer mixture to a food processor or blender and pulse until well blended. Strain through a fine-mesh sieve into a mixing bowl, pressing solids with the back of a wooden spoon to remove all seeds. Discard pulp.

1¼ pounds (about 5 cups) fresh blackberries, rinsed and patted dry, or unsweetened frozen blackberries, thawed

½ cup plus 2 tablespoons granulated sugar

2 teaspoons unflavored gelatin

2 tablespoons water

1 large egg yolk

1 cup whipping cream, chilled

◆ Meanwhile, sprinkle gelatin over the water in a small, heavy saucepan. Let gelatin stand 10 minutes, or until softened, and stir over low heat just until melted. Whisk gelatin mixture into blackberry puree. Refrigerate 45 minutes, or until cold but not set, stirring occasionally.

◆ Whisk egg yolk and the remaining 2 tablespoons sugar in a small bowl until thick and pale. Fold into berry mixture. Whip cream in large bowl until soft peaks form. Carefully fold whipped cream into berry mixture. Divide mixture among 6 balloon goblets and chill 3 hours, or until set. The mousse can be prepared 1 day ahead. Cover and refrigerate until ready to serve, then garnish with mint sprigs and serve with the Lemon Madeleines.

Serves 6

Lemon Madeleines

◆ Preheat oven to 375°F. Butter 12 madeleine molds and set aside.

◆ Beat egg yolks and granulated sugar with electric mixer 5 minutes, or until pale yellow in color and slowly dissolving ribbons form when beaters are lifted. Fold in lemon zest and lemon juice. Fold in flour.

◆ Place half of batter in a small bowl; fold in butter. Gently fold batters together. Divide batter among madeleine molds and bake 15 minutes, or until toothpick inserted in center of madeleines comes out clean.

◆ Turn madeleines onto a wire rack and cool completely. Sift confectioners' sugar over madeleines before serving. The madeleines can be prepared 6 hours ahead. Store at room temperature in an airtight container until served.

Makes 12 cookies

Mint sprigs or edible flowers, for garnish

Lemon Madeleines (recipe follows)

Lemon Madeleines

6 large egg yolks

½ cup granulated sugar

2 tablespoons grated fresh lemon zest

1 tablespoon freshly squeezed lemon juice

1 cup all-purpose flour, sifted

6 tablespoons unsalted butter, melted, lukewarm

Confectioners' sugar

Raspberries with Honey-Almond Cream

Tim's Fine Berries

This is a simple yet elegant raspberry dessert. Serve it on your finest china with silver spoons, and pretend you're at a manor house in England.

◆ Rinse berries lightly and quickly pat dry so they do not become mushy.

◆ With a rotary mixer, whip cream in a small mixing bowl until it forms a thick liquid. Add the almond extract and honey and whip until soft peaks form—do not whip until stiff.

◆ To serve, divide raspberries among dessert plates, spoon 2 or 3 dollops of whipped cream on the berries, sprinkle with almonds, and garnish with mint leaves.

Serves 4

4 cups red raspberries

2 cups whipping cream

½ teaspoon almond extract

1½ tablespoons good-grade raw honey

¼ cup toasted, slivered almonds

Fresh mint leaves, for garnish

Hazelnut Chocolate Chip Cookies

Holmquist Hazelnut Orchards

These big cookie-jar cookies, brimming with hazelnuts and chocolate, are perfect to pack in a lunchbox or to save for after-school snacks. If possible, use Holmquist roasted hazelnuts; they're lower in fat and sweeter than normal hazelnuts, don't need to be toasted and de-skinned before baking, and make a sweet, less greasy, more flavorful cookie.

◆ Preheat oven to 350°F. Spray two baking sheets with nonstick cooking spray.

◆ In a large mixing bowl, whisk eggs until frothy and light. Add sugars and vanilla and whisk until well blended and smooth. Add oil and beat until thoroughly incorporated.

◆ Sift flour with salt and baking soda into wet ingredients and mix thoroughly with a large spoon (the dough will be sticky). Fold in nuts and chocolate chips.

2 large eggs

½ cup granulated sugar

1½ cups firmly packed brown sugar

2 teaspoons pure vanilla extract

1 cup light vegetable oil, such as canola, corn, or soy

2½ cups all-purpose flour

1 teaspoon kosher salt

1 teaspoon baking soda

1 cup toasted, chopped hazelnuts (see Techniques section)

1 cup semisweet chocolate chips

- ◆ Drop by rounded tablespoons onto baking sheets, leaving about 2 inches between dough balls so cookies can spread as they cook. Bake 10 to 12 minutes, or until golden brown around edges.

- ◆ Place baking sheets on wire racks and cool 1 to 2 minutes, then, with a spatula, carefully remove cookies to wire racks to cool completely.

Makes 32 cookies

HOLMQUIST HAZELNUT ORCHARDS

Holmquist Hazelnut Orchards was founded in 1928 and is one of Washington State's largest hazelnut producers. Located just a short drive from the Dutch community of Lynden, Washington, the orchard nudges the Canadian border and has sweeping views of Mount Baker and the Canadian coastal range. It is owned by Gerald Holmquist, whose grandson is the sixth generation to live on the farm.

"Washington State grows about 3 percent of the hazelnuts in the United States, compared to Oregon's 97 percent," Gerald explains. "Hazelnuts grow on bushes that are cultivated into trees. If Mother Nature does not cooperate by blowing the nuts to the ground when they're ripe, we'll sometimes hire a helicopter to do the job. As the air currents from the blades beat the branches of the trees together, the hazelnuts fall to the ground. The grass under the trees is mowed like a golf-course putting green so that the nuts can be easily raked up, sorted, washed, dried, sized, and bagged."

The Holmquists grow the DuChilly variety, which is slimmer, more tapered, and lower in fat than the more common type of hazelnut (imagine an almond-hazelnut hybrid). Another advantage to the DuChilly is that it doesn't have the dark, sometimes bitter skin of other hazelnuts.

Holmquist hazelnuts are available in the shell, natural, dry-roasted (the top seller), or lightly salted. They also come in flavors—barbecue, ranch, Southwestern, and orange-honey. For bakers and cooks, the family's chopped and sliced hazelnuts, hazelnut oil, and hazelnut flour are useful options. But the Belgian milk chocolate—and dark chocolate—covered hazelnuts are undoubtedly the most decadent items in the Holmquists' rich product line.

You'll find a member of the Holmquist family selling hazelnuts in the North Arcade seven days a week during the summer months, and several days a week the rest of the year.

Sour Cream Cranberry Pie

Mech Apiaries

F resh cranberries come into the Market's highstalls from October through December, and this delicious pie makes a grand finale to any fall or holiday meal—a pleasant change from pumpkin and mince pies. The tartness of the cranberries makes a nice contrast to the smooth, sweet, custardy filling.

◆ Preheat oven to 425°F.

◆ With an electric mixer, beat eggs in a small mixing bowl until thick. In a large mixing bowl combine honey, sour cream, and cranberry juice. Stir eggs in carefully by hand.

◆ Mix salt and flour together with cranberries and add to egg mixture, stirring gently. Pour into pie shell and sprinkle walnuts over the top.

◆ Bake 10 minutes at 425°F, then turn oven down to 375°F and continue baking 25 minutes more or until lightly browned on top. Cool completely on a rack before slicing.

Serves 8

2 large eggs

¾ cup honey

1 cup sour cream

2 tablespoons cranberry juice

¼ teaspoon kosher salt

2 tablespoons all-purpose flour

1 cup raw cranberries

One 9-inch pie shell, unbaked

1 cup chopped walnuts

Breads

Blueberry Coffee Cake
Sourdough Fresh Herb Bread
Fresh Dill Beer Bread
Foccacia Bread with Sun-Dried Tomatoes
Honey-Orange Rye Bread
Strawberry-Nut Bread
Banana-Nut Bread/Cake
Seattle's Best Sour Cream Coffee Cake

Blueberry Coffee Cake

Canter-Berry Farms

This Sunday morning breakfast favorite tastes the "berry best" when served warm from the oven and slathered with softened sweet butter or even honey butter.

◆ Preheat oven to 400°F. Lightly grease a 9-by-9-inch baking pan or spray with nonstick cooking spray. In a small mixing bowl stir together brown sugar, the 2 tablespoons flour, and salt, and reserve.

◆ In a large mixing bowl sift together the 2 cups flour and baking powder. Whisk flour to incorporate baking powder completely. In a medium mixing bowl whisk eggs until slightly beaten. Add granulated sugar, milk, and canola oil and whisk thoroughly. Make a well in center of dry ingredients, add wet ingredients, and stir with a fork until mixed. The dough will be a bit lumpy.

◆ Turn batter into prepared pan, then press it evenly into corners. Evenly distribute blueberries over batter, keeping berries ½ inch away from the sides of the pan so berries do not burn. If using frozen berries, remove any stems and break apart any berries that stick together.

◆ Sprinkle reserved brown sugar mixture evenly over batter all the way to edges of pan. Cut butter into small pieces and dot batter with butter.

◆ Bake 30 to 40 minutes (the longer time will be necessary if using frozen berries), or until the butter and brown sugar have melted on top of the cake and appear liquidy. Do not worry; the cake will absorb the liquid as it cools. The cake is done when it turns golden around the corners, shrinks away from sides of pan, and gives off a strong, sweet blueberry aroma. Cool 10 minutes over a rack, run a knife around sides to release cake, then cut into slices and serve while still warm.

Serves 8

Cook's Hint: Clarissa Metzler Cross and Doug Cross, who own Canter-Berry Farms, suggest choosing blueberries that are

1 cup firmly packed brown sugar

2 tablespoons plus 2 cups all-purpose flour

½ teaspoon kosher salt

1 tablespoon baking powder

2 large eggs

½ cup granulated sugar

¾ cup whole milk

½ cup canola or vegetable oil

1½ cups fresh blueberries or frozen blueberries (Note: If using frozen blueberries, do not thaw before adding to the batter)

2 tablespoons unsalted butter

uniform in size, firm, and dry. The berries should be indigo blue in color with a silvery frost. Shiny berries are old. When you get your berries home, pick through them and discard any that are shriveled or moldy. Place the berries in a moistureproof container in the refrigerator, where they should stay fresh for at least one week. Do not rinse blueberries until just before you are ready to use them.

Sourdough Fresh Herb Bread

Cinnamon Works

Although it requires a little planning to prepare the sourdough starter a few days before you actually want to make this bread, it's worth it for the subtle sourdough/ cheese taste and dense texture. You can purchase sourdough starter at MarketSpice in the Pike Place Market or at some upscale grocery stores. It is important to use fresh, not dried, herbs in this recipe.

◆ Grease four 5-by-9-inch loaf pans, or 2 large baking sheets, depending on whether you want loaves or rounds of bread.

1 package sourdough starter, prepared as the package directs

2 tablespoons active dry yeast

2¼ cups warm whole milk

2 tablespoons granulated sugar

1 tablespoon unsalted butter, melted

CINNAMON WORKS

In the wee hours of the morning and throughout the day, the rich smell of cinnamon hovers over the east side of Pike Place. When the aroma is particularly strong, you can bet that another tray of mammoth cinnamon buns has just been hoisted from the ovens at Cinnamon Works.

Customers jockey for position in line and queue up two and three deep to claim their share of the booty at this natural foods bakery that uses real vanilla, maple syrup, butter, and eggs from free-running hens in its baked-on-the-premises goodies. Specialties include cinnamon rolls of all varieties (whole-wheat is the best-selling favorite), whole-wheat scones, and *fragassa*, an Italian vegetable-cheese bread. Desserts include oat bars made with seasonal fresh fruit, pumpkin cookies, and pecan bars. Vegan cookies and muffins are wildly popular, as is the "secret-formula" granola. Quick breads, such as carrot, zucchini, and banana, are available seasonally.

◆ In a large mixing bowl, whisk together 2½ cups of prepared sourdough starter, yeast, milk, and sugar and let stand 2 minutes, or until bubbly. Add butter and stir until mixed thoroughly. Add flour and salt and blend until a soft, smooth dough forms.

◆ Add arugula, basil, garlic, and cheese to dough and mix until well incorporated. Turn out dough onto a well-floured board and knead 5 minutes, or until smooth and satiny, adding additional flour if breadboard or your hands become sticky.

◆ Place dough in a lightly greased mixing bowl, turning it over once to grease surface. Cover with a dish towel and allow to rise in a warm place 1 to 1½ hours, or until doubled in size. Punch down dough, cut into fourths, and allow to rest 10 minutes. Shape loaves to fit in loaf pans, or form loaves into rounds and place on greased baking sheets. Cover and allow loaves to rise ½ to 1 hour, or until doubled in size. After 15 to 20 minutes, preheat oven to 350°F.

◆ Brush loaves with egg wash (the beaten egg). Place loaves in oven and bake 30 to 40 minutes, or until loaves turn golden on top and bread pulls away from sides of loaf pan. To test for doneness, tap loaf; if it sounds hollow, it's done. Remove loaves from loaf pans or baking sheets and place on a wire rack to cool. Slice and serve.

Makes 4 loaves or rounds

Cook's Hint: Sourdough starter can be tricky to make. For best results, use a glass bowl to mix, and use a wooden or plastic spoon to stir it. Cover the glass bowl *loosely* with plastic wrap. (Do not use a snug-fitting lid, or the sourdough could die due to lack of oxygen.) Place the sourdough starter in a warm, dark, draft-free area for about 2 days. When the sourdough is ready it will be thick, wispy, and cream-colored. Put it to rest in the refrigerator, loosely covered, but return it to room temperature when ready to use. After you've used the amount you need, replenish the starter by adding ¾ cup flour, ¾ cup water, and 1 teaspoon granulated sugar or honey, and return it to a warm, dark, draft-free space for 24 hours. If you don't use the starter within 10 days, add another 1 teaspoon granulated sugar or honey, and repeat every 10 days unless replenished.

6 cups unbleached white flour, plus extra for the breadboard

2 teaspoons kosher salt

2 tablespoons chopped arugula

2 tablespoons chopped fresh basil

3 cloves garlic, minced

1 cup grated Parmesan cheese

1 large egg, beaten

Fresh Dill Beer Bread

Chef Nancie Brecher, who trained at the Culinary Institute of America in Hyde Park, New York, and La Varenne in Burgundy, France, has taught thousands of Seattleites to cook over the past dozen years at Cook's World,* her cooking school and kitchenware shop in the University District. She presents everything from basic and intermediate courses to one-night classes focusing on divergent ethnic styles such as regional French, Vietnamese, Spanish, and Japanese. In her Fresh Herbs class, Nancie shows students how to build layers of flavor with herbs rather than salt and fat, and she suggests keeping at least three fresh herbs in the refrigerator at all times. "Easy access to fresh herbs makes them available to experiment with in your home cooking," she reasons. During class she demonstrated this easy-to-make dill bread, a crowd-pleaser I have made at home many times since, using fresh dill purchased from Market farmers.

1 large egg

2 teaspoons kosher salt

3 cups unbleached all-purpose flour

1 tablespoon plus 1 teaspoon baking powder

3 tablespoons firmly packed light brown sugar

3 tablespoons minced fresh dill

½ teaspoon baking soda

1 can or bottle (12 ounce) inexpensive beer (such as Miller High Life or Coors), room temperature

◆ Position oven rack in lower third of oven, then preheat oven to 350°F. Generously grease an 4-by-8-inch loaf pan.

◆ To make egg wash, pulse egg and ½ teaspoon of the kosher salt in a food processor. Remove from processor and reserve. Do not clean work bowl.

◆ Add flour, baking powder, brown sugar, dill, baking soda, and the remaining 1½ teaspoons kosher salt to work bowl and pulse 2 seconds. Add half the beer and blend using 4 on/off turns. Add remaining beer and mix using 8 to 10 on/off turns, or just until the batter is blended, scraping down sides of work bowl as needed. The dough will be sticky, but do not overmix or the bread will be tough.

◆ Transfer dough to reserved pan, press into the corners with a spatula, and brush the top lightly with egg wash. Bake 35 to 45 minutes, or until loaf turns golden brown and a toothpick inserted into the middle comes out with only a few crumbs. Cool bread on a wire rack for 10 minutes, then turn it out of pan. For easier cutting, allow to cool completely and use a serrated knife.

Serves 8

*Outside of the Market Historic District.

Foccacia Bread with Sun-Dried Tomatoes

Sur La Table

Foccacia, a large, flat Italian bread sprinkled before baking with olive oil, salt, and herbs, has become a favorite of many artisan bread bakers throughout the country. This easy-to-prepare version for home cooks features sun-dried tomatoes, but you can personalize it even further with the addition of fresh or dried herbs, garlic, or onions. I used chopped fresh Walla Walla onions and dried oregano.

◆ Preheat oven to 450°F. Lightly grease an 11-by-17-inch baking sheet with a rim (often referred to as a jelly-roll pan) or spray with nonstick cooking spray, and set aside.

◆ Place flour, salt, yeast, the 2 tablespoons olive oil, and sun-dried tomatoes in a large mixing bowl and stir well with a large spoon. Add 1¾ cups hot water and stir until dough forms a ball. If dough seems too dry, add a bit more hot water.

◆ Flour breadboard and turn out dough onto board. Knead until smooth, adding the minimum amount of flour to keep dough from sticking to your hands and board. The dough will be soft, almost the consistency of biscuit dough.

◆ Place dough in a lightly greased bowl, turning it over once to grease surface. Cover with a clean towel and let dough rise in a warm place for at least 30 minutes, or until doubled in size.

◆ Punch down dough and knead a couple of times, then press it into prepared baking sheet until it is ¼ to ½ inch thick. Cover dough with a clean kitchen towel, and let rest in a warm place about 20 minutes, or until it rises slightly. Drizzle with olive oil and sprinkle the top of the dough with herbs, garlic, and/or onions. Finish by sprinkling with pepper to taste.

◆ Bake 12 to 15 minutes, or until lightly browned and puffy. Serve while still warm, cut into slabs, with additional olive oil or softened butter, if desired.

Makes 16 to 20 slices

4 cups all-purpose flour, plus extra for the breadboard

2 teaspoons kosher salt

2 packages quick-rise yeast

2 tablespoons olive oil, plus extra for drizzling

¼ cup oil-packed sun-dried tomatoes, chopped

1¾ to 2¼ cups hot water

Fresh or dried herbs of your choice (such as oregano, rosemary, thyme, chives, parsley, or basil) and/or garlic, onions, sautéed onions, or a mixture of several (optional)

Freshly ground black pepper

Unsalted butter, softened (optional)

Cook's Hint: To make a warm place for dough to rise, fill a large baking pan with hot water and put it on the lowest rack in an unheated oven. Place the covered bread in a mixing bowl on an oven rack above the water, and close the oven door.

MECH APIARIES

Doris and Don Mech have been busy as bees since 1973, when they left their careers as a teacher and an electrical engineer, respectively, to begin Mech Apiaries, their honey farm in Maple Valley. Doris, a helpful, patient woman with wire-rim glasses, brings all the products of the beehive to the North Arcade every Saturday throughout the year.

Her stall is a visual knockout, with hand-carved beeswax sculptures of teddy bears, Christmas trees, and bees in flight. Jars of honey in shades from gold to brown march across her table and you'll also find bee pollen, honey taffy, and Doris's cookbook, *Joy with Honey*.

"Our honey is raw—pure and old-fashioned. As a result of simple straining and careful processing it comes to you with the original vitamins, minerals, enzymes, and pollen intact," Doris explains. "Many people don't realize that everything in the hive is useful, from bee pollen to the sweet honeycomb to the wax."

Like other types of farming, bee farming runs seasonally and depends heavily on the presence or absence of rain. In May, the bees gather nectar from the flowers of broadleaf maple trees in Maple Valley to produce a robust-tasting honey. In June, the Mechs truck the beehives to Harstene Island, where the bees gather nectar from wild huckleberry bushes to produce a light amber honey in the middle range of flavor intensity. July sees the Mechs trucking the beehives back to the lowlands of the Green River Valley, where the bees feast on wild blackberries, which yield a light, delicate, slightly fruity honey.

Snowberry bushes blossom in August, when the Mechs move some of their bees over the Cascade Mountains to the farmland near Cle Elum and Ellensburg. Snowberry honey is mild, with a slight tang. Fireweed honey, a very mild and pale honey, is also produced in August, when the Mechs take their bees to the Cascades near the foothills of Mount Rainier. Here black bears sometimes fight the Mechs for the rich honey.

In late summer, Doris and Don move the bees to the Kittitas Valley, where they feast on strawberry clover and produce a mild, delicate honey with the same flavor as strawberry clover flowers. "Since we have to move the hives at night in search of the finest nectars, during harvest season my husband and I are a lot like the worker bees—we never sleep!" Doris says.

Honey-Orange Rye Bread

Mech Apiaries

Baking bread is so soothing and therapeutic—every time I make it I wonder why I don't do it more often. And this dense, solid bread has a wonderful orange taste and a slight crunch from the rye grain. It's particularly suitable for peanut-butter-and-jelly sandwiches, especially if you spread them with orange marmalade!

- ◆ Grease four 4½-by-8½-inch loaf pans.

- ◆ Soften yeast in the ½ cup warm water. In a large mixing bowl, mix together honey, molasses, salt, and oil. Stir in the 3 cups hot water, then stir in rye flour and beat well. Add softened yeast and orange zest and mix well. Stir in enough of the unbleached white flour to make a soft dough. Cover with a kitchen towel and allow to rest 10 minutes.

- ◆ Turn out dough onto a well-floured breadboard and knead for 10 minutes, adding additional unbleached white flour if breadboard or your hands get sticky. Place dough in a lightly greased mixing bowl, turning it over once to grease surface. Cover and allow to rise in a warm place about 1½ hours, or until doubled in size, then punch down.

- ◆ Turn dough out onto a lightly floured board, divide it into four equal portions, and shape each portion into a smooth ball. Cover and allow to rest 10 minutes, then shape into four loaves and place in loaf pans. Cover and return to a warm place to rise about 1 hour, or until doubled in size.

- ◆ Preheat oven to 375°F. Bake 30 minutes, or until golden brown and hollow sounding when tapped, then cool on wire racks.

Makes 4 loaves

Cook's Hint: For a softer-crusted bread, brush with soft margarine or butter before baking. Home-baked bread will slice well while still warm if you use an electric carving knife or a very sharp bread knife.

---

2 packages active dry yeast

½ cup warm water

½ cup honey

½ cup molasses

2 tablespoons kosher salt

½ cup vegetable oil

3 cups hot water

3 cups rye flour

¼ cup grated orange zest

8 to 9 cups unbleached white flour, plus extra for the breadboard

Strawberry-Nut Bread

Biringer Farm Country Store

This quick bread, redolent of cinnamon and packed with nuts, is great to make around the Thanksgiving and Christmas holidays instead of banana-nut bread, and a good way to use up the extra strawberries you froze during the summer.

◆ Preheat oven to 350°F. Lightly grease two 5-by-9-inch loaf pans or spray with nonstick cooking spray.

◆ In a large mixing bowl, sift together flour, baking soda, salt, cinnamon, and sugar, then whisk until cinnamon is dispersed throughout flour. In a separate large bowl, whisk eggs, then mix in the oil, strawberries, and pecans with a fork.

◆ Make a well in the center of the dry ingredients and add wet ingredients, stirring just enough to moisten dry ingredients. Divide batter between prepared loaf pans and bake 1 hour, or until a toothpick inserted in the center comes out clean.

◆ Cool 10 minutes on a wire rack. Turn out loaves, slice into 8 slices per loaf, and serve as desired (see Cook's Hint below).

Makes 2 loaves

Cook's Hint: In the spring or summer, I prefer to make this recipe with fresh berries and toasted hazelnuts in place of the pecans. If you use fresh berries, make sure they are very ripe and juicy. Halve or quarter the berries, then gently mash them with a fork to start the juices flowing. Let the berries sit at room temperature for 1 hour before adding to the wet ingredients. You can also substitute frozen, sweetened berries, but reduce the 2 cups sugar to 1½ cups. Once baked, slices of Strawberry-Nut Bread make a scandalously rich base for strawberry shortcake or strawberry sundaes. To serve, just put a slice in the bottom of a deep dish and add a scoop of strawberry ice cream or frozen yogurt, additional sliced strawberries or strawberry syrup, whipped cream or whipped topping, and top with a whole strawberry.

3 cups sifted all-purpose flour

1 teaspoon baking soda

1 teaspoon kosher salt

1 tablespoon ground cinnamon

2 cups granulated sugar

4 large eggs

1¼ cups light vegetable oil, such as canola, corn, or soy

2 cups frozen, unsweetened, sliced strawberries, thawed

1¼ cups chopped pecans

In a prime location fronting Pike Place, the Biringer Farm Country Store offers a little taste of the country in the midst of the big city. Owned and operated by Melody Biringer, a third-generation berry farmer affectionately known as "the farmer's daughter," the store is an offshoot of the Biringer Farm U-Pick in Marysville, Washington, which is run by Melody's parents, Dianna (a.k.a. "The Strawberry Lady") and Mike Biringer.

The Pike Place store carries the complete line of Biringer Farm products, including prizewinning berry jams, farmhouse cookies in alluring flavors (hazelnut, orange-vanilla, pumpkin pecan, and raspberry), scone and muffin mixes, and flavored teas. The raspberry and strawberry cocoa mixes, tea cookies, and raspberry brownie mix make especially welcome gifts, and you're invited to sample the products before you buy.

Banana-Nut Bread/Cake

Sur La Table

This recipe is unlike any banana-nut bread I've ever tried. It can't seem to make up its mind—is it a cake masquerading as a bread, or a bread disguised as a cake? You decide, based on the type of pan you choose to bake it in.

◆ Preheat oven to 350°F. Lightly butter two 5-by-9-inch loaf pans (for banana-nut bread) or one 9-by-13-inch baking pan (for banana-nut cake), or spray with nonstick cooking spray.

◆ In a large mixing bowl, mix sugars, flour, and baking powder until well blended and set aside. Mix eggs, baking soda dissolved in buttermilk, and vanilla in a medium mixing bowl and blend thoroughly. Add bananas and nuts to wet ingredients and stir.

◆ Make a well in center of dry ingredients and add wet ingredients, stirring just enough to moisten dry ingredients. Spoon batter into pan(s) of your choice.

◆ Bake 25 to 35 minutes, depending on baking pans used. The bread/cake is done when it pulls away from the sides of the pan and turns golden brown on top, and when a toothpick inserted in the middle comes out almost clean (a few crumbs

½ cup firmly packed brown sugar

1 cup granulated sugar

2 cups all-purpose flour

1 teaspoon baking powder

2 large eggs, beaten

1 teaspoon baking soda, dissolved in ½ cup buttermilk

1 teaspoon pure vanilla extract

3 or 4 ripe bananas, mashed

1 cup walnuts, chopped

should remain). Cool bread/cake on a wire rack about 10 minutes, then turn out of the pan to finish cooling. If desired, frost with Cream Cheese Icing (page 148).

Makes 2 loaves or 1 cake

Seattle's Best Sour Cream Coffee Cake

Seattle's Best Coffee

Y ou won't be able to resist this rich, eggy coffee cake, and not just for breakfast. The hazelnuts throughout the batter, the coffee glaze, and the finely ground coffee on top are unusual touches that make this a recipe to treasure.

◆ Preheat oven to 350°F. Lightly grease a 12-cup Bundt pan or spray with nonstick cooking spray.

◆ In a large mixing bowl, whisk together butter and sugar. Beat in eggs one at a time until well blended. Stir in brewed coffee and vanilla.

◆ Mix together flour, baking powder, baking soda, and salt and add dry ingredients to wet ingredients, alternating with sour cream, until well blended. Combine brown sugar, hazelnuts, and nutmeg in a small bowl.

◆ Spread one-half of the batter into bottom of prepared Bundt pan. Sprinkle one-half of hazelnut mixture over batter. Pour remaining batter over the top, then finish with remaining hazelnut mixture.

◆ Bake 35 to 45 minutes, or until a toothpick inserted in the middle comes out clean. Cool coffee cake on a wire rack for 15 minutes before removing from pan.

◆ Drizzle Coffee Glaze over cake while it is still warm, then let cake rest 15 minutes to absorb glaze. Just before cutting and serving, dust cake with confectioners' sugar and ground coffee.

Serves 8 to 10

½ cup unsalted butter, softened

1 cup granulated sugar

2 large eggs

1 tablespoon freshly brewed double-strength Seattle's Best Blend coffee or espresso

1 teaspoon pure vanilla extract

1¾ cups all-purpose flour, sifted

2 teaspoons baking powder

1 teaspoon baking soda

½ teaspoon kosher salt

1 cup sour cream

⅓ cup firmly packed light brown sugar

⅓ cup chopped hazelnuts, toasted (see Techniques section)

½ teaspoon ground nutmeg

Coffee Glaze (recipe follows)

Confectioners' sugar, sifted

Coffee Glaze

◆ In a small bowl, whisk confectioners' sugar, coffee, half-and-half, and vanilla extract until smooth.

Pinch of finely ground coffee (Turkish grind) (Note: You can use any variety of coffee you wish in this recipe, so long as it is ground Turkish-style)

Coffee Glaze

1 cup confectioners' sugar

3 tablespoons freshly brewed double-strength Seattle's Best Blend coffee or espresso

½ teaspoon half-and-half

¼ teaspoon pure vanilla extract

Sauces, Relishes & Dips

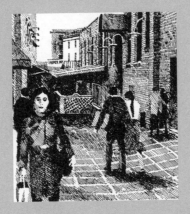

Honey-Berry Vinaigrette
Salmon Spread
Spicy Cherry Catsup
Arugula Pesto
Triple Hot Seafood Glaze
Cranberry-Apple Sauce
Poppy Seed Dressing with Honey
Marinara Vegetable Sauce
Indo-Afro-Tex-Mex Culture-Shock Dip
Red Raspberry Chutney

Honey-Berry Vinaigrette

DISH D' LISH

Chef Kathy Casey suggests tossing this luscious, jewel-colored vinaigrette with mixed baby greens or baby spinach leaves, then sprinkling with toasted hazelnuts, additional fresh berries, and fresh, chèvre-style goat cheese.

◆ Combine all the ingredients in a blender or food processor and pulse until smooth. Serve immediately, or cover and refrigerate up to 3 days.

Makes ½ cup vinaigrette

¼ cup fresh berries, such as strawberries, raspberries, blackberries, marionberries, or a mixture

2 tablespoons red wine vinegar

1 tablespoon honey

1 teaspoon Dijon mustard

3 tablespoons canola oil or light olive oil

Pinch of cayenne pepper

¼ teaspoon kosher salt

◆

Salmon Spread

The Crumpet Shop

This recipe epitomizes real Northwest comfort food. It's a wonderful light lunch or late-afternoon treat on a cold, cloudy day, and it also makes elegant appetizers.

◆ Blend lox in a food processor until creamy. Add cream cheese, a few cubes at a time, until it is all processed and the mixture is pale pink and smooth.

◆ Spread on warm, buttered crumpets (as they do at The Crumpet Shop) and garnish with cucumber, tomato, and/or onion slices. For appetizers, serve on crackers of your choice with cucumber, tomato, and/or onion slices, a few capers, and a sprig of dill.

Makes about 1½ cups; 8 servings as a light lunch, or 24 appetizers

6 ounces Nova lox, coarsely chopped

8 ounces cream cheese, cut into ½-inch cubes

Crumpets or crackers of your choice

Cucumber, tomato, and/or onion slices, capers, and sprigs of dill, for garnish

THE CRUMPET SHOP

Crumpets hail from the British Isles, and The Crumpet Shop opened in 1976 when owners Nancy McFaul and Gary Lassater, a husband-and-wife team, acquired a crumpet recipe from the owner of a bakery in Victoria, BC, who had brought the recipe from England. They opened for business in the Market for a mere $12,000. Since then, the little shop has gained fame throughout the United States (including a mention in *Saveur* magazine) and across the world for its crumpets and scones.

Every morning through the big plate-glass windows along First Avenue you can watch Gary (the baker) make "unsweetened, yeast-raised English griddle cakes," a.k.a. crumpets. During the daily ritual, the baker pours crumpet batter into stainless-steel crumpet rings that have been arranged on a hot griddle. The crumpets are "baked" on the stovetop until the bottoms are smooth and brown and the tops are pitted with tiny holes, much like English muffins. Once cool enough to handle, they're popped from their rings, the edges snipped by hand, and they're ready to go.

Although traditionally served with butter and jam, crumpets at The Crumpet Shop can be ordered with all sorts of savory and sweet toppings, including scrambled eggs and ham, fruity preserves, nut butters, and pesto. Everything is baked in-house, and in addition to crumpets the shop serves scones, soups, sandwiches on Scottish groat bread, and a perfect espresso or "cuppa" freshly brewed premium tea or chai.

Spicy Cherry Catsup

Chukar Cherry Company

That all-American favorite, catsup, rises to new heights when infused with dried cherries and jalapeño peppers. Serve the catsup the conventional way (over hot dogs or hamburgers) or as suggested in *The Chukar Cherry Recipe Collection*, with grilled chicken skewers threaded with kumquats and additional dried cherries.

◆ Soak cherries in enough apple juice to cover for 10 to 20 minutes, then drain well and discard juice.

◆ Place cherries, tomato paste, vinegar, peppers, sugar, salt, and pepper in a blender or food processor and pulse until fairly smooth, scraping down the sides of the work bowl as needed.

◆ In a small saucepan, bring cherry mixture to a boil, cover, and simmer 5 to 10 minutes, or until catsup thickens and darkens slightly, stirring frequently. Transfer catsup to a nonreactive bowl or jar with a lid and allow to cool. Cover and refrigerate up to 1 week.

Makes about ⅔ cup

½ cup Chukar dried sweet or tart cherries

4 to 6 tablespoons apple juice or water

¼ cup tomato paste

¼ cup red wine vinegar

2 jalapeño peppers, seeds and membranes removed, chopped

1 tablespoon granulated sugar

Pinch of kosher salt

Pinch of freshly ground black pepper

CHUKAR CHERRY COMPANY

The Chukar Cherry Company came into existence when Pam and Guy Auld, successful real estate and management professionals in Seattle, underwent "a classic case of urban flight" in 1985. In search of a better life for themselves and their three young daughters, the Aulds moved east of the mountains to small-town Prosser, Washington. They purchased a 350-acre farm with a large cherry orchard in the bountiful Yakima Valley.

At first the Aulds sold on the farmers' tables at Pike Place, but they soon realized that fresh cherries have a short season and shelf life, so they searched for a way to market their crop throughout the year. The result was "the year 'round cherry and berry company," which they started in 1988. Cherries are a difficult and demanding crop to grow, so the Aulds named their company after the beguiling and swift-flying Chukar bird. Its image reflects characteristics similar to Northwest cherries—tempting and sweet, fleeting in season, and challenging to capture.

However brief cherry season may be, Chukar Cherries has created an extensive and ever-growing product line that includes dried and pitted sweet Bing, honey-golden Rainier, and Columbia River tart cherries; dried cranberries, strawberries, and blueberries; trail mixes; chocolate-coated cherries, berries, and nuts; cherry jam and peach preserves; dessert toppings and pie fillings; cherry sauces, glazes, and salsa; cherry herb tea; and cream scone mix. The Cabernet Chocolate Cherries (dried tart cherries coated in pure dark chocolate) are outstanding, and make a decadent dessert when paired with a bottle of Washington state Cabernet Sauvignon.

At Chukar's permanent space in the Main Arcade, you'll find fresh cherries for sale during the season, along with free samples of their dried products every day of the week. There's even a self-published cookbook, *The Chukar Cherry Recipe Collection*, which contains recipes using both fresh and dried cherries. Quite impressive for small family farmers whose successful business began because they had too many fresh cherries on hand.

Arugula Pesto

Pike Place Market Basket CSA

The nutty, spicy flavor of fresh arugula inspired this pesto recipe from Rena Langille, who spent a summer working for the Market Basket CSA. Rena likes adding the pesto to rice and pasta dishes, or using it as a spread for toast, crostini, or crackers. If you use the pesto in a pasta dish that already contains a lot of cheese, Rena suggests omitting the Parmesan from the recipe.

◆ Place arugula leaves, garlic, and nuts in a food processor and pulse eight or 10 times, or until the ingredients are coarsely chopped. With the motor running, add olive oil in a thin, slow stream until a thick paste forms.

◆ Transfer arugula mixture to a small bowl, stir well, and add salt, pepper, and cheese. Taste and adjust seasonings as needed. Use immediately, cover and refrigerate and use within one to two days, or freeze for later use (see Cook's Hint below).

Makes about 1½ cups

Cook's Hint: Pesto is incredibly versatile. Serve it over steamed new potatoes, broiled fish, or grilled chicken. Add butter or cream cheese to make a bread spread or chip/vegetable dip. A couple of tablespoons in your favorite minestrone soup recipe add an extra-special flavor. To freeze the pesto, spoon it into an ice cube tray, freeze the cubes, then pop them out and store them in a heavy-duty freezer-safe bag. Use the frozen cubes to make a quick sandwich filling or cocktail spread by mixing one thawed pesto cube with a three-ounce package of softened cream cheese.

½ *pound arugula leaves, rinsed, drained, spun dry, and coarsely torn if large*

2 to 3 cloves garlic, coarsely chopped

¼ *cup pine nuts, hazelnuts, or walnuts, coarsely chopped*

¼ *cup extra virgin olive oil*

Pinch of kosher salt

Pinch of freshly ground black pepper

¼ *cup grated Parmesan cheese (optional)*

PIKE PLACE MARKET BASKET CSA

(COMMUNITY SUPPORTED AGRICULTURE)

One of the most innovative, life-sustaining programs the Market has introduced in recent years is known as the Pike Place Market Basket CSA. A grassroots food delivery system that started in Japan and Europe in the 1960s, Community Supported Agriculture (CSA) operates on a simple premise. Consumers, often called shareholders, sharers, or subscribers, buy a "share" from a local farm, which entitles them to weekly deliveries of fresh produce throughout a designated season. Sharers pick up their produce at the farm or a convenient drop site.

It's a win-win situation for everyone: Farmers are assured a reliable market and a direct relationship with their customers; sharers gain access to the freshest produce available at reasonable prices; and many subscribers develop a connection with "their" farm through attending potluck dinners, work parties, and harvest festivals.

The Pike Place Market Basket, which started in 1997, is a variation on the basic CSA model called a "cooperative" CSA, in which several farms join together to pool their produce. Rena Langille, a longtime Market shopper, worked at the Market Basket one summer and shared her indelible memories. "It felt good to get up early in the morning and pedal downtown to the big, shiny coolers along Western Avenue. Soon the staff and volunteers would be lined up filling the baskets, and the alluring aromas of fresh greens, berries, tomatoes, melons, squashes, and summer dust would fill the air.

"We got to know the farmers too. It put real faces on the products we were working with, the products we went home with at night. Everyone had a good feeling about being together doing something productive, something that made sense. And the people who came to get their baskets were so happy to get all the nice produce."

Paul Dunn, a longtime Market resident, president of Friends of the Market, and Market Basket volunteer, adds another perspective. He says, "This program is a small link between the farmers, who get a weekly check, and the Market Basket subscribers, who make the Market relevant and enduring as it moves into the 21st century. Volunteering reassures me there will be farms in our future and a dependable generation of farmers and consumers in closer commerce than ever before. The CSA concept is growing in all regions of the country and may be leading to a different form of 'family farm' in America."

Triple Hot Seafood Glaze

Four Seasons Olympic Hotel

The Market is a special place for Gavin Stephenson, executive chef of the historic Four Seasons Olympic Hotel* in downtown Seattle, where he oversees The Georgian Room, Shuckers, and The Garden. A native of Britain and a 20-year veteran of the culinary industry, Gavin says, "I visit the Market at least three times a week. Going there and talking with the vendors helps to refuel my culinary engine. Every time I go I discover something new, and inevitably come away with fresh ideas. This region offers a remarkable abundance of fresh produce throughout the year. Every season in the Market is a sensory experience." One of Gavin's discoveries was the wide array of hot pepper jellies available at Micks Peppouri (page 13). The jellies tenderize, season, and glaze in one easy step, and are a boon to the home cook as well as the professional chef.

◆ Place the wine, lime juice, and habanero, jalapeño, and chipotle peppers in a small, nonreactive saucepan and bring to a boil. Cook 15 to 20 minutes, or until pan is almost dry, stirring occasionally. Remove pan from heat and stir in pepper jelly and gingerroot until jelly is melted. Allow glaze to cool, then transfer glaze to a small mixing bowl or jar with a tight-fitting lid.

◆ To use glaze, preheat the grill or broiler. Pour a few tablespoons of glaze into a small bowl, and with a clean pastry brush, brush the tops of fish steaks or the flesh side of fish fillets or a whole side of salmon with the glaze. Transfer the fish to a broiling pan or baking sheet and cook until desired doneness is reached. Sprinkle with cilantro just before serving, if desired. Cover and refrigerate any leftover glaze for up to 2 weeks.

Makes about 1 cup glaze

Cook's Hint: Habanero peppers are extremely hot, so wear thin, disposable rubber gloves and do not touch your eyes or nose when working with them.

*Outside of the Market Historic District.

1 cup dry white wine

½ cup freshly squeezed lime juice

1 tablespoon minced fresh habanero peppers, seeds and membranes removed

1 teaspoon minced fresh jalapeño peppers, seeds and membranes removed

1 teaspoon ground chipotle pepper

1 cup Micks Mild Red Pepper Jelly or sweet pepper chutney

2 tablespoons minced gingerroot

Minced cilantro (optional)

Cranberry-Apple Sauce

Catering by Phyllis

As the owner of Catering by Phyllis and a volunteer member of the Pike Place Market Preservation and Development Authority (PDA) Council, Phyllis Rosen knows a thing or two about food and using the Market's culinary resources, especially the wide variety of produce from the organic farmers. Phyllis suggests using this savory-sweet sauce with its brilliant pink color as a condiment with poultry, especially locally raised duck or turkey, or spicy chicken sausage, which is available at Uli's Famous Sausage (page 57).

◆ In a large, heavy-bottomed, nonreactive saucepan, bring the cranberries, apple, sugar, and wine to a boil over medium-high heat. Stir well, lower heat, and simmer 10 to 15 minutes, or until the berries begin to pop and the apple is very tender, stirring occasionally.

◆ Remove the pan from the heat; then, using an immersion blender, a stand-up blender, or a food processor, purée the sauce. If using a blender or food processor, cover the top with a kitchen towel and process using short pulses at first so that the hot sauce doesn't overflow when the machine is turned on. Strain through a fine-mesh sieve placed over a large bowl, pressing out the solids with the back of a large spoon.

◆ Add the salt, pepper, orange zest, and 1½ teaspoons of the mustard, and stir well. Taste and add the additional 1½ teaspoons of mustard, plus more salt and pepper, if desired. Use the sauce immediately, or allow to cool, cover, and refrigerate, or freeze for later use.

Makes about 1½ cups

Cook's Hint: If you prefer a more rustic, less elegant sauce, simply omit the puréeing and sieving step. Also, Phyllis suggests that to make a quick version of the sauce (or when cranberries are out of season), you can use 2 cups of canned cranberry sauce in place of the fresh cranberries and omit the sugar.

2 cups (about ½ pound) fresh cranberries, rinsed and picked over for bruised berries

1 large tart apple, such as Gravenstein or Granny Smith (about ½ pound), peeled, cored, and coarsely chopped

¾ cup granulated sugar

½ cup dry red wine or freshly squeezed orange juice

¼ teaspoon kosher salt, or to taste

½ teaspoon freshly cracked black pepper, or to taste

½ teaspoon minced fresh orange zest

1½ to 3 teaspoons Dijon mustard

Poppy Seed Dressing with Honey

Mech Apiaries

Try this dressing as a delicious accompaniment to any tossed green salad or fruit salad. It also pairs well with a composed salad of sliced avocados, grapefruit, and apples on a bed of crisp romaine.

◆ Place honey, dry mustard, salt, vinegar, and grated onion in a blender or mixing bowl and process or whisk by hand until smooth.

◆ Start blender, gradually add oil in a slow stream, and process until thoroughly blended. Stop blender and sprinkle poppy seeds on top, then flip blender on and off three or four times until seeds are mixed in. Alternatively, whisk in oil by hand, then whisk in seeds.

◆ Place dressing in a serving bowl or pitcher and let your family and guests serve themselves.

Makes just under 2 cups

½ cup mild honey

1 teaspoon dry mustard

1 teaspoon kosher salt

⅓ cup apple cider vinegar

1 tablespoon finely grated Walla Walla onion or other sweet onion, such as Vidalia or Maui

1 cup light vegetable oil (soy oil recommended)

1½ tablespoons poppy seeds

LOPRIORE BROTHERS PASTA BAR

There's both a casual atmosphere and a sense of immediacy at LoPriore Brothers Pasta Bar, where customers sit at the counter and watch as their selections are cooked right before their eyes. Fettuccine Alfredo, sausage sandwiches, Italian subs, soups, and salads are specialties here, as is the first and only 28-ounce bowl of pasta in the Market. It's served with bread and a choice of sauce—meat, marinara, Alfredo, pesto, or olive-oil-and-garlic. The LoPriore brothers (Dave, Brian, and Paul) have a robust Italian background and use recipes passed down through their family in both their catering and on-site businesses.

Marinara Vegetable Sauce

LoPriore Brothers Pasta Bar

You'll enjoy this rich, garlic-filled sauce over fresh pasta cooked al dente. Add cooked shrimp, scallops, crab, and shellfish for a lusty version of seafood pasta. The recipe makes a lot of sauce, but leftovers can be easily frozen for later use.

◆ Place a large saucepan or stockpot over medium heat and add olive oil. When oil is hot, add onions, garlic, and shallot and cook 1 to 2 minutes. Add mushrooms and cook 1 to 2 minutes more. Add wine, Worcestershire sauce, tomatoes and their juice, and tomato paste and stir well.

◆ Add basil, cilantro, granulated garlic, pepper, and oregano and stir well. Add 2 cups of the water, stir well, cover, and simmer about 1 hour. If the sauce gets too thick, add the remaining 1 cup water during the last 20 minutes of cooking time.

Makes 8 cups

2 tablespoons olive oil

2 white or yellow onions, chopped

1 bulb garlic, cloves separated and minced

1 shallot, chopped

1 pound button or cremini mushrooms, chopped

1 cup good-quality red table wine, such as Burgundy

¼ cup Worcestershire sauce

1 can (14½ ounce) whole tomatoes, diced, plus their juice

1 can (12 ounce) tomato paste

½ cup chopped fresh basil

1 cup chopped cilantro

3 tablespoons granulated garlic

1 tablespoon freshly ground black pepper

2 tablespoons dried oregano, crumbled

2 to 3 cups water

Indo-Afro-Tex-Mex Culture-Shock Dip

World Class Chili

Joe started cooking at the age of 14, when he was tending cattle and preparing his own meals. He devised this unusual yet delicious dip from recipes he learned in Cameroon, West Africa, while visiting his niece in the Peace Corps. West Africa is a region where Indonesian and Arabian cuisines mix, and Joe merged these diverse cuisines with his own specialty: Tex-Mex. As you might expect of this pepper aficionado, while in Cameroon, he organized a chili cook-off!

◆ Combine all the ingredients in a food processor and pulse until smooth. Chill overnight, then serve at room temperature as desired (see Cook's Hint below).

Cook's Hint: You can use this dip in many ways. Serve it with tortilla chips, spread it on squares of nine-grain bread for a quick lunch, or serve it on crackers or crusty bread slices for easy-to-prepare appetizers. Add another chopped chipotle pepper to a few tablespoons of the dip, carefully pull up the skin of a roasting chicken, and rub the dip over the flesh before placing in a hot oven (450°F) for a quick and delicious dinner. The dip is also good on grilled hamburgers spread with hot mustard.

Makes 2 cups

1 cup plain yogurt

1 cup smooth peanut butter (Jif brand recommended)

8 mild green chile peppers, such as New Mexico or Anaheim, roasted, peeled, and chopped (Note: You can substitute canned peppers, but the flavor won't be the same; see Techniques section for roasting instructions)

4 hot green chile peppers, such as jalapeños or serranos, roasted, peeled, and chopped (see Techniques section)

1 chipotle pepper in adobo sauce, chopped (Note: Chipotle peppers in adobo sauce are available at Mexican specialty markets, such as El Mercado Latino in the Pike Place Market)

Pinch of kosher salt, or to taste

Pinch of granulated sugar

Joe Canavan, "The Chili Man," has been whipping up four kinds of chili every day of the week except Sunday since 1986. Joe jokingly claims that chili was invented by his Uncle Bill one Saturday afternoon in March, 1863, near Butte, Montana.

Regardless of who invented chili, Joe is reinventing it with his bubbling cauldrons of Texas chili (made with beef); California-style chili (chicken); Cincinnati-style chili (pork and beef); and vegetarian chili. The chili is served in varying degrees of heat, with macho being the hottest. As Joe says, "It ain't the kind your mother used to make."

No matter your preference, each variety is served straight up or over your choice of rice, pinto or black beans, shell pasta, or any mixture of the four. Sides include oyster crackers, tortilla chips, or sweet, cakelike corn bread. Daily specials round out the menu, and it's all served up in the Economy Market Atrium under the watchful eye of a life-sized statue of Big Foot, while a life-sized copper squid flies overhead.

More humor from Joe when he recounts the time Al McGuire, a famous basketball coach, shared the following advice: "You understand life when you know why there's a hooker on the corner, a wino in the hall, and when you're in a really good chili joint, the waitress has dirt on her ankles."

Red Raspberry Chutney

Tim's Fine Berries

If you like chutney, you'll become as addicted to this hearty version as I am—serve it with meat or nonmeat dishes, swordfish, Indian dishes, or on toast, crackers, biscuits, or crumpets. It would even be good on ice cream, frozen yogurt, or sherbet.

◆ Place all the ingredients in a large saucepan and bring to a boil. Reduce heat to low and simmer, uncovered, until mixture thickens and darkens, 1 to 2 hours, depending on the flavor desired. (Taste after 1 hour and, if you desire a richer, heartier flavor and denser texture, continue cooking.) Chill and serve as desired. You may also increase or decrease any of the dried

8 cups (2 quarts) red raspberries

2¼ cups firmly packed brown sugar

1 cup golden raisins

1 cup unsulfured dried apricots

1 cup water (use less or eliminate completely if berries are very soft)

½ cup toasted, chopped almonds (see Techniques section)

¼ cup freshly squeezed lemon juice

fruits or flavorings, depending on your taste and use for the chutney. The chutney can be kept in the refrigerator for 1 to 2 weeks and also freezes well.

Makes about 4 cups

2 tablespoons freshly squeezed lime juice

1 tablespoon of a mixture of grated fresh lemon, lime, and orange zest

1½ teaspoons kosher salt (optional)

1 teaspoon grated white or yellow onion

¼ teaspoon ground cloves

TIM'S FINE BERRIES

Since 1948, Tim Johannes's family has been in the berry business, selling blueberries, blackberries, and raspberries. But since taking over the business a few years back, Tim has added to the product line and currently brings 15 varieties of fruit to the Market. His table glistens with jewel-like boxes of everything from strawberries to blueberries, tayberries to black raspberries. Even exotic gooseberries and currants are often for sale. But about one-quarter of his business is devoted to fresh raspberries, and they remain a customer favorite.

"People love raspberries, but sometimes they don't realize the many varieties available," Tim explains. "Meekers are an all-round berry—large, firm, and rich red in color, with a high sugar content and excellent flavor. Chilliwacks, named after the town in British Columbia, are a big, hearty berry, very firm and sweet. Sumners are a small, round, bright berry, fairly firm, very sweet and delicious. Tulameens are the king of all raspberries. They're very large and sweet with a perfect balance of tartness to sweetness."

Tim picks his berries fresh each morning, trucks them to the Market from his farm in McMillan, Washington, and sells them in the North Arcade daily June through August.

Beverages

Iced Caffe Crema
Caffe Marrakech
Fresh Fruit Smoothie
Winter Spirits
Teatime Tips
A "Real" New York Egg Cream
Spanish Table Sangría
The Perfect Cup of Coffee
Chai
Iced Berry Spice Tea

STARBUCKS COFFEE COMPANY

The story of Starbucks Coffee Company could be (and probably is) a chapter in a business-school casebook, and it all began in 1971 in the Pike Place Market, where three San Francisco–area college graduates began selling roaster-fresh, whole-bean coffee to retail customers. They named their company Starbucks, after the first mate in Herman Melville's *Moby Dick*, although "Starbo" had been another early possibility.

Additional Starbucks branches opened, and the men started selling coffee wholesale to restaurants, other espresso houses, and coffee retailers throughout the United States. When Howard Schultz, a sales and marketing expert, joined the company in 1982, Starbucks was already a local, highly respected roaster and retailer of whole-bean and ground coffees.

A business trip to Italy in 1983 opened Schultz's eyes to the rich tradition of the espresso beverage, and espresso drinks became an essential element of his vision for the young company. In 1984, Schultz convinced the founders of Starbucks to test the coffeehouse concept in downtown Seattle, where the first Starbucks caffe latte was served.

With the help of local investors, Schultz purchased Starbucks in 1987 and opened locations in Chicago and Vancouver, BC, for a total of 17 stores by year-end. The number of locations continued to double over the next five years, and by 1992 the company had completed its initial public offering. Its stock traded on the NASDAQ National Market under the trading symbol "SBUX." Since then the stock has split several times, and Starbucks stores have continued to multiply across the United States and throughout the world, influencing cultures and lifestyles across the globe.

The Pike Place Market outlet remains a venerated touchstone, although visitors may be a bit underwhelmed by its narrow, unassuming storefront and creaky, rough-hewn floors. It's funky and nostalgic, with just a couple of stools for seating, nothing like the palatial Starbucks coffeehouses of recent years.

But the staff is ever-friendly, the souvenir coffee mugs are worth owning, the caffe lattes are still among the best in town, and the commemorative bronze plaque that marks the site of the worldwide coffee chain's inception is worth a photograph. Market musicians like to set up just outside the door, so you'll often be regaled while waiting to pick up your coffee beverage of choice.

Iced Caffe Crema

Starbucks Coffee Company

1 cup chilled, strong coffee

½ cup half-and-half

2 rounded tablespoons confectioners' sugar

2 cups crushed ice

A well-prepared iced coffee is like a magical potion that can simultaneously refresh and rejuvenate the mind and body. For the most pleasing results, choose a coffee with a tangy, almost effervescent acidity and medium body. To vary the flavors in this iced coffee recipe, try adding one of the following: 2 teaspoons malt powder, 1 teaspoon cinnamon, 1 teaspoon cocoa powder, or a garnish of whipped cream dusted with grated chocolate.

◆ Combine the ingredients in a blender and mix until creamy. Pour into tall glasses and serve at once.

Serves 4

Cook's Hint: To make good iced coffee, start with your favorite Starbucks coffee brewed double-strength to compensate for the dilution from the ice. Starbucks recommends Gazebo Blend (a blend of African coffees), Latin American coffees such as Starbucks House Blend or Colombia, or most of the coffees in its Mild coffee family. Use a filtered drip brewing method and 4 tablespoons of coffee for every 6 ounces of water. Instead of merely allowing the coffee to cool, the experts at Starbucks suggest that you immediately pour the coffee over a pitcher of ice, which instantly cools and dilutes the coffee. Serve the coffee over additional ice.

Caffe Marrakech

Starbucks Coffee Company

2 cinnamon sticks (each 3 inches long)

4 whole cloves

4 whole allspice berries

4 whole cardamom pods

4 cups hot, strong, freshly brewed coffee

Milk (optional)

Brown sugar (optional)

E xotic spices can really perk up an iced coffee, and the variety of combinations is almost endless. For example, Starbucks suggests that to make a "Caffe Rio," simply substitute 4 strips of orange zest, 4 strips of lemon zest, and 8 whole cloves in place of the spices called for below, then proceed with the recipe as written.

- In a glass carafe, combine cinnamon sticks, cloves, allspice berries, and cardamom pods. Immediately after brewing the coffee, pour it directly into the carafe. Steep spices in the coffee until it comes to room temperature; then strain spices and discard. Cover coffee and place in refrigerator to chill.

- Pour coffee into tall glasses filled with ice and serve with milk and brown sugar, if desired. The addition of milk and sugar intensifies the spices, so taste as you go.

Serves 4 to 6

Winter Spirits

Chukar Cherry Company

This creative cocktail is the brainchild of Michael Beaver, an award-winning bartender who now works as a manager at McCormick's Fish House & Bar in downtown Seattle. Mike describes his creation as "big and bold and a great drink for the winter months."

- Fill a martini shaker with ice, add the whiskey and Madeira, and shake for 15 to 30 seconds (at least 15 shakes), or until the shaker is frosty cold. Strain the liquid into a martini glass and garnish with cherries.

Serves 1

Cook's Hint: Like port and sherry, Madeira is a fortified wine that contains 18 to 20 percent alcohol. It hails from Portugal and comes in four distinct styles ranging from quite dry to very sweet, with Malmsey being "the richest, darkest, and sweetest of the Madeira wines," according to *Wine Lover's Companion*.

2 ounces Bushmills 10- or 16-year-old single-malt Irish whiskey or other good-quality single-malt whiskey

Splash of Madeira (Malmsey style recommended)

2 dried tart Chukar cherries, for garnish

SHY GIANT FROZEN YOGURT

A berry smoothie—frozen yogurt mixed with sliced bananas, fresh berries, and low-fat milk or fruit juice, all buzzed in a blender—is a specialty at Shy Giant Frozen Yogurt, and it's also a healthful lunch on the run. When it opened in 1976, Shy Giant was the first frozen yogurt shop in the Pacific Northwest and only the second on the West Coast. Paul Billington owned the shop from 1983 until 2002, when longtime employee Celeste Poff-Shafer and her husband Bruce bought the business.

Along with Shy Giant's famous fresh fruit smoothies, you'll find custom-flavored frozen yogurts, nonfat yogurts, and (if you're feeling more indulgent), premium ice creams by the scoop.

Fresh Fruit Smoothie

Shy Giant Frozen Yogurt

Half a fresh banana

1 cup fresh blueberries, raspberries, or strawberries, rinsed and patted dry

1 cup frozen yogurt of your choice

¼ cup low-fat milk or fruit juice of your choice

With its alternating layers of yogurt and fruit, this is an eye-pleasing concoction, a light meal-in-a-glass, and a delicious, healthful treat.

◆ In a blender, pulse fruits until smooth, pour into bowl, and reserve. In the same blender, liquefy yogurt and milk.

◆ Pour one-third of yogurt mixture into a tall glass. Pour one-half of fruit purée over yogurt. Repeat layers, ending with yogurt.

◆ Serve with a straw and a long spoon, and watch the smiles come out.

Serves 1

THE PERENNIAL TEA ROOM

From its location on a narrow stretch of Post Alley, to the window-box planters filled with pansies out front, to the whimsical teapots that line its windows, The Perennial Tea Room looks like a shop plucked straight out of the British Isles. It is owned by Sue Zuege and Julee Rosanoff, savvy businesswomen who have doubled their space since opening in the Market in 1989. "For over 10 years we have 'served' the tea community of the United States, both in person and by mail," Sue explains. "We consider ourselves an oasis of tea in 'Latte Land.'"

Here you'll find an ever-changing roster of 60 estate teas and tisanes in bulk, imported English tea bags, tea cozies and tea towels imported from Britain and Ireland, books on tea, sugars and creamers, electric kettles, children's tea sets, and all the necessities for afternoon tea, such as tea strainers and silver serving trays. Several types of domestic and imported shortbread and tea biscuits are offered, as are daily samples of four freshly brewed teas available in small sampler sizes, by the cup, or by the pot.

Part of the fun of visiting this homey shop is the opportunity to delight at the staggering array of teapots. From England comes Sadler's reliable if homely Brown Betty, a workhorse teapot for everyday use. Cast-iron pots in classic designs hail from Japan, where they have been used for centuries in traditional tea ceremonies. Luxurious blue-and-gilt Lomonosov porcelain teapots are collector's items first manufactured in 1744 in St. Petersburg for the Czar and his court. It's like a round-the-world tour of tea vessels that are both artistically crafted and useful.

Teatime Tips

The Perennial Tea Room

For the perfect pot of tea, bring fresh, cold water to a full boil. Place 1 level teaspoon of loose tea per cup directly into pot. Pour in water to fill, steep 3 minutes, then stir. Strain directly into cup or decant into serving pot. Use tea cozy only after tea leaves have been removed. Add milk or lemon and sugar or honey to taste, and enjoy.

- For a perfect cup of tea, bring fresh, cold water to a full boil. Place 1 level teaspoon of tea into strainer or infuser, or loose into a cup. Pour in water to fill, cover with a saucer, and steep 3 minutes. Add milk or lemon and sugar or honey to taste.

- To decaffeinate tea, bring fresh, cold water to a full boil. Place 1 level teaspoon of loose caffeinated tea per cup directly into pot. Pour in water to fill, and steep only 30 seconds. Pour off water in pot, then pour in fresh boiling water to fill, steep 3 minutes, and stir. Strain directly into cup or decant into serving pot. Use tea cozy only after tea leaves have been removed. Add milk or lemon and sugar or honey to taste.

A "Real" New York Egg Cream

Danny's Wonder Freeze

½ cup whole milk

¼ cup chocolate syrup (Fox's U-bet brand recommended)

Soda water

Egg creams have been a favorite New York City soda fountain drink since the 1930s. They don't contain eggs; they're so named because the froth on the top looks like beaten egg whites. "There are 73 different ways to make an egg cream, and it all has to do with what neighborhood you grew up in," Danny explains. "When egg creams first began in New York City, you'd freeze whole milk, then chip it into chunks, add chocolate syrup and 'fitzer' [soda] water, and stir. The key is Fox's U-bet Chocolate Syrup, which is popular in the neighborhoods of Brooklyn. I'm one of the only people in Seattle who uses it, and it makes quite a difference."

- Place milk and chocolate syrup in a large (16 ounce), tall glass. Stir well, then top off the glass with soda water. Serve immediately with a long spoon and a straw.

Serves 1

DANNY'S WONDER FREEZE

An oversized plastic soft-serve vanilla ice cream cone signals Danny's Wonder Freeze, an unpretentious place that's reminiscent of a New York hot dog stand from the 1950s. That's not too surprising given that it started in the Market in 1952, back when soft-serve ice cream machines really were considered a "wonderful" novelty.

Danny McCullem, the tanned, fit guy who runs around the Market in a Bronx baseball cap, red sports shirt, and khakis, mans the counter. He looks more like an athletic director than the owner of a hot dog stand, but that's been his occupation since he took over from original owner Mas Kajioka in 1986.

"The key thing here is hot dogs. I run Danny's Wonder Freeze like a New York hot dog stand," Danny explains. "I can tell what part of the United States a customer is from based on what condiments they ask for on their hot dog."

According to the 'dog expert, Southerners ask for "slaw" (coleslaw), New Englanders request celery salt, and New Yorkers demand spicy New York red onion sauce, "hold the chili." No matter where you come from, mustard, relish, grilled onions, and sauerkraut are standard options at Danny's; homemade chili or cheese costs extra.

In a nod to more vegetarian-leaning times, Danny will also fix you a tofu hot dog or tofu corn dog. Corn dogs are a Southern specialty, invented in 1942 by Texan Neil Fletcher for the country's largest state fair . . . the State Fair of Texas. Danny's version features a vegetarian hot dog skewered on a stick for easy eating, then dipped in heavy corn-bread batter and deep-fried.

After your weiner, don't miss out on a soft-serve ice cream cone, a chocolate-dipped cone with or without nuts, or a "real" New York egg cream.

Spanish Table Sangría

The Spanish Table*

D o you like your sangría dry or sweet? Prebottled versions available in America and at many restaurants in the United States are definitely on the sweet side, but this rendition from Steve Winston (which isn't so much a strict recipe as a formula) is definitely on the dry side. In his informative newsletter, Steve , who owns The Spanish Table, advises:

"For me, sangría is often a totally spontaneous reaction to the presence of ripe fruit, and winter is the best season for citrus fruits, when the variety of oranges ranges from satsumas to Clementines to Valencias. I just quarter the fruit—limes, oranges, a grapefruit for tartness, plus a juicy apple or pear. I give the citrus fruits a little squeeze to release the juice as I drop them in the pitcher, add the apples or pears, then the wine. I use red wine, but white wine lovers can use white. I put the pitcher in the refrigerator. When ready to serve, I add up to a can of carbonated soda or (to be more authentic) a bottle of *La Casera*, which is similar to seltzer water with a spritz of lemon. To serve, pour the sangría into glasses filled with ice, adding slices of fruit as garnish. Since my friends are usually thirsty, I make an extra pitcher for refills."

When I tested this recipe during the winter months, I followed Steve's suggestions, then added kumquats and sliced star fruit to the finished sangría for a festive touch.

*Just outside the Market Historic District.

THE SPANISH TABLE

The Spanish Table opened for business in 1995 on the Pike Place Hillclimb and specializes in food, wine, and cookware from Spain and Portugal. The store is a lifelong dream for the husband-and-wife team of Steve Winston and Sharon Baden, who made numerous trips to Spain, fell in love with the food and culture, and decided to open up shop. The concept has been so successful that Steve and Sharon opened satellite stores in Berkeley, California, and Santa Fe, New Mexico, in 2001 and 2002, respectively.

The two-level space boasts a small deli upstairs with a handful of stools and outside seating on the terrace. You can eat your *bocadillo* (Spanish sandwich) or *torta española* (a wedge of potato, onion, and egg frittata) on the premises or take them away. Espresso cut with sweetened condensed milk (the potent *bomba*), cured meats (such as *jamón serrano*), and cheeses (such as manchego, Cabrales, or the "Drunken Goat," which is cured in red wine) are also available.

But don't get so involved in lunch that you miss a stroll through the impressive wine grotto and the shelves full of Spanish products that await you down the stairs. The Spanish Table is the ultimate resource for *cazuelas* (terra-cotta baking dishes), hand-painted ceramics, Iberian cookbooks and travel guides, Spanish green recycled glass objects, olive-wood spoons, and copper *cataplanas* (dome-shaped, hinged copper pots for cooking clams and mussels). Twin-handled *paelleras* (paella pans) feed from one to 200!

The Perfect Cup of Coffee

Seattle's Best Coffee

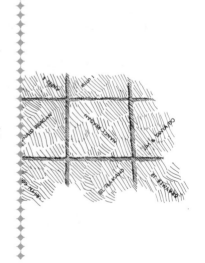

- ◆ Always use the correct grind of coffee for the particular brewing method you are using.

- ◆ Always start with filtered, cold tap water for brewing. Hot water tends to flatten taste.

- ◆ Always measure the water correctly according to the brewing system you have.

- ◆ Never guess amounts. The recommended proportions for brewed coffee: 1 tablespoon ground coffee per one 6-ounce cup of water.

- ◆ Never reheat coffee. Keep coffee warm in a thermos or vacuum container for best results.

SEATTLE'S BEST COFFEE

With its foamy caffe lattes, indoor and outdoor seating, and excellent people-watching opportunities, Seattle's Best Coffee cafe, at the intersection of Post Alley and Pine Street, is an ideal Market meeting place. If you're lucky enough to get a seat at the counter, you can take full advantage of Seattle's clean, bracing air and get a good view of the sky, the tops of the Olympic Mountains, and the tips of the totem poles in nearby Victor Steinbrueck Park.

Seattle's Best Coffee traces its history back to 1968, when Jim Stewart opened the Wet Whisker, an ice cream and coffee shop, in the sleepy seaside town of Coupeville, Washington. In 1969, Jim bought his first roaster from a peanut vendor on a beach in southern California, hauled the machine back to Coupeville, and learned the ins and outs of roasting coffee beans in the Northern European style, a lighter roast than the full-city roast favored by other major coffee purveyors about town.

Jim sold the Coupeville store and soon opened a new place on Seattle's waterfront, where he quickly established a good tourist trade. In 1971 he opened the Pike Place Market location, which served as a significant milestone in the foundation of Seattle's coffee boom.

Soon Jim became known as *Bwana Kahowa*, or Mr. Coffee, in Africa, one of the many places he visits in search of the highest-grade coffees. "We look for the small producers who use the old methods and practice coffee handling as an art," Jim explains.

In 1983, Jim moved the company to Vashon Island, a short ferry ride from downtown Seattle, in order to expand his roasting facilities. In 1998, Seattle's Best Coffee was purchased by AFC Enterprises, Inc. in Atlanta, Georgia—one of the world's largest restaurant companies.

More than 30 years after Jim Stewart first carted that 12-pound peanut roaster back from California, Seattle's Best Coffee stores have spread across the United States from Hawaii to Pennsylvania, and into foreign countries such as Japan, Bahrain, and the Philippines. And Mr. Coffee still travels the globe to maintain the strong relationships he has developed over the years with individual coffee farmers and their families.

TENZING MOMO

Tenzing Momo is the kind of place where phrases like "heavy karma" and "good vibes" seem as much at home as the antique glass jars of dried herbs and flowers that line its walls. Since 1977 this herbal apothecary has dispensed herbal alternatives, along with brewing and dosage instructions, to help people stop smoking, dull toothaches, and get over colds and flu.

Located in the Economy Market Atrium, Tenzing Momo was one of the first herbal apothecaries on the West Coast and is modeled after a Tibetan pharmacy. Its name means "illustrious food," and the store specializes in herbs and dried flowers (the largest collection on the West Coast), tinctures (300 different kinds, with intriguing names such as women's tonic, liver detoxify, and lights out), essential oils (370 varieties, everything from bitter almond to heliotrope to ylang-ylang), bulk teas, Tibetan and Buddhist statuary, and specialty incense (Egyptian musk and patchouli sound yummy).

Here you'll find ear candles (which rely on suction to draw out ear wax), ginseng (the "king of the herbs"), tarot cards, crystals, and natural shampoos, soaps, and lotions. Floor-to-ceiling bookcases are filled with 500 weighty tomes featuring theories from Tibetan, Ayurvedic, Hindu, Central and South American, Asian, European, and North American herbology. You can even have your future read by Chief Thundercloud, the resident Native American psychic and shaman.

Chai

Tenzing Momo

Since this recipe was first printed more than 10 years ago, chai, or spiced black tea, has become all the rage at local coffee and tea shops. You can make it yourself using the formula below, or buy the prepackaged dry tea mix at Tenzing Momo.

◆ Mix together cassia chips, ginger, cloves, cardamom seeds, and peppercorns to make tea mix. Weigh 3 to 5 ounces of mix and simmer in the water 45 minutes, covered. Add black tea and steep 5 minutes. Strain, add milk, and serve. Add sugar to taste.

Makes 3 cups tea; when prepared with milk, the recipe serves 18 (the proportion is 1 part tea to 2 parts milk)

12 ounces cassia chips (American cinnamon bark)

6 ounces ginger, cut and sifted

2 ounces whole cloves

2 ounces whole cardamom seeds

¾ ounce black peppercorns

4 cups water

2 tablespoons black tea, such as Ceylon orange pekoe

6 cups whole or low-fat milk

Granulated sugar, brown sugar, or honey

Iced Berry Spice Tea

MarketSpice

This berry-rich tea is flavored with cranberry juice, cinnamon, and cloves. When combined they make a fruity, spicy brew. I also like to serve the tea hot for soothing sipping during the winter months.

- ◆ Pour water over tea leaves, stir, and steep 5 minutes. Strain tea into a large pitcher and add cinnamon sticks and cloves. Cover and cool.

- ◆ Strain out cinnamon and cloves and discard. Add cranberry juice, sugar, and lemon juice and stir until sugar dissolves.

- ◆ To serve, pour tea over ice and garnish with lemon slices.

Serves 6

Cook's Hint: To clear tea that has become cloudy, slowly add boiling water, stirring until the tea clears.

3 cups boiling water

1 rounded tablespoon MarketSpice Northwest Breakfast or other good-quality black tea blend, or 4 MarketSpice Northwest Breakfast tea bags

3 cinnamon sticks (each 3 inches long)

15 whole cloves

1½ cups cranberry juice

⅓ cup granulated sugar

3 tablespoons freshly squeezed lemon juice

Lemon slices, for garnish

MARKETSPICE

"Spice is the variety of life" at MarketSpice, which started as a small tea and spice shop on one of the lower levels of the Market in 1911 and has been at its present location under the Market clock for more than 40 years. As in days gone by, MarketSpice teas and spices are still blended in small batches by hand on an as-needed or as-ordered basis so they stay as fresh as possible.

The shop sells well over 100 spices in bulk from around the world, 50 bulk loose-leaf black teas, more than 50 green and herbal teas, more than 50 bulk coffee varieties, many salt-free seasonings, and a wide variety of spice blends. The spice blends are unique to MarketSpice and are often accompanied by recipe suggestions.

One of MarketSpice's most popular products is its eponymous MarketSpice tea, a black tea flavored with spices and essential oils (especially noticeable is the rich flavor of orange). It was developed in the early 1970s by a former owner of the store who was married to a pharmacist. Her husband used oils to flavor the medicines he dispensed, so she tried the same method of camouflage to perk up the taste of tea.

The fruit of her efforts? The most famous tea blend in the Northwest. There's always a pot perking in the back of the store (the preferred way to brew this tea because the longer it perks, the sweeter and more flavorful it gets), plus cups for sampling. There are even candles, flavored honey, and tea cookies infused with the essence of the well-loved tea for those who just can't get enough of a good thing.

Appendixes

Techniques
Produce Availability Chart
Mail-order Information
Index
About the Author

Techniques

One of the things that has pleased me most since the publication of the original *Pike Place Market Cookbook* is when readers tell me they like the book because the recipes always work! I chalk that up to the fact that I am similar to many cookbook buyers: I am a good home cook who has taken lots of cooking classes, read many cookbooks and cooking magazines, and put my kitchen to good use over the years. However, I have no formal culinary training as a chef, nutritionist, or dietician; therefore, I have no biases in any of these areas.

Since I'm not a professional chef and don't test my recipes in a commercial kitchen, I rely on my own common sense, my instincts, and my residential-grade kitchen equipment to see me through. I have tested all the recipes myself under such normal, everyday conditions and modified them to reflect the same.

I assume that readers use these recipes in much the same way as I do, and that you already have an understanding of the fundamentals of cooking or have a good basic cookbook in which to look up answers to questions that might arise. However, I have included the following descriptions of a few unusual techniques and concerns mentioned within these pages that might be unfamiliar or difficult to find elsewhere.

Bouquet garni: To make a bouquet garni, cut out an 8-by-8-inch square of clean cheesecloth and fill with fresh herbs of your choice, the classic combination being thyme, parsley, and bay leaf. Pull up the ends of the cheesecloth and tie with kitchen string. Use the bag to flavor stews or soups, removing and discarding the bouquet garni before serving the dish.

Bread crumbs: To make unseasoned soft (fresh) bread crumbs, tear slices of white or whole-wheat bread into chunks and place them in a food processor. Process until crumbs of the desired size form. Fresh bread crumbs can be stored in the refrigerator for up to a week; in the freezer, tightly wrapped, they keep for about 6 months.

To make unseasoned dry bread crumbs, place a single layer of white or whole-wheat bread slices on a baking sheet, and bake at 300°F for about 10 minutes, or until the bread turns light brown and dries completely, turning once. Allow the bread to cool, then place in a food processor or blender and process until the crumbs reach the desired texture.

Chiffonade: Pull basil leaves from the stem, stack them neatly one on top of the other, and roll them tightly like a cigar. Using a very sharp knife, cut the leaves into thin slivers. Unroll the basil slivers and fluff.

Citrus zest: Although the "peel," "rind," and "zest" of citrus fruits are sometimes thought to be the same thing, they are not. The "zest" is the vibrantly colored, thin outer layer of the peel. It has a bright, clean, sometimes perfumy taste and isn't bitter. The remainder of the peel, the white portion called the albedo, is often quite bitter in taste, pithy in texture, and doesn't have the same aromatic flavor of the zest. Handy tools for removing the zest of citrus fruits include a citrus zester, paring knife, or a sharp vegetable peeler.

Clarified butter (also referred to as *ghee*): Melt unsalted butter in a nonstick skillet over low heat. As the white foam rises to the top, skim and discard it. The clarified butter is the heavy yellow butter that remains in the bottom of the pan.

Deglazing: After sautéing or roasting a food, a flavorful residue of browned juices and food particles sticks to the bottom and sides of the pan. To make a delicious sauce from these caramelized pan juices, remove the meat or seafood, then add a small amount of liquid (such as wine, broth, or water) to the hot pan. Heat on the stovetop over medium-high heat and, with a wooden spoon or spatula, scrape the bottom and sides of the pan to loosen the browned particles and crusted juices. The sauce can be served as is, or additional ingredients can be added.

Kosher salt: I use kosher salt in my cooking and specify it in the recipes in this book for two reasons. First, common table salt contains chemicals and additives that give it a harsh, cloying taste. Kosher salt tastes clean and fresh. Second, because of its larger crystals, kosher salt is easier to feel as it passes between your fingers, and easier to see when you season food with it.

Mise en place: This French cooking term (pronounced Meez ahn plahs) refers to having all the ingredients necessary for making a dish prepared and ready to combine before starting to cook. It is useful for any dish, but it's an absolute necessity for sautés, stir-fries, and other dishes that are cooked over high heat in a very short amount of time.

Ovens: Knowing how your oven operates, its capabilities and special features, and even its hot spots can make roasting a turkey or baking a cake less intimidating. Particularly if you own a convection or complicated gas oven, I recommend reading the instruction manual thoroughly, taking classes through the appliance distributor, and/or having a technician make a service call to your home to explain how the oven operates.

Plumping dried fruits, such as dried cherries, apricots, raisins, or apples: Add fruits to a small saucepan and cover with water, stock, or liqueur. Bring to a boil, cover, and remove from heat. Allow to stand 10 to 20 minutes, or until the fruit is plumped. To speed the plumping process, pour ½ cup water into a microwave-safe glass dish. Add the fruit and microwave on HIGH 30 seconds. Stir and repeat. When the fruit begins to plump, remove from the microwave oven and cover. Let rest 5 minutes, drain water, and use the fruit as directed.

Raw eggs: Concerns about salmonella poisoning have called into question the use of raw eggs in food preparation. Two of the recipes in this book call for using raw eggs (Blackberry Mousse with Lemon Madeleines and Salmon Soup with Aïoli). Although I have experienced no ill effects when testing these recipes, I would encourage all readers to use the freshest eggs available and to thoroughly wash and dry the eggs' outside shells before use. Pregnant women, the very young and the very elderly, and any individuals with chronic or autoimmune diseases should be informed of the uncooked eggs before sampling these recipes and may opt to forgo them.

Raw finfish: One of the recipes in this book (Tahitian Poisson Cru) calls for the use of raw fish that is "cooked" in a citrus marinade. Because the fish is still essentially raw even after marination, it is of the utmost importance to use the freshest fish available from your most trusted fishmonger or other reliable source. Pregnant women, the very young and the very elderly, and those with certain health problems, which include liver disease (cirrhosis or chronic alcohol abuse), diabetes mellitus, immune disorders (AIDS or cancer), and gastrointestinal disorders should be especially watchful and may opt to forgo this recipe.

Reading the recipe: Before beginning to cook, read through the recipe a couple of times to familiarize yourself with the cooking techniques, steps involved, and ingredients required. Thoroughly understanding the road map of a recipe *before* diving in can help you avoid wasted effort and poor results.

Reducing sauces: Reducing, or cooking down liquids that have been added to a pan in which a sauce is made, concentrates the flavors and thickens the sauce to the right consistency. Do not salt a liquid or sauce that is to be reduced, or the final sauce may end up oversalted. Season to taste after the sauce has been reduced.

Roasting bell or chile peppers: Roast peppers in one of these four ways: Char the outside of the peppers with a propane blowtorch until black; roast over a gas burner on high heat, turning frequently with kitchen tongs, until well charred on all sides; broil under a hot broiler several inches from the heat, turning frequently, until brownish-black blisters form; or roast in a preheated 400°F oven 10 to 15 minutes, turning frequently, or until brownish-black blisters form. Put the roasted peppers in a paper or plastic bag, close the top, and let stand 10 minutes. Remove the peppers from the bag and scrape off the skin; cut away seeds and ribs. Wipe away any remaining black particles with a damp cloth, then slice or chop as needed. If desired, use thin plastic or rubber gloves to protect your hands while preparing the peppers.

Roasting garlic: Preheat oven to 375°F. Slice ½ inch off the top of the garlic bulb, wrap in aluminum foil, and bake 35 minutes, or until garlic is very tender and easily squeezed from the garlic cloves.

Sea salt: Sea salt is often used to highlight or "finish" dishes; therefore, it is often added at the end of cooking. "Finishing" refers to the technique of applying a key ingredient after a dish is cooked (or after it is dressed, in the case of a salad) and immediately before it is served. I use a variety of sea salts from around the world, including Fleur du Sel from France, Maldon from England, and Alaea from Hawaii.

Spices: Nothing beats whole spices freshly ground in a mortar and pestle or an electric coffee grinder (just make sure to dedicate a grinder exclusively to spices; do not alternate between spices and coffee beans!). But even if you don't commit to grinding your own, you should clean out your spice rack at least once a year so your ground spices remain fresh and potent. At a minimum, use freshly ground black pepper when seasoning your food.

Stock: Although homemade vegetable, chicken, and beef stocks are always preferred over canned stocks in cooking, I realize that many home cooks don't have time to spend making their own. Therefore, in most of the recipes in this book where stock is called for, I give a substitute using canned broth mixed with water.

Toasting nuts and seeds: To toast hazelnuts, arrange them on a cookie sheet in a single layer and place in a preheated 375°F oven for 10 minutes. Remove from the oven and allow to cool slightly. Place the nuts between two rough terry-cloth towels and rub off as much of the nuts' brown skins as you can, or rub a handful of nuts between your palms (or a single difficult-to-skin nut between forefinger and thumb). Alternately (particularly for small quantities of nuts), use the toasting method described below.

To toast sesame, mustard, coriander, pumpkin, and cumin seeds, Szechwan peppercorns, or nuts, heat them in a dry skillet over medium heat for about 3 to 5 minutes, or until they begin to turn light brown and/or give off their aroma (mustard seeds begin to pop), shaking the pan back and forth often so the ingredients do not burn. Remove from heat, cool, and add to your recipe or grind as directed.

Tomato peeling and seeding: To peel a tomato, cut a shallow "X" in the bottom end and drop it into boiling water for 15 to 20 seconds. Remove and transfer to a bowl of ice water. After 15 to 20 seconds, remove the tomato, pat dry, and slip off the skin with a sharp knife. To seed, cut the tomato in half horizontally and gently squeeze the halves over a bowl to force out the seeds. Fingers or a small spoon work well to remove any remaining seeds.

Produce Availability Chart

Produce	Jan	Feb	Mar	Apr	May	Jun	July	Aug	Sept	Oct	Nov	Dec
Apple cider (fresh)	❖	❖	❖	❖	❖	❖	❖	❖	❖	❖	❖	❖
Apples (fresh picked)							❖	❖	❖	❖	❖	❖
Apricots							❖	❖				
Arugula							❖	❖	❖			
Asparagus				❖	❖							
Basil						❖	❖	❖	❖	❖		
Beans, green							❖	❖	❖	❖		
Beets						❖	❖	❖	❖	❖	❖	❖
Blackberries							❖	❖	❖			
Blueberries							❖	❖	❖			
Bok choy						❖	❖	❖	❖	❖	❖	
Boysenberries							❖	❖	❖			
Broccoli						❖	❖	❖	❖	❖	❖	
Brussels sprouts									❖	❖	❖	
Cabbage, Chinese							❖	❖	❖	❖		
Cabbage, green							❖	❖	❖	❖	❖	❖
Cabbage, red							❖	❖	❖	❖	❖	
Cabbage, Savoy							❖	❖	❖	❖		
Carrots			❖	❖	❖	❖	❖	❖	❖	❖	❖	❖
Cauliflower			❖	❖			❖	❖	❖	❖		
Celery								❖	❖	❖	❖	
Chard									❖	❖		
Cherries (pie)							❖	❖				
Cherries (sweet)						❖	❖					
Chile peppers									❖	❖		
Collard greens							❖	❖	❖	❖	❖	
Corn							❖	❖	❖	❖		
Cucumbers, pickling							❖	❖	❖			

Produce	Jan	Feb	Mar	Apr	May	Jun	July	Aug	Sept	Oct	Nov	Dec
Cucumbers, slicing								❖	❖			
Currants						❖	❖	❖	❖			
Daikon							❖	❖	❖	❖	❖	
Dill							❖	❖	❖			
Eggplant								❖	❖			
Garlic							❖	❖	❖	❖	❖	❖
Gooseberries							❖	❖	❖	❖		
Gourds, ornamental									❖	❖	❖	
Grapes									❖	❖	❖	
Herbs				❖	❖	❖	❖	❖	❖			
Honey	❖	❖	❖	❖	❖	❖	❖	❖	❖	❖	❖	❖
Horseradish								❖				
Kale									❖	❖	❖	
Kohlrabi							❖	❖	❖	❖	❖	❖
Leeks	❖	❖	❖						❖	❖	❖	❖
Lettuce, head					❖	❖	❖	❖	❖	❖	❖	
Lettuce, leaf					❖	❖	❖	❖	❖	❖	❖	
Loganberries							❖	❖				
Marionberries							❖	❖				
Melon, bitter							❖	❖				
Melons							❖	❖	❖			
Mint						❖	❖	❖				
Mizuna				❖	❖	❖						
Mushrooms, wild										❖	❖	
Mustard greens					❖	❖	❖	❖	❖	❖	❖	
Nectarines							❖	❖	❖			
Nuts										❖	❖	
Onions, green				❖	❖	❖	❖	❖	❖	❖	❖	

Produce	Jan	Feb	Mar	Apr	May	Jun	July	Aug	Sept	Oct	Nov	Dec
Onions, Walla Walla							❖	❖	❖			
Onions, yellow							❖	❖	❖	❖	❖	❖
Parsley							❖	❖	❖			
Peaches							❖	❖	❖			
Pears								❖	❖	❖		
Peas, green					❖	❖	❖					
Peas, snow					❖	❖						
Peppers							❖	❖	❖	❖	❖	
Potatoes, Finnish								❖	❖	❖	❖	
Potatoes, German									❖	❖	❖	
Potatoes, red									❖	❖		
Pumpkins									❖	❖		
Quince										❖		
Radishes					❖	❖	❖	❖	❖			
Raspberries						❖	❖	❖	❖			
Rhubarb				❖	❖	❖						
Rutabaga									❖	❖	❖	❖
Shallots									❖	❖	❖	❖
Spinach				❖	❖	❖	❖	❖	❖	❖		
Sprouts (alfalfa, bean, etc.)	❖	❖	❖	❖	❖	❖	❖	❖	❖	❖	❖	❖
Squash, summer								❖	❖	❖		
Squash, winter								❖	❖	❖	❖	❖
Strawberries						❖	❖					
Tomatoes							❖	❖	❖	❖		
Turnips							❖	❖	❖	❖	❖	❖
Watercress						❖	❖	❖	❖	❖		
Zucchini							❖	❖	❖	❖		

Mail-order Information

A number of the recipes in this book call for specialty foods or products available only at the Pike Place Market. To make it easier to try these recipes, the following is a list of businesses that will send you their products via overnight air service, United Parcel Service, or through the U.S. mail. Some will send fresh produce, seafood, or foodstuffs; others can transport only certain of their products (preserved items, such as herb vinegars, jams, and jellies). The businesses have varying policies on credit cards; some accept them, while others will take only a check or money order, so inquire before placing your order.

Note: The Pike Place Market also maintains a retail directory on its website: www.pikeplacemarket.org.

Alm Hill Gardens
3550 Alm Road / Everson, WA 98247 / (360) 966-4157
Raspberry vinegar, jams and jellies, flowers, berries, vegetables, herbs, evergreen wreaths

Bavarian Meat Delicatessen
1920 Pike Place / Seattle, WA 98101 / (206) 441-0942
Bacon, smoked meats, German specialty foods

Biringer Farm Country Store
1528 Pike Place / Seattle, WA 98101 / (206) 467-0383 / (800) 448-8212 / www.biringers.com
Berry jams; farmhouse cookies; scone, muffin, and brownie mixes; flavored tea and cocoa

Canter-Berry Farms
19102 SE Green Valley Road / Auburn, WA 98092 / (253) 939-2706 / (800) 548-8418 / www.canterberryfarms.com
Blueberry jam, syrup, vinegar, chutney

Chukar Cherry Company
PO Box 510 / 320 Wine Country Road / Prosser, WA 99350-0510 / (509) 786-2055 / (800) 624-9544 / www.chukar.com
Dried cherries, berries, trail mixes, chocolate-covered dried cherries, fruit preserves and sauces

City Fish
1535 Pike Place / Seattle, WA 98101 / (206) 682-9329 / (800) 334-2669 / www.cityfish.com
Fresh seafood market

Cook's World*
2900 NE Blakeley Street / Seattle, WA 98105 / (206) 528-8192 / www.cooksworld.net
Kitchenware shop and cooking school
*Outside the Market Historic District

DeLaurenti Specialty Food & Wine
1435 First Avenue / Seattle, WA 98101 / (206) 622-0141
Italian specialty products, wine, cheeses, deli meats

Dilettante Chocolates

1603 First Avenue / Seattle, WA 98101 / (206) 328-1530 / (800) 482-0281 / www.dilettantechocolates.com

European-style truffles, buttercreams, caramels, toffee, marzipan; molded chocolates, chocolate bars, and sauces; chocolate couverture and chocolate chips

DISH D' LISH

Pike Place Market / Seattle, WA 98101 / (206) 223-1848 / www.kathycasey.com

Kathy Casey sauces, seasonings, and cookbooks; gift baskets including Northwest wines and microbrews

Duffield Farm

PO Box 66925 / Seattle, WA 98166 / (206) 246-8266

Organic vegetables, fruits, herbs, and edible flowers; herbal vinegars

El Mercado Latino

1514 Pike Place / Seattle, WA 98101 / (206) 623-3240 / www.latinofoods.com

Latin American, South and Central American, African, Creole, Spanish, and some Asian specialty foods and fresh produce

Etta's Seafood

2020 Western Avenue / Seattle, WA 98121 / (206) 443-6000 / www.tomdouglas.com

Tom Douglas products, including cookbooks, spice rubs, and barbecue and teriyaki sauces

Exotic Meats*

17532 Aurora Avenue N / Shoreline, WA 98133 / (206) 546-4922 / www.exoticmeats.com

Specialty meats and seafood, including alligator, crawfish, possum, and bear
*Outside the Market Historic District

Frank's Quality Produce

1508 Pike Place / Seattle, WA 98101 / (206) 624-5666

Local and regional fruits and vegetables in season, as well as produce from around the world; fruit baskets

Grand Central Baking Company (Corporate Office)*

4634 East Marginal Way S, Suite C110 / Seattle, WA 98134 / (206) 768-0320 / www.grandcentralbakery.com

Artisan breads, baked goods, and catering
*Outside the Market Historic District

Holmquist Hazelnut Orchards

9821 Holmquist Road / Lynden, WA 98264 / (360) 988-9240 / www.holmquisthazelnuts.com

Raw, roasted, salted, and chocolate-covered hazelnuts; hazelnut oil, butter, and flour; chopped and sliced hazelnuts

Ivacco Foods

1501 Pike Place / Seattle, WA 98101 / (206) 223-9582

Grains, beans, pasta, coffee, tea, olive oil, balsamic vinegar, and many other bulk items; health foods

Jack's Fish Spot

1514 Pike Place / Seattle, WA 98101 / (206) 467-0514 / www.jacksfishspot.com

Fresh seafood market

Kells Irish Restaurant & Pub

1916 Post Alley / Seattle, WA 98101/ (206)728-1916 / www.kellsirish.com

Kells logo merchandise, Irish music CDs, Claddagh rings and charms, gift certificates

Kitchen Basics
1514 Pike Place #10 / Seattle, WA 98101 / (206) 622-2014 / (800) 233-2014 / www.fiestatable.com
Kitchenware, kitchen gadgets, plus a wide assortment of Fiestaware

Cynthia Lair*
www.feedingfamily.com
Cooking teacher and author of Feeding the Whole Family *and* Feeding the Young Athlete
*Outside the Market Historic District

Lina's Produce
Arcade #7 / Pike Place Public Market / Seattle, WA 98101 / (206) 622-5952
Local and regional fruits and vegetables in season, as well as produce from around the world; fruit baskets

Market Cellar Winery and Home Brew Supplies
1432 Western Avenue / Seattle, WA 98101 / (206) 622-1880 / www.marketcellarwinery.com
Red and white wines made on-site; beer and wine brewing supplies, magazines, books

The Market Foundation
85 Pike Street, Room 500 / Seattle, WA 98101 / (206) 682-PIKE (682-7453) / www.pikeplacemarket.org
Market- and Rachel the Pig–related merchandise, such as books, tote bags, note cards, and jewelry; information on the Market Foundation Travel Auction and other events

MarketSpice
85A Pike Place / Seattle, WA 98101 / (206) 622-6340
Dried herbs, spices, coffee, and tea in bulk; a wide array of specialty food items; teacups and tea sets

Mech Apiaries
PO Box 452 / Maple Valley, WA 98038 / (206) 432-3971
Raw honey, honey products, beeswax candles, and Joy with Honey cookbook

Micks Peppouri
PO Box 8324 / Yakima, WA 98908 / (509) 966-2328 / (800) 204-5679 / www.micks.com
Pepper jellies, flavored-pepper jellies, and wine jellies

The Perennial Tea Room
1910 Post Alley / Seattle, WA 98101 / (206) 448-4054 / (888) 448-4054 / www.perennialtearoom.com
Tea in bulk, tea-making accessories, whimsical teapots, tea-related books

Pike Place Fish
86 Pike Place / Seattle, WA 98101 / (206) 682-7181 / (800) 542-7732 / www.pikeplacefish.com
Fresh seafood market

Pike Place Market
85 Pike Street, Room 500 / Seattle, WA 98101 / (206) 774-5239 / www.pikeplacemarket.org
Visit the website or call for information on receiving FreshWire, the Market's electronic newsletter; joining the Market Basket Community Supported Awgriculture (CSA); accesing Market shopping directories and more

The Pike Place Market Creamery
1514 Pike Place #3 / Seattle, WA 98101 / (206) 622-5029
Unrefrigerated items only, such as jams, jellies, honey, and soy milk; T-shirts

Pike Place Nuts
97-A Pike Street #2 / Seattle, WA 98101 / (206) 623-8204
Roasted cashews and peanuts available through the Pike Place Cashew Club

Pike and Western Wine Shop
1934 Pike Place / Seattle, WA 98101 / (206) 441-1307 / www.pikeandwestern.com
Wine and wine accessories; weekly wine tasting

Pure Food Fish Market
1511 Pike Place / Seattle, WA 98101 / (206) 622-5765 / (800) 392-3474 / www.freshseafood.com
Fresh seafood market

Quality Cheese
1508 Pike Place / Seattle, WA 98101 / (206) 624-4029
Fresh cheeses from the Northwest, the United States, and around the world; 2-pound minimum on mail orders

Seattle's Best Coffee
413 Pine Street, Suite 500 / Seattle, WA 98101 / (206) 254-7200 / (800) 722-3190 / www.seattlesbest.com
Coffee beans, espresso makers and supplies, coffee-related specialty items

Snoqualmie Valley Honey Farm
10052 416th Avenue SE / North Bend, WA 98045 / (425) 888-9021 / (800) 643-1995 / www.honeyexpress.com
Liquid and cream honey, honey products, beeswax candles

Sosio's Fruit & Produce
1527 Pike Place / Seattle, WA 98101 / (206) 622-1370
Local and regional fruits and vegetables in season, as well as produce from around the world; fruit baskets

Sotto Voce
211 171st Street S / Spanaway, WA 98387 / (253) 539-0730 / (800) 487-0730 / www.sottovoce.com
Flavored olive oils and vinegars

The Souk
1916 Pike Place / Seattle, WA 98101 / (206) 441-1666
Indian and Pakistani herbs, spices, and lentils in bulk; frozen halal meats; chapati bread

The Spanish Table
1427 Western Avenue / Seattle, WA 98101 / (206) 682-2827 / www.spanishtable.com
*Iberian specialty foods, wines and liqueurs, and take-out foods; glassware and porcelain; paella pans (paelleras)
and cookware; cookbooks and guidebooks*

Stackhouse Brothers Orchards
13501 Cogswell Road / Hickman, CA 95323 / (209) 883-2663 / (800) 382-7654
Raw, roasted, and flavored almonds; dried fruits

Starbucks Coffee Company
PO Box 3717 / Seattle, WA 98124-3717 / (800) STARBUC (782-7282) / www.starbucks.com
Coffee beans, espresso makers and supplies, coffee-related specialty items

Sur La Table
84 Pine Street / Seattle, WA 98101-1573 / (206) 448-2244 / (800) 240-0853 (Pike Place Market store) / (800) 243-0852 (catalog division) / www.surlatable.com

12,500 items in stock, including kitchenware, kitchen gadgets, French copperware, table settings, and cookbooks

The Tasting Room
1924 Post Alley / Seattle, WA 98101 / (206) 770-9463

Tasting room that highlights Washington's boutique wineries and encourages customers to try the wines before they buy

Tenzing Momo
93 Pike Street / Seattle, WA 98101 / (206) 623-9837 / www.tenzingmomo.com

Medicinal herbs and dried flowers; tinctures and essential oils; natural soaps and shampoos; incense; tarot cards and crystals

Totem Smokehouse
1906 Pike Place / Seattle, WA 98101 / (206) 443-1710 / (800) 972-5666 / www.totemsmokehouse.com

Smoked salmon, oysters, scallops, trout, and tuna; wood chips for grilling; cookbooks

Uli's Famous Sausage
1511 Pike Place Market / Seattle, WA 98101 / (206) 839-1000 / www.ulisfamoussausage.com

A wide assortment of handmade sausages, including bratwurst, andouille, salmon, and chicken

Washington Wine Center
93 Pike Street, Suite 315 / Seattle, WA 98101 / (206) 667-9463 / www.washingtonwine.org

Educational materials on Washington wines and touring the wine country; information on Taste Washington (which bills itself as "the ultimate food and wine event") and the Auction of Washington Wines

Whistling Train Farm
27112 78th Avenue S / Kent, WA 98032 / (253) 859-5197 / www.whistlingtrainfarm.com

Organic produce, herbs, and flowers; naturally raised eggs, poultry, and pork

Woodring Orchards
P.O. Box 707 / Monroe, WA 98272 / (360) 794-9778 / (800) 848-2554 / www.woodringnorthwest.com

Apple and fruit ciders; specialty products such as jams, jellies, and glazes made from apples and other fruits; caramel and chocolate sauces

World Merchants Spice, Herb, & Teahouse
1509 Western Avenue / Seattle, WA 98101 / (206) 682-7274 / www.worldspice.com

Dried herbs, spices, spice blends, and tea in bulk; cookbooks

Uwajimaya, Inc.*
600 Fifth Avenue S / Seattle, WA 98104 / (206) 624-6248 / (800) 889-1928 / www.uwajimaya.com

Fresh seafood market, Asian produce and specialty items, kitchenware, cookbooks

*Outside the Market Historic District

Index

About the Author

Braiden Rex-Johnson is the Seattle-based author of four books, including *Inside the Pike Place Market: Exploring America's Favorite Farmers' Market* (Sasquatch Books, 1999). She is the food editor for *Seattle Homes and Lifestyles* magazine and the "Market Grapevine" columnist for *Wine Press Northwest.* Rex-Johnson is a former columnist for both the print and online versions of *CityFood,* has been a frequent contributor to *Northwest Palate,* and has written articles for the *Seattle Times, Simply Seafood, Alaska* and *Horizon Airlines* magazines, and *Health.*

Rex-Johnson specializes in Northwest cuisine, with an affinity for farmers' markets, organic farming, and farmers' concerns. Seafood is another specialty, with particular interest in Northwest species and Asian treatments of seafood.

Spencer Johnson

She and her husband, Spencer Johnson (an architect and the illustrator of her books), live in a condominium a tomato toss from Seattle's beloved Pike Place Market, a food lover's paradise whose farm stalls, fishmongers, and specialty food stores she visits several times a week for sustenance and inspiration.

Rex-Johnson is a member of the International Association of Culinary Professionals, the American Institute of Wine and Food, Women Chefs and Restaurateurs, the Seattle Convivium of Slow Food, and Friends of the Market.

Rachel is a life-sized bronze piggy bank. The bronze casting, by Whidbey Island sculptor Georgia Gerber, was modeled on a real pig named Rachel who outweighed the statue by 200 pounds! The bronze Rachel has become a Market icon. In her central location under the Market clock and in front of Pike Place Fish (the spot where visitors gather to watch the singing fishmongers "throw the fish"), Rachel has also become a meeting place for locals and tourists from across the globe. But this is a porker with a purpose: Rachel collects donations for the Market Foundation. Proceeds benefit human service agencies and programs in the Market serving the nearly 10,000 low-income and elderly residents of downtown Seattle.